Contract Law in India

Contract Law in India

Third Edition

Nilima Bhadbhade

This book was originally published as a monograph in the International Encyclopaedia of Laws/Contracts.

General Editors: Roger Blanpain, Frank Hendrickx
Volume Editor: Jacques Herbots

Wolters Kluwer

Published by:
Kluwer Law International B.V.
PO Box 316
2400 AH Alphen aan den Rijn
The Netherlands
Website: www.wklawbusiness.com

Sold and distributed in North, Central and South America by:
Wolters Kluwer Legal & Regulatory U.S.
7201 McKinney Circle
Frederick, MD 21704
United States of America
Email: customer.service@wolterskluwer.com

Sold and distributed in all other countries by:
Turpin Distribution Services Ltd.
Stratton Business Park
Pegasus Drive, Biggleswade
Bedfordshire SG18 8TQ
United Kingdom
Email: kluwerlaw@turpin-distribution.com

ISBN 978-90-411-6852-8

This title is available on www.kluwerlawonline.com

The Author

Nilima Bhadbhade, Ph.D. practices law at Pune, Maharashtra State, India, and had been Associate Professor at ILS Law College in Pune, Maharashtra, India. She studied law at the ILS Law College, Pune, and later LL.M. at the University of Pune. She topped the LL.B. class of 1982, joined the bar immediately, practiced in the Civil and Appeal Courts and Tribunals in Pune, and also taught law. In 1993, she left the profession for full-time teaching at the ILS Law College. She had been teaching laws of contracts, insurance, evidence, and intellectual property and has trained students for moot courts and presentation skills. She now practices contracts, commercial and arbitration laws.

Her areas of interest are Laws of Contract, Insurance, and Intellectual Property. She has been invited to seminars and workshops to speak on these subjects and has also conducted workshops and seminars on teaching methods. She conducts training programmes for persons in industry about contracting.

In 2012, she thoroughly revised the fourteenth edition in two volumes of the 100-year old treatise – *Pollock and Mulla's Indian Contract and Specific Relief Acts*, with an updated edition in 2014. She has also written a book in 2014 – *Specific Performance of Contracts: The Tests of Inadequacy and Effective Enforcement.*

Her works are available at <http://ilslaw.academia.edu/NilimaBhadbhade>.

The Author

Table of Contents

Table of Contents

List of Abbreviations

AC	Appeal Cases
AIR	All India Reporter
All	Allahabad
All ER	All England Reports
All ER Rep	All England Reports (Reprint)
AP	Andhra Pradesh
Bom	Bombay
Bom LR	Bombay Law Reporter
Cal	Calcutta
Ch	Chancery
Del	Delhi
FB	Full Bench
FC	Federal Court
Guj	Gujarat
Hyd	Hyderabad
IA	Indian Appeals
ibid.	*ibidium* (in the same place)
ILR	Indian Law Reports
ITR	Income-Tax Reports
KB	King's Bench
Ker	Kerala
Lah	Lahore
LR	Law Reports
Mad	Madras
Mad LJ	Madras Law Journal
MIA	Moore's India Appeals
MLJ	Madras Law Journal

List of Abbreviations

MP	Madhya Pradesh
Mys	Mysore
Nag	Nagpur
Ori	Orissa
Pat	Patna
PC	Privy Council
Pesh	Peshawar
PIL	Public Interest Litigation
Pun	Punjab
QB	Queen's Bench
Raj	Rajasthan
SC	Supreme Court
SCC	Supreme Court Cases
SCR	Supreme Court Reports
SCW	Supreme Court Weekly
Supp	Supplement
UK	United Kingdom
UNCITRAL	United Nations Commission on International Trade Law
US	United States of America
WTO	World Trade Organization

Preface

This monograph presents the Indian law of contracts for a foreign lawyer. It discusses important principles of contract law as found in the Indian Contract Act 1872 and other special laws and precedent. At first sight, a reader might be tempted to think that Indian law follows English law. This is to some extent true, because the Act draws heavily on the English common law prevalent when it was enacted. Yet Indian law differs on many important aspects; the difference have been highlighted at suitable places. Contracts are governed by many other statutes. These statutes and their application are stated at appropriate places. Reference to case law is also indispensable for interpretation of the Act. Many case laws decide principles on which the Act is silent. The statutes and judgments, especially of the Supreme Court of India, are available on the Internet for anyone wanting to know the details.

The law stated here is updated as of August 2015.

Nilima Bhadbhade, Ph.D., Pune.

General Introduction

§1. The General Background of the Country

I. Geography

1. India, that is *Bharat*, is the seventh largest country in the world. Delhi is its capital.

Located towards the south of Asia, she stands apart from Asia, marked off by the Himalayas to her north. Spread across 3,287,263 sq. km,[1] she measures 3,214 km from north to south and 2,933 km from east to west. The land frontier is 15,200 km, and her coastline is 7,516 km.

She has common borders with Afghanistan and Pakistan to the northwest; China, Bhutan, and Nepal to the north; and Myanmar and Bangladesh on the east. Sri Lanka is to the south, separated from India by the narrow Palk channel of the Indian Ocean.

2. There are four distinct zones. The Himalayas form the great mountain zone to the north and have the world's highest peaks, along with fertile and scenic valleys. The plains of the Ganges and Indus, formed from three rivers – the Indus, Ganges, and Brahmaputra – are fertile and densely populated. The desert region is to the west and northwest. The peninsular plateau has mountains and hill ranges, with ranges running near the coasts leaving a beautiful narrow coastal strip.

India is fed by its rivers – perennial snow-fed rivers flowing from the Himalayas and peninsular and coastal rivers fed by rainfall.

3. India has a tropical monsoon-type climate. She is affected by seasonal winds – the northeast winter monsoon and the southwest summer monsoon. There are four seasons – winter, hot-weather summer, rainy south-western monsoon, and post monsoon.

With such varied geographical features and climatic conditions, she is blessed with rich and varied vegetation. She has 47,000 species of plants in areas surveyed and 89,451 varieties of fauna.

1. For all data in paras 1–5: < http://india.gov.in/india-glance/profile > visited 15 Aug. 2015.

II. Population

4. India's population on 1 March 2011 (according to 2011 census) was 1,210 million, with 623.7 million males and 586.4 million females. Although India has 2.4% of the world surface area, it holds 16.7% of the world's population, making a population density of 324 per sq. km. The literacy rate, including persons who can read and write with understanding in any language, is 74.04%.

III. National Symbols and Calendar

5. The national flag is a horizontal tricolour with saffron, white, and green bands and a navy blue wheel in the centre of the white band. The State emblem depicts three lions on an abacus with a horse and bull and the words '*Satyameva Jayate*' (Truth Alone Triumphs) inscribed. The national anthem *'Jana-gana-mana'* is in the Hindi language, and the national song '*Vande Mataram'* is in the Sanskrit language. The tiger is the national animal, the peacock is the national bird, the Indian fig tree is the national tree, the mango is the national fruit, and lotus the national flower.

The national calendar is based on the *Saka* era, with *Chaitra* (falling in March) as its first month. It is adopted along with the Gregorian calendar.

IV. The Political System

6. India is a Union of states. It is a Sovereign Socialist Secular Democratic Republic. The Republic is governed by the Constitution, which came into force on 26 January 1950. She has a parliamentary form of government, and a federal structure with strong unitary features.

A. The Constitution

7. India has a written Constitution. It is a lengthy, elaborate, and detailed document. Its Preamble gives direction and purpose to the Constitution. The Constitution broadly deals with the following:

(i) Organization and structure of the Central government and its three branches.
(ii) Organization and structure of the states and three branches.
(iii) Federal structure, that is, Centre-state relations.
(iv) Procedure and powers of legislatures.
(v) Collective responsibility of Council of Ministers.
(vi) Safeguards to citizens and persons, particularly minorities.
(vii) Directive Principles of State Policy directed toward social welfare.
(viii) Other administrative details such as languages, government services, elections, citizenship, and high officers such as Comptroller and Auditor General of India and Attorney General of India.

Along with these details in its provisions, the Constitution provides for growth and development of conventions.

B. The Three Branches of Government

1. The Legislature

8. Parliament: The Parliament of India is bicameral. The lower House has 552 members[2] elected from the people, directly from territorial constituencies and on basis of adult suffrage. It is the House of the People – the *Lok Sabha.* The Upper House has 250 members elected by proportional representation and nominated members. It is the Council of states – the *Rajya Sabha.* These two Houses and the President constitute Parliament. The President has to discharge important functions in relation to the two Houses. The two Houses are constituted on different bases, and do not enjoy co-equal status. Each House and its members individually enjoy privileges and immunities.

The Council of Ministers is responsible to the *Lok Sabha*. The *Lok Sabha* exercises final authority in matters of taxation and expenditure of public money.

The legislative powers of the Parliament are expressly made subject to provisions of the Constitution.

State legislatures: The state governments also follow closely the model at the Centre. Each state has a Legislative Assembly – *Vidhan Sabha* – with members elected directly by adult suffrage. Seven states have a Legislative Council – *Vidhan Parishad.* Laws are made by the Legislative Assembly. The Council has only a recommending role.

2. The Executive

9. Central Executive: The Central Executive consists of the President and the Council of Ministers, headed by the Prime Minister. The Cabinet is a smaller body of Ministers that determines policy of the government and governs the country. The Council of Ministers is responsible to the *Lok Sabha.* The government must maintain a majority in the *Lok Sabha* as a condition of survival.

The President is the Head of State and the formal executive. All executive action at the Centre is expressed to be taken in his name, yet he cannot function on own his discretion or individual judgment. He has to act on the advice of the Council of Ministers and is bound by that advice.

The Central Executive appoints judges of Supreme Court and High Courts. It makes subordinate legislation, can declare Emergency, and issues Ordinances.

State Executive: The state Executive consists of the Governor, who is the Head of state, and the Council of Ministers, which is headed by a Chief Minister. The Council is accountable to the Legislative Assembly.

2. 2 nominated members.

The Governor is the link between the state and the Centre.

3. The Judiciary

9.1. India has a unified judicial system.[3] With the Supreme Court at the apex, every state also has a High Court. Lower courts are subordinate to the High Courts. Specialized courts and tribunals decide specified matters.

C. The Federal Structure

10. India comprises twenty-nine states and seven union territories. The states are Andhra Pradesh, Assam, Arunachal Pradesh, Bihar, Chhattisgarh, Goa, Gujarat, Haryana, Himachal Pradesh, Jammu and Kashmir, Jharkhand, Karnataka, Kerala, Madhya Pradesh, Maharashtra, Manipur, Meghalaya, Mizoram, Nagaland, Orissa, Punjab, Rajasthan (largest by area), Sikkim, Tamil Nadu, Telangana, Tripura, Uttarakhand, Uttar Pradesh (largest by population), West Bengal.

Jammu and Kashmir is the only state having its own Constitution and enjoys a special status. Its permanent residents enjoy special rights.

Union territories[4] are Andaman and Nicobar Islands, Chandigarh, Dadra and Nagar Haveli, Daman and Diu, Delhi, Lakshadweep and Puducherry. Delhi is a National Capital Territory.

The Constitution establishes a dual polity, with governments at the Centre and in the states. It delineates a very elaborate scheme of distribution of legislative, executive, and financial powers between the two,[5] and the one cannot encroach into the field assigned to the other.

There is considerable centralization within this federal framework. The Parliament enjoys legislative and financial powers on matters enumerated in Lists I (Central List) and III (Concurrent List) of Schedule VII the Constitution. It can in certain situations also legislate on the exclusive state lists. Residual power also vests with the Parliament.

In cases of emergency, the whole system transforms into a unitary system. The Governor, who is the Head of a state, is a nominee of the Centre.

D. Fundamental Rights

11. The Constitution guarantees to the people certain basic rights and freedoms, such as the following:

---

3. See paras 18–23 *infra*.
4. These are centrally administered units not forming part of any state. They are separate and distinct on account of historical, cultural and political reasons. They are administered directly by the Central Executive – by the President through an Administrator.
5. See para. 39 *infra*.

(i) equality and equal protection of laws, non-discrimination on the basis of religion, race, caste, sex etc.;
(ii) freedoms – of speech and expression, forming association, moving freely within the territory of India, acquiring property in India, carrying on any business, trade or profession;
(iii) freedom of the person – of life and liberty;
(iv) freedom against jeopardy and ex post facto laws;
(v) freedom of conscience, to practice and propagate any religion.

Some of these rights are available only to citizens.

These rights are guaranteed. The State cannot take them away, even by legislation. The State can impose only some specified restrictions in the interest of law and order, social controls, and so on. If the State restricts these rights or takes them away, even by legislation, such action is struck down by the judiciary. The right to enforce these rights is also a fundamental right.

The contents of these rights have widened and expanded over the years as a result of a very liberal construction of the Constitution. They can be restricted or suspended only when the President has proclaimed emergency.

E. Citizenship

12. There is a single citizenship for the whole of India, acquired by birth, descent, registration, or naturalization.[6] All Indians, therefore, enjoy same political and civil rights of citizenship throughout the country, no matter in which state they reside.

F. Elections

13. The Lower Houses at the Centre and the states consist of members elected on the basis of universal adult suffrage. Every citizen, male or female, who has reached age of 18 years or over, has a right to vote, without discrimination.

The President is elected by elected members of the Parliament and state legislative assemblies.

A general election to the Parliament is one of the largest electoral exercises in the world. Election to Parliament and the *Vidhan Sabha* occurs once in five years. Members are elected from territorial constituencies, the division of which is done by a Delimitation Commission.

An autonomous Election Commission[7] supervises and conducts elections to the Parliament and states, as well as the President and Vice President.

6. See the Citizenship Act 1955.
7. Visit http://eci.nic.in.

Political parties are an indispensable part of any democracy. India has a multi-party system. There are more than fifty political parties in the country. Regional parties exceed national parties.[8] All political parties must get registered with the Election Commission.

G. Languages

14. India is a multilingual country having numerous languages, with Hindi as the official language. English can be used for official purposes and is widely used for communication.

Twenty-two languages are expressly recognized in the Constitution for use of intrastate official transactions. The states can adopt these as their official languages, for purposes of legislation, and for use in High Courts. Besides these twenty-two languages, there are 844 different dialects.

V. Cultural and Social Values

15. India is a country home to many religious communities. She is a secular State. Secularism is the basic feature of her Constitution. There is no official, State-organized religion. Every individual enjoys freedom of conscience. The State cannot discriminate on the ground of religion. Festivals of all religious communities are public holidays. Festivals such as Christmas, *Divali* (festival of lights), *Holi* (festival of colours), and *Eid* are celebrated by everyone irrespective of religion.

Indians speak different and dissimilar languages belonging to two major linguistic families – the *IndoAryan* (derived from Sanskrit) and *Dravidian*. The nation binds together a much larger number of linguistic and cultural groups than any other federation. Because languages are prevalent in compact areas, the division of the Union into states is essentially based on language. Some school children comfortably learn four languages. Citizens can move freely and acquire immovable property throughout the territory of India. Differences in language, culture, and religion do not hamper the exercise of this freedom. Persons from all states, speaking altogether different languages and of different cultures intermingle and coexist peacefully, despite occasional incidents of disharmony.

Music, dance, and theatre have a tradition of more than 2000 years. *Karnatic* and *Hindustani* are two main schools of classical music practiced, preserved, and promoted. Classical dance takes many forms. Traditional and folk dance and music fascinate one and all. Mumbai and Chennai have a huge film industry. Culture and its expression form a large industry.

There is no social security system as in advanced countries like the United Kingdom or the United States. The aged and the disabled are naturally cared for within the family. Despite the trend toward forming nuclear families in cities and urban areas, families are joint. One might find a family of four or five generations living together.

8. A national party is one which secures 6% of the votes polled in four or more states.

India is a socialist State, but has a mixed economy. Her participation in the World Trade Organization (WTO) required her to open up her economy and allow private and foreign enterprise in areas hitherto in the public sector exclusively, and also in other sectors.

§2. Indian Law Belongs to Common Law Tradition

16. The English common law was applied initially by the East India Company for administration of overseas settlements and applied to English servants employed by the Company. As Indians joined that service, the mayor's courts then established were empowered to resolve disputes according to justice and right, which meant the English law. Supreme Courts, which replaced mayor's courts later, were to apply the common law, but in litigation between Mahomedans and Hindus, their law applied in matters of family or succession. Other matters were to be decided according to 'justice, equity and good conscience'. This term conveniently meant common law, because that was the law the judges knew. The Privy Council once observed:

> the matter must be decided by equity and good conscience, generally interpreted to mean the rules of English law if found applicable to Indian Society and circumstances.[9]

When codification began in the early nineteenth century, the codes and Acts drew on the principles of English common law. These laws still continue with modifications made after independence. Court procedure also follows the common law. Features of the common law model found in India are as follows:

(i) binding role of precedent;
(ii) positions of judges;
(iii) adversary system in procedure;
(iv) importance of procedure in legal remedies.

§3. Primacy of Legislation

17. The Constitution gives full legislative freedom to the legislatures. They are absolutely free in their respective fields. The power of legislatures to make laws is subject to provisions of the Constitution. There is a presumption in favour of constitutionality of a law.

The Supreme Court and High Courts enjoy the power of judicial review. This means that they ensure that laws passed by the legislature and orders of the executive do not contravene the Constitution, in which case they are struck down as unconstitutional.

---

9. *Waghela Rajsanji v. Sheikh Masludin* (1887) 14 IA 89.

The struggle of supremacy between the legislature and the judiciary became apparent when the Parliament made laws to overcome the effect of judgments. In 1967, the Supreme Court decided[10] that the authority of the Parliament was absolute and permanent and that it could amend the Constitution in any manner and to any extent. In 1973, in a very significant judgment[11] in a case challenging a constitutional amendment, the Supreme Court conceded the right of amendment to the Parliament, but decided that the Parliament could not amend the basic structure of the Constitution. The question whether any amendment would violate the basic structure would be decided by the courts. The Constitution has been amended one hundred times.

§4. Position of the Judiciary

18. The Judiciary adorns a crucial position under the Constitution. It dispenses justice between persons and also between the State and persons. It interprets the Constitution and ensures that all authorities of the State act within its bounds. It is the protector of fundamental rights guaranteed under the Constitution.

The Constitution contains provisions to safeguard judicial independence. This enables the judges to act impartially without fear and favour.

19. India has a unified judicial system. Courts stand in hierarchy with the Supreme Court at the top. There are High Courts below the Supreme Court and courts subordinate to the High Courts.

20. The Supreme Court is at the apex and sits at Delhi. Presently it has twenty-eight judges. It enjoys very wide powers and an extensive jurisdiction. It is the ultimate arbiter in constitutional matters and the protector of fundamental rights. It interprets the Constitution, and it decides disputes between states or between the Centre and the states. The jurisdiction of the Supreme Court can fall broadly in the following heads:

(i) enforce fundamental rights;
(ii) exercise original jurisdiction to decide intergovernmental disputes;
(iii) preside as the highest court of appeal in all matters;
(iv) exercise extensive appellate jurisdiction from any court or tribunal in the country;
(v) commit a person for contempt;
(vi) exercise power to make any order necessary for doing complete justice in any case;
(vii) exercise advisory jurisdiction.

10. *L C Golak Nath v. State of Punjab* AIR 1967 SC 1643.
11. *Keshavananda Bharati v. State of Kerala* AIR 1973 SC 1461; later *Minerva Mills Ltd v. Union of India* AIR 1980 SC 1789.

The principles of law laid down by the Supreme Court in deciding cases are binding as precedent.[12]

21. The state judiciary consists of a High Court and a system of subordinate courts.

Each state has a High Court. The High Court stands at the head of a state's judicial administration. There are twenty-four High Courts.[13] They have power to issue writs for enforcing fundamental rights as well as for correcting any errors of jurisdictions of lower courts.

The jurisdiction and procedure of many High Courts are governed by the provisions of the Letters Patent of the nineteenth century by which they were constituted.

High Courts enjoy the following:

(i) original jurisdiction in testamentary, matrimonial, and guardianship matters;
(ii) original jurisdiction in many matters under various statutes;
(iii) appellate jurisdiction;
(iv) writ jurisdiction for enforcement of fundamental rights;
(v) supervisory powers over subordinate courts;
(vi) powers to punish for contempt of itself and other courts;[14]
(vii) admiralty jurisdiction in some High Courts.

22. The subordinate courts, civil and criminal, are not under control of the Executive, but under the control of the concerned High Court. There is a district judge in each district of a state. Below him are subordinate judges. They all belong to state judicial services.

The structure and functions of subordinate courts are generally the same throughout India. Criminal courts are governed by the Criminal Procedure Code. Civil courts are set up under the separate laws of each state. Orders and judgments of any competent court at any place can be enforced by any other court in India.

23. Disputes about specific subject matters are decided by tribunals established under the Constitution. Many laws provide for adjudication or trial of disputes about specified matters by tribunals, that is, disputes regarding government services, taxation, labour disputes, land reforms, elections, and so on. This has lightened the workload of the courts and improved disposal of cases.

Lok Adalats are voluntary agencies monitored by the State Legal Aid and Advice Boards. They assist in resolving disputes through the conciliatory method. Set up under the Legal Services Authorities Act 1987, their order is final and binds parties.

I. The Legal Profession

24. The Advocates Act 1961 recognizes only one single class of practitioners and sets up a common roll of advocates having the right to practice in all the courts,

---

12. See paras 85, 93, 94.
13. Some High Courts have jurisdiction over more than one state.
14. See Contempt of Courts Act 1971.

including the Supreme Court. The Bar Council of India is an autonomous body that prescribes standards of professional conduct and etiquette for advocates, safeguards the rights and interests of advocates, promotes and lays down standards for legal education, and performs other functions. The Bar Council of India and the State Bar Councils maintain discipline among advocates.

Advocates have a right of hearing before all courts. In certain matters (e.g., family courts and consumer courts) an advocate can appear only with permission of the court.

II. Locus Standi and Public Interest Litigation (PIL)

25. People who come to court must show that they have an interest to protect. This is the rule of *locus standi*. They must show that a right of their own has been adversely affected or that breach of duty has occurred; otherwise, they are non-suited. This rule prevents spurious claims and speculative litigation by busybodies.

Public interest litigation (PIL) is a term used to describe proceedings filed by a person not directly injured or affected, agitating a matter of public interest, usually in writ jurisdiction of a High Court or the Supreme Court. The two concepts of *locus standi* and justiciability have been expanded to accommodate petitions raising issues of public interest, involving violations of human rights of powerless people, harm to ecology and environment, and bad governance, which also resulted in denial of human rights to the silent majority of people.[15]

The petitioner, who may be an individual or social action group, espouses some public cause, often the cause of the underprivileged who were otherwise unable to come to court. To ensure that PIL is not misused, the court will ensure that the petitioner is not doing so for personal gain, private profit, or political motivation.

The High Courts and the Supreme Court have special PIL cells.

§5. Distinction between Public Law and Private Law (Administrative Contracts)

26. If contracts are classified according to rights and obligations of parties, all contracts are private contracts and subject to one law – the Indian Contract Act. If they are classified according to parties, those to which the government is a party are government contracts and must comply with special formalities.[16] The government has the same rights and obligations under such contracts as any other party, and disputes arising of such contracts are decided by ordinary courts or arbitration. The government enjoys a special period of limitation of thirty years for all suits.

Administrative law applies to contracts in certain aspects, however. The principles in administrative law have been applied to prevent arbitrariness in awarding contracts by public authorities (including government) to contractors. In effect, the

15. S.P. Sathe, *Administrative Law* (7th edn, Lexis Nexis 2004).
16. Article 299 of the Constitution of India.

special principles apply to those aspects of contract that arise before it is formed. Once it is formed, such a contract is like any other.

This is done by way of writ petition in a High Court or Supreme Court in the exercise of the fundamental right guaranteeing equality before law and equal protection of laws. This aspect is discussed in detail in Part II – Chapter 11.[17]

§6. Commercial Contracts

27. Commercial contracts are those made between two or more parties who are in business for the purpose of trade and are contracting for such purpose. All other contracts are non-commercial contracts.

The contract law does not make any distinction between commercial contracts and other contracts. The law applicable to all contracts is the same – the Indian Contract Act. The rights and obligations do not differ.

An important distinction emerges in interpretation of a contract. Because interpretation involves ascertaining the intention of parties, the intention of commercial parties would take a shape different from that of other parties. When the express contract is silent, the terms implied will be different in commercial and non-commercial contracts. Customs and usages of their trade get attracted.

Another important distinction relates to the rate of interest awarded by the court where parties have not agreed on any rate. Commercial contracts will attract commercial rate of interest, that is, the bank lending rate.

17. See paras 768–780 *infra*.

Introduction to the Law of Contracts

§1. DEFINITION OF CONTRACT

I. A Contract under the Indian Contract Act 1872

28. A contract is an agreement enforceable by law. An agreement is a promise or set of promises. A promise is an accepted proposal. A contract is defined in this manner under the Indian Contract Act in the traditional analysis of offer and acceptance. A contract may result by other modes also, but the offer-acceptance analysis is a useful method to ascertain whether a contract has indeed resulted from negotiations between persons.

An agreement is enforceable by law if it is made by free consent of parties competent to contract, for lawful consideration and object, and is not expressly declared to be void by law. Formal requirements such as writing, registration, and so on might be required by other laws.

The effect of a contract may be an obligation to perform an act or to abstain. It may also result in transfer of property.

A contract can be substituted, or cancelled, or in some cases, only its terms altered in the same manner as a contract is made, and is subject to the same tests for enforceability as a contract. These cannot be done unilaterally; it requires the consent of both or all parties. A promisee under a contract can, however, unilaterally dispense with or remit the performance of any promise partly or fully or can accept any other satisfaction from the promisor. Some powers under a contract can be exercised unilaterally, like an option, right of pre-emption, right of termination, withholding money or property, and set-off. These must be exercised strictly in the manner and to the extent provided in the contract.

29. Although an intention to create legal relations is not expressly stated in the Act as a requirement of contract, the necessity of such intention is implicit in the requirement of a valid proposal,[18] which when accepted becomes a promise. A proposal will result in a contract if it is made with an intention to be legally bound by the acceptance, if given.

18. The Indian Contract Act uses the word 'proposal' for an offer.

II. Bargain and Reliance

30. The basis of a contract in the Indian law is not reliance. Unlike contracts under the civil law systems, it is not enough to have an intention to create legal relations. Indian law requires consideration. A unilateral declaration of will cannot result in a binding obligation under contract, but if acted on by the person to whom it is made, it might amount to an estoppel. The principle of estoppel is restricted to representations of existing facts; it does not apply to promises.

III. Promissory Estoppel

31. The doctrine of promissory estoppel,[19] which binds a person to his promise if acted on, is recognized in a leading case decided by the Supreme Court, which held that it did afford a cause of action. Where a person makes a promise knowing that it would be acted on by the person to whom it is made, and it is so acted on, the person making the promise cannot be allowed to go back on it. The promise can then be enforced, although doing this seriously dilutes the requirement of consideration.

This doctrine has been applied in the field of administrative law to promises made by government and governmental institutions, but has not yet been applied between private parties.

IV. Source of Obligations

32. A contract is a source of obligations. It creates a legal bond between the parties to the contract by which one, the 'promisor', is bound in favour of the other, the 'promisee', to do the promised act or abstain from doing it, the 'promise'. This would include the promise to transfer ownership of property or an interest in property, or pay money.

The terms 'creditor' and 'debtor' are used in the Indian law and practice to refer to parties in a transaction involving a debt or a promise to pay money, and the term 'debt' is used to describe the subject matter of such promise and the term 'payment' to the performance of this obligation. When referring to contractual obligation in general, the equivalent words in the Indian law are 'promisee', 'promisor', 'promise' and 'performance'.

The Indian Contract Act uses the word 'promise' for the obligation and provides: 'The parties to a contract must either perform or offer to perform, their respective promises'[20] unless it is excused or dispensed with under the provisions of law. The promisee can dispense with the obligation fully or in part.

The promisee's right under a contract is a personal right against the promisor; it is not a right in rem. The doctrine of privity[21] prevents the promisee from enforcing

19. See paras 142–143 *infra*.
20. Section 37 of the Indian Contract Act.
21. See paras 354–380 *infra*.

it against any other person, even though directly involved in the performance of the contract. The promisee is entitled to enforce the promise by filing a suit for an appropriate remedy, unless the contract or the law enables him to take action or remedies without recourse to courts, by exercising his 'self-help' remedies.[22]

V. Contractual Obligations as Assets and Liabilities

33. Although a contract creates obligations as distinct from property rights, rights and liabilities created by contracts are assets and liabilities of persons. These obligations are not a charge over the property of the promisor unless such obligations have been secured over specific properties by an instrument or by law, by creating a charge, mortgage, lien, and so on.

Claims arising out of contract, including those in the nature of unliquidated damages, are 'debts' provable against a debtor in insolvency proceedings. If the claim is unliquidated, the promisee-creditor will be required to have the amount ascertained by judgment or decree in proceedings against the debtor.

Although amounts due under a contract are mere obligations and not property, ascertained amounts due under a contract to a person, or due by him to others, are reflected in his books of accounts, respectively, as assets or liabilities, so are goods receivable or deliverable under contract of purchase or sale of goods. Continuing obligations under contracts in force or claims for unliquidated amounts or damages might not be reflected in the balance sheet. However, obligations that are the subject matter of pending proceedings might be shown as contingent liabilities. Standard or prescribed accounting norms and practices will determine treatment of obligations for accounting purposes.

§2. Historical Background of the Law of Contracts

I. Law of Contract before the British Rule

34. In the ancient and medieval period, Indian society was developed. The Hindu and the Mahomedan law provided rules for agreements affecting personal relations and business, commercial transactions, and transfer of property.

Principles relating to contracts were not codified under Hindu law. The sources of law were numerous, in the nature of commentaries. Two good sources are the *Vyavahārmayukha* and *Arthashāstra*. The latter is a renowned treatise about politics and government. One finds, for example, elaborate rules governing competency, denying power of contracting to minors, persons addicted to vices, persons without limbs, persons who had renounced the worldly affairs, married women, and dependants. Married women could not bind their husbands or family properties. Various sources of law differ in the categories of incompetent persons. As regards consent, all sources agreed that a transaction vitiated by fraud or force could be declared unenforceable by the King.

22. See 505–514, 516 *infra*.

Unlike Mahomedan or Christian systems, Hindu law recognized the occupation of money-lending and had detailed provisions about interest and repayment. A creditor could not charge exorbitant interest. Money could be lent against security of pledge or sureties, and interest could be higher where the debt was not secured. The rule of *dāmdupat* prevented a creditor from recovering at any time whether toward principal or interest an amount more than double the money lent. This rule is still prevalent as a custom.

The obligation to repay debts has been an essential aspect of Hindu religion and law, urged by spiritual exhortation. Failure to repay a debt meant rebirth as a slave or servant or a woman in the house of the creditor. A Hindu son is, therefore, liable to repay the lawful debts of his father irrespective of whether he has inherited property from his father or not.

Contract rules are secular principles under Mahomedan law, which had a very comprehensive law relating to contract. One finds in Islamic law rules governing various commercial relations, such as bailment, guarantee, indemnity, partnership, and agency. Islamic law, however, forbade usury or lending against interest.

During the Mughal period, the Mahomedan criminal law and law affecting trade and business applied to both Mahomedans and non-Mahomedans. The latter were governed by their personal law only in personal matters.

II. The British Period

35. Initially, Queen Elizabeth's Charter of 1600 gave limited legislative authority to the London East India Company, (predecessor of the East India Company) to make laws and orders necessary for good government of the Company, which were to be reasonable and not repugnant to the laws of England. Later Charters of the seventeenth century also recognized this power. The company administered courts in the seventeenth century under a fairly exhaustive system of laws in Bombay, Madras, and Bengal. Charters of the seventeenth century required courts to decide cases according to principles of equity and good conscience and according to laws and customs of merchants.

Royal Charters in the eighteenth century established courts of Justice in the Presidency-towns of Calcutta, Madras, and Bombay and made applicable within the jurisdictions of these courts the English law, common law and statutory law in force at that time. After this the courts applied the English common and statutory law as existing in England in 1726, the year of the Royal Charter. These were applicable so far as necessary for Indian circumstances. Therefore, some provisions such as forfeiture for suicide or about maintenance and champerty were excluded as not applicable to Indian circumstances.

The Regulating Act of 1773 empowered the Governor-General and Council to make Rules, Ordinances, and Regulations for good governance in Bengal, and by 1807 the same powers belonged to Bombay and Madras governments. The Act of 1833 gave power to the Governor-General in Council of India the power to legislate for India.

Initially, the Hindu and Mahomedan law applied to transactions between persons to whom these laws applied outside the Presidency-towns, but the English law applied within the jurisdictions of the High Courts. To remedy the inconvenience caused by this situation, statutes of 1781 and 1797 empowered these Courts to decide all matters of contract among Mahomedans by laws and usages of Mahomedans, and in case of Hindus, by Hindu laws and usages, and where one party was a Mahomedan or a Hindu, by the laws and usages of the defendant. Application of English law was excluded to that extent. This continued also after High Courts were established in these towns in 1862. The Hindu or Mahomedan law of contract was thus applied until the enactment of the Indian Contract Act 1872. Customs of other communities were also recognized.

III. Eighteenth Century: Areas Outside Presidency Towns

36. Outside the Presidency-towns, that is, in the other villages and towns, the old system of courts and procedures was retained. Regulations required the judges of district and city courts to act according to justice, equity, and good conscience where no specific usage or rule existed. The expression 'justice, equity, and good conscience' was interpreted to mean the rules of English law so far as applicable to the Indian society and circumstances.[23] The application of English law did not raise much objection because there might not be any rule of personal law in cases relating to transactions made by natives with the British counterparts.

IV. Application of Hindu or Mahomedan Law

37. The courts applied the law of contract of Hindus and Mahomedans under various Statutes, Charters, and Regulations. New texts and writings on these laws emerged. Hindu and Mahomedan scholars were sought to express their views on the respective laws. Law scholars were attached to courts. Thus, English laws prohibiting usury applied at that time only to British subjects and not native lenders. Trade usage of the Hindu community had the force of law. Minority was determined with reference to these laws, as were the rights and disabilities of minors. The English law applied as between British subjects. Application of all laws, Hindu, Mahomedan, or English common law, was subject to rules of equity, at times also deviating from the principles of English common law of contract.

V. Contract Legislation in British India

38. The Indian Legislature established for the whole of British India by the Charter Act of 1833, made a number of Acts on various areas involving contract matters, that is, interest, usury, bills of lading, merchant shipping, carriers, and insurance assignment. These laws affecting business and commercial transactions were applicable until their repeal after enactment of the Indian Contract Act in 1872. Soon after its enactment a question arose about validity of an agreement in restraint

23. *Waghela Rajsanji v. Sheikh Masludin* (1887) 14 IA 89.

of trade, valid under the Hindu law of contract, but void under the Act. It was held that the Act applied to all persons.

The Indian Contract Act of 1872 originates from a Bill drawn in England in 1866 by the Third Indian Law Commission functioning in England. It was then circulated into the Council of the Governor-General, and then referred to a Select Committee and published and circulated to the local governments. Controversy arose between the Secretary of State and Commissioners on one side, and the Home and the Indian authorities on the other on certain aspects of the proposed law. The Secretary of State permitted the Government of India to alter the Bill. The Commissioners resigned. The Bill was then carried through the Council with important amendments made by Sir Fitzjames Stephen.

For its most part it draws on the English law of that time. The first draft of the Act was made by the Third Indian Law Commission constituted in England in 1861. This incorporated the principles of English law. The Commission resigned on differences with the Indian Legislature at that time. With some portions borrowed from the draft of the New York Code of 1862 then being discussed, the draft of the present Act was finalized. It also borrows from laws of other countries.

VI. Indian Contract Act 1872

39. The Indian Contract Act 1872 applied universally within India to all contracts. It saved, however, usages and customs of trade or incidents of contract that were not inconsistent with it. It continues to operate in independent India by virtue of Article 372(1) of the Constitution of India, which saves laws made before 1950.

The Constitution of India divides legislative powers between the Parliament at the Centre, and the states in India.[24] The subject of contract falls within the concurrent list of subject areas, on which both the Parliament and state legislatures can make law, the latter can make law or amend to the extent it is not repugnant with any law made by the Parliament. Some states have made minor amendments in the Indian Contract Act in the exercise of these powers. However, to the extent the subject belongs to the Central List, on which only the Parliament can make law (e.g., forward contracts, insurance, banking, and so on), the state legislatures lack legislative powers. Only the Parliament can make laws with extraterritorial operation.

The Act has not been amended extensively. Important amendments were made in 1899 about the effect of undue influence on enforcement of a contract, in 1988 rendering void those agreements that seek to extinguish rights or discharge any party from liability, and in 2012 to except from this provision guarantees given by banks. Some states have made minor amendments.

The later trend is to make separate legislation governing particular contracts. Accordingly the provisions relating to sale of goods and partnership were removed from the Indian Contract Act and put into separate enactments. Acts were made before Indian Independence (1947) dealing with negotiable instruments, transfer of

24. Schedule VII of the Constitution of India has three lists. List I – the Central List – gives the subjects on which the Parliament can make laws, List II – the State List – gives the subjects for the States, and List III – the Concurrent List – gives the subjects on which both can make laws.

property, and carriage by air, sea, and railways. After 1947, the Parliament of India enacted laws affecting forward contracts, multimodal transportation of goods, hire-purchase, conditions of employment, consumer protection, information technology, and so on.

VII. Recommendations of Law Commission of India

40. The law reform process was institutionalized by the government setting up Law Commissions after 1834. The first Law Commission was established in that year, which recommended codification of the Penal Code. Later Commissions have contributed to legislation based mainly on the then prevailing English laws. The Indian Contract Act and the Indian Evidence Act, both of 1872, and the Transfer of Property Act of 1882 were enacted based on such recommendations.

After Independence in 1947, the Government of India established the First Law Commission in 1955. Twenty Law Commissions[25] constituted since then have suggested law reform from time to time, making 257 reports[26] on issues and subjects spanning all areas of law and government.

In 1958 the Second Law Commission considered exhaustively the provisions of the Indian Contract Act, and in its thirteenth report, recommended some amendments, which included dilution of the doctrine of privity, recognizing doctrine of promissory estoppel, and permitting reasonable restraints on the right to carry on trade. These did not become law. Its recommendations in 1984 made in its ninety-seventh report were accepted and the Act amended to invalidate prescriptive clauses in contracts. Its 103rd report of 1984 enabling the Courts to refuse enforcement to unfair terms in contracts, was not accepted, nor its 108th report recognizing promissory estoppel. Its 199th report of 2006 seeks to define procedural and substantive unfairness in formation of contracts, and provides guidelines for such determination, and recommends that courts and arbitral tribunals shall grant certain reliefs to relieve parties from the effect of such unfairness.[27]

§3. Classification of Contracts

I. Consensual Contracts

41. The basis of contract under the Indian law is an agreement. An agreement results from an accepted proposal, and it is enforceable as a contract if the consent is free, the parties competent, the consideration and object are lawful, and it is not expressly declared void. It does not require any formality for validity unless required by some other law.

The terms agreement and contract differ in law. A contract is an agreement enforceable by law. It is usual to state an aphorism: 'All contracts are agreements,

---

25. Visit website of Law Commission of India at, <http://lawcommissionofindia.nic.in>.
26. Until August 2012.
27. See para. 257.1 *infra*.

but all agreements are not contracts'. Yet, it is common to use the term agreement to describe a contract. Parties making a written contract will routinely call it an 'agreement'.

II. Formal or 'Solemn' Contracts

42. Although the Indian Contract Act does not require that an agreement be in writing, or subject to any formal requirement, it expressly saves any other law requiring formalities. Where any other law requires any formality, such as writing, attestation, or registration to make a contract enforceable, lack of such formality will affect the contract. The extent to which the lack of formality affects the contract would depend on the precise effect and interpretation of that statutory provision.[28]

III. Valid and Voidable Contracts, and Void Agreements

43. A valid contract is enforceable. An agreement with free consent of competent parties, with lawful object and consideration and not expressly declared void by law, and satisfying the formalities, if any, prescribed by any other law, is a valid contract.

A voidable contract is one that is enforceable by one of the parties, but not the other. It is valid until its rescission is communicated. If the consent of a party is caused by coercion, undue influence, misrepresentation, or fraud, such contract is voidable at his option. A contract is also voidable under the Indian Contract Act if one party has repudiated his obligations under the contract and other breaches discussed later.

A void agreement is not enforceable by law. The Act expressly declares some agreements void, that is, agreements with unlawful consideration of object, agreement in restraint of marriage, trade or legal proceedings, wagers, and so on.

A valid contract 'becomes void' on the happening of a contingency or a supervening event making its performance impossible. When it becomes void, it ceases to be enforceable.

IV. Real Contracts

44. The Indian law does not make any distinction between contracts. A 'real contract' that is made by delivery of property is just like any other contract. Where money is lent it is a contract of loan. Where goods are delivered with a specific purpose on condition that they are to be resumed or delivered when a purpose is fulfilled, it is a contract of bailment. The general principles of contract apply to it, as do special provisions in the chapter of bailment in the Indian Contract Act. Pledges

---

28. See paras 156–169 *infra*.

are contracts of bailment in which goods are delivered as security for payment or for performance of a promise.

An agreement to transfer property is as much a contract as any other. The actual transfer of property will be made by delivery of possession of property or any other mode intending to transfer ownership, and in cases of immovable property, by a registered instrument.

V. Bilateral and Unilateral Contracts

45. An agreement is either a promise or a set of promises forming consideration for one another. The terms bilateral or unilateral are not familiar to the Indian contract law.

The 'bilateral' contract is under Indian law an agreement consisting of reciprocal promises imposing future obligations on both or all parties. It forms by proposal and acceptance, and the promise of one party is the consideration of the other's promise. If one promise (second promise) is dependent on the other (first promise) for its performance, or is to be performed before the first promise, and if the first promise is not performed, the second promise also need not be performed. This right of the promisee of the first promise is in addition to his rights to claim compensation for its breach.

In a unilateral contract, the outstanding obligation is all on one side. The consideration for a promise can be a present or past act or abstinence. Unlike English law, the Indian law recognizes past consideration.

VI. Onerous and Gratuitous Contracts

46. A gratuitous promise is one for which there is no exchange at all, for example, a promise to gift an amount or a thing. It is given without expectation of compensation[29] or any element of self-interest.[30] Indian law does not categorize contracts as gratuitous or otherwise. In regard to enforceability, what matters is not whether the transaction is gratuitous, but lack of such consideration as is defined by law.

The fact that a transaction is gratuitous matters in that third-party interests created gratuitously are not protected. The insolvency law does not invalidate in the case of an insolvency any transfer by the insolvent for valuable consideration or any contract or dealing by or with the insolvent for valuable consideration.[31]

An agreement made without consideration is void, but is enforceable[32] in three cases: (i) a signed and registered agreement between near relations made out of

29. *Lala Man Mohan Das v. Janki Prasad* AIR 1945 PC 23.
30. *Babu Bhagwati Saran Singh v. Maiyan Murat Mati Kuer* AIR 1931 Pat 394; *Ram Pratap Kamalia Mills v. State of Bihar* AIR 1963 Pat 153.
31. Sections 53, 54, 55 of the Provincial Insolvency Act 1920.
32. Section 25 of the Indian Contract Act, see para. 139 *infra*.

natural love and affection; (ii) a promise to pay a time-barred debt; and (iii) a promise to pay for a past voluntary act. These promises are not gratuitous, but without consideration as contemplated in the Act. A gratuitous promise or promise without consideration will not be enforceable, except in the above three cases. However, a gift once made and completed cannot be recovered on the grounds that there was no consideration.

Where a person does an act or delivers a thing to another without intending to do so gratuitously, that the other is bound to return the thing or compensate for the act or the thing. This obligation arises out of *quasi-contract.*[33] This obligation to compensate arises from acceptance and enjoyment of benefit of that act or thing, even though there was no request.

VII. Aleatory: 'Contingent' Contracts

47. A contingent contract is a contract to do or not to do something, if some event, collateral to such contract, does or does not happen.[34] In such contracts, performance by one party depends on a future uncertain event. The Indian Contract Act devotes one chapter to such contracts. Contracts of insurance, indemnity, and guarantee are contingent contracts. So is a contract of wagering; the Indian Contract Act specifically declares it void. Depending on the obligation undertaken based on the uncertain future event, the performance will become due on its happening, or the contract will become void. Whether any liability under a contract is contingent or absolute is often a matter of interpretation of its terms.

VIII. Personal Contracts

48. It is usual to call contracts personal contracts in which the intention of the parties is that its performance shall be effected by the party himself and not by anyone else. The Indian Contract Act leaves it to be determined by the intention of the parties[35] whether any promise contained in it should be performed by the promisor himself, in which case such promise must be performed by the promisor. In other cases the promisor or his representatives may employ a competent person to perform it. Such vicarious performance differs from assignment of contract. The promisor is liable to the promisee for the non-performance or defective performance by the person so employed.

Where the contract requires personal performance, death of the promisor ends the contract and frees the other party from liability. In other cases, the contract can be enforced against legal representatives of the promisor.

33. Section 70 of the Indian Contract Act.
34. See paras 346–348 *infra*.
35. Section 40 of the Indian Contract Act.

IX. Standard Form Contracts

49. Contracts in standard form are valid contracts. The vice in them lies in that the party drafting the contract is able to incorporate into them unfair, onerous terms, sometimes seeking to limit or even exclude liability. Often contract documents containing such terms are handed over to the other party, who may agree to them without having read them or understood them or because he lacks bargaining power and has no other alternative source for obtaining the necessary goods and services.

The courts have evolved various strategies to limit mischief caused by such terms. The first question is whether these terms can be said to have been agreed to and having contractual effect. It is important to find whether these terms have been effectively communicated to the party whom they seek to bind and have been fully accepted by him. Second, if they are indeed part of the contract, they are subject to strict interpretation against the party who seeks its protection. Third, the court has the power to nullify the term as void and unenforceable, being against public policy.[36]

§4. Contract and Torts

I. Nature of Obligation

50. Both contract and tort belong to the law of obligations, but the obligations are essentially different.

The function of the law of torts is to provide compensation for harm, and that of contract law is enforcement of agreements. Obligation arises in contract by consent of parties to it and out of an agreement between them. It is owed by one party to the other party of the contract. Obligations in tort are independent of any agreement, are imposed by law on persons, and are owed to persons generally. A tort is defined as a duty other than a contractual duty.[37] A tort is a violation of a right in rem – owed to persons generally, whereas breach of contract is an infringement of a right in personam – toward specific person or persons.

Motive for breach is irrelevant in determining whether there is breach of contract or in determining amount of compensation; it is relevant in tort.

If the plaintiff's claim depends on proof of contract, he cannot sue in tort. If his claim is independent of contract, he can choose to sue in tort, though he could have alternatively pleaded in contract.[38]

II. Damages and Other Remedies

51. Damages in contract and in tort are compensatory. They are awarded to compensate the plaintiff's actual loss. The tests of burden of proof, remoteness,

36. See paras 256, 319 *infra*.
37. *Sachs v. Henderson* [1902] 1 KB 612.
38. *Rajkot Municipal Corporation v. Manjulaben Jayantilal Nakum* (1997) 9 SCC 552.

causation, and mitigation are similar. Damages in both cases are assessed with reference to the date of the wrong – the breach in the case of contract and the breach of duty in case of tort.

The plaintiff claiming damages for breach of contract has to show the loss flowed naturally and in the usual course of things from the breach or was within the reasonable contemplation of the parties at the time of making of the contract,[39] whereas the plaintiff in tort must show only that the loss was reasonably foreseeable by the defendant.

The function of awarding compensation differs. Damages in contract are awarded to compensate the plaintiff for expectation losses, and are calculated to place the plaintiff in a position as if the contract has been performed. Damages in tort protect the reliance or status quo interest of the plaintiff and must put the plaintiff in a position as if the tort had not been committed.

Damages to compensate for mental pain and suffering, distress, vexation, or loss of enjoyment are more rarely awarded in contract than in tort. Punitive or exemplary damages are awarded in tort, but not in contract.

Other remedies such as injunction, restitution, and self-help are available in tort. These are also available in contract. Parties may provide for means to enforce their rights within the framework of contract and without recourse to courts. These are often called 'self-help' remedies.

III. Claims in Tort

52. Persons such as bailees, carriers, doctors, or other professionals undertake to discharge duties and may also make contracts promising to perform them. They may be liable in negligence in contract to the party, and in tort to any person not party who has suffered by it. Where a party to a contract has agreed, expressly or impliedly, to take reasonable care or exercise skill in the performance of its promise, the promisee can have an option to sue in tort or contract.[40] A tortious claim can lie in respect of matters occurring before formation of contract, for example, for fraud. Persons who are not parties to contract can sue in tort if the contract affects them.[41]

IV. Consumer Protection Act

53. In the Indian law, the state of mind of the party breaking the contract is irrelevant, whether in fixing liability or in assessment of damages, unless the state of mind is essential to the obligation (e.g., obligation to use reasonable care or skill). However, a consumer can claim compensation if goods are defective or service deficient only if he has suffered loss or injury as a result of negligence of the

39. Section 73 of the Indian Contract Act.
40. *S Chatterjee v. Dr K L Bhave* AIR 1960 MP 323.
41. See para. 362 *infra*.

opposite party. In this case, the relationship between parties arises out of contract, but the liability for compensation arises only in case of negligence.[42] Other reliefs such as refund of price or charges can be ordered without the need to show the state of mind of the opposite party.

§5. CONTRACT AND QUASI-CONTRACT

54. Some situations may require that a person be held liable to another without any agreement for money or benefit received by him, to which that other person is better entitled. These give rise to *quasi-contractual* obligations, which aim at preventing unjust enrichment. The principle of unjust enrichment is stated: 'A person who has been unjustly enriched at the expense of another is required to make restitution to the other'. The principle contains three things: (i) that the defendant has been enriched by the receipt of benefit; (ii) he must have been so enriched at the plaintiff's expense; and (iii) it would be unjust to allow him to keep the benefit.[43] These are obligations imposed by law.

Situations arise apart from contractual relations, where relief must be given to remedy situations of unjust enrichment. Some of these are directly dealt with in the Indian Contract Act.

I. Under the Indian Contract Act

55. Even in 1872, long before the English law recognized obligations in the nature of restitution, Indian Contract Act itself distinguished between obligations arising from contractual relationship and those arising from 'relations resembling those created by contract', which is how it terms *quasi-contracts*. These are described in sections 68–72 of the Act, which describe the circumstances in which such obligation arises and the obligation itself.[44]

The Act describes five situations in which the *quasi-contractual* obligation of restitution arises, as follows:

(i) A person supplying necessaries to a minor or another incompetent person is entitled to reimbursement from his property.
(ii) A person paying money that another is legally bound to pay, is entitled to reimbursement.
(iii) A person who lawfully does something for another or delivers something, without the intention to do so gratuitously, is entitled to restoration or compensation.
(iv) A finder of goods is responsible for them as a bailee.
(v) A person who has paid money or delivered something to another by mistake or under coercion is entitled to its repayment or return.

42. Section 14(d) of the Consumer Protection Act 1986.
43. *Mahabir Kishore v. State of Madhya Pradesh* AIR 1990 SC 313.
44. See paras 791–819 *infra.*

The courts have at times stretched the interpretation of sections 68–72 for accommodating similar situations. Situations requiring relief in restitution may be many, and not restricted to these five. The Law Commission of India saw the need in 1958 and hence recommended for amending the Act to include all diverse situations in which restitutionary relief becomes necessary.

II. Compensation

56. If a person obligated in any of the above five cases fails to discharge his obligation, any person injured by such failure is entitled to receive the same compensation from the party in default as if such person had contracted to discharge it and had broken his contract.[45]

III. Other Situations Entitling Restitution

57. Even apart from cases discussed above, relief against unjust enrichment is granted in certain situations, some arising in the course of contractual relations. These are actions for money had and received, claims for contribution, and claims of subrogation.

§6. Contract and the Law of Property

58. The Indian law makes a distinction between interests in property (which are property) and personal obligations arising out of contractual relationship. Contracts bind only parties to it,[46] and cannot be enforced against transferees even if the obligations are concerned with rights in property. The exceptions to the operation of this principle are discussed later.

I. Property

59. The word *property* has a subject and an objective content. It may either be a thing over which certain rights exist or of certain rights over a thing.

Property is not only the thing that is the subject matter of ownership. The word has dual significance – the thing and the legal concept. It also includes the *dominium*, or the right of ownership, which may be partial or full. It is indicative and descriptive of every possible interest a party can have. The term is nowhere described in various statutes governing property. But in enactments, the term is used in its wider sense, as including not only property strictly so-called, but also any

45. Third paragraph of s. 73 of the Indian Contract Act.
46. See paras 355–380 *infra*.

interest or right therein. It has been used in a dual sense of the thing as well as the right to the thing.

Ownership of property consists of a bundle of rights. It is, therefore, possible that various rights and interests be vested in different persons. For example, in a leased property that is subject to mortgage and has three 'owners', the owner owns the property and the mortgagee and lessee own the mortgagee's right and leasehold right, respectively; all these interests are capable of further transfer. This is because a transfer of property is either a transfer of absolute ownership or a transfer of one or more of such subordinate rights.

II. Legal and Equitable Ownership

60. The Indian law does not distinguish between legal and equitable estates.[47] Under the Indian law, unlike English law, trust property is vested in the trustee. The beneficiary does not have an equitable estate or interest in the trust property, but merely a right against the trustee as owner of property. Similarly, a contract of sale does not create any interest in any property or any equitable interest in the purchaser. It is an executory contract creating personal obligations, capable of specific performance. Section 40 of the Transfer of Property Act describes such a contract as an obligation arising out of contract and annexed to the ownership of property. It does not by itself create any interest in the property. It can be enforced by seeking compensation or specific performance.

III. Kinds of Interests in Property

61. Property may be tangible or intangible. Leasehold rights, that is, rights that a lessee has in the property taken by him on lease, are interests in property in Indian law, and hence, capable of being transferred. Goodwill, trademarks, patents, and debts (called actionable claims) are also property.

A benefit arising out of land is an interest in land and, therefore, immovable property under the Transfer of Property Act. These would include hereditary allowances, rights of way, rights to fishery, and right to ferry. From time to time certain rights, some of which resemble the right of usufruct under the Belgian law, have been recognized as immovable property and, therefore, transferable and also liable to registration. Some of them are right to collect dues for fair or market held on a plot of land, life interest to income from a property, right to enter – land and carry away fish from a lake or to remove trees, right to graze cattle over the land of another, and right to collect rents from tenants of a land.

Property to be produced and manufactured is not in existence and cannot be transferred. Even if transferred, it operates as a contract to be performed in the future and is specifically enforceable as soon as it comes into existence. One can make a

47. *J M Tagore v. G M Tagore* (1872) 47 IA Supp 18; *Webb v. Macpherson* (1903) 30 IA 238; *Chhatra Kumari Devi v. Mohan Bikram Shah* AIR 1931 PC 196.

contract to transfer it. Future property differs from future interest in property. These are called reversions and remainders in the English law.

The Indian law recognizes vested interests and contingent interests in property. An interest is vested when it is created without specifying the time when it is to take effect, or where it is to take effect on happening of a condition, which is certain to happen. Thus, a gift by A to B on death of C creates a vested interest in B that is capable of being inherited and transferred. When an interest is vested, the transfer is complete. An interest is contingent if it is to take effect on happening of an event that is uncertain. Thus, a gift by A to B on marriage of C is contingent, because C may never marry. B's interest is contingent and cannot be transferred until C marries. When C marries, it becomes vested.

IV. Acquisition and Transfer of Property

62. Any property or rights or interest in property can be acquired by the following: (i) agreement; (ii) inheritance or bequest; (iii) prescription; (iv) operation of law.

V. Property and Contract

63. The law relating to transfer of property is itself a branch of the law of contracts in its wide sense as dealing with the extinction of obligations created by contract.

There is a clear distinction between a completed conveyance and an executory contract. All transfers of property other than gifts, that is, sales, mortgages, leases, and exchanges, necessarily imply a contract to transfer such property.[48] A lease contains obligations of a contractual nature.

Transfers being *executed* contracts, their validity depends on the same principles as those applicable to contracts. It is for this reason that the Transfer of Property Act 1882 states that the chapters and sections of that Act relating to contract shall be taken as part of the Indian Contract Act 1872 enacted earlier.[49] Therefore, a sale, mortgage, lease, or exchange will be void or voidable if the contract in pursuance of which the transfer has been made is void or voidable, that is, where the agreement is without consideration,[50] or made under a bilateral mistake of fact, or where the consent of any of the parties is caused by fraud, misrepresentation, or undue influence.[51] A lease or a mortgage when registered and completed is a transfer of property and cannot be avoided on the ground of breach by any party, even if the

48. *Narayan Laxman Kottewar v. State of Bombay* AIR 1960 Bom 126.
49. Section 4 of the Transfer of Property Act 1882.
50. *Tatia v. Babaji* (1896) ILR 22 Bom 176.
51. *Rani Kunwar v. Mahbub Baksh* AIR 1930 All 252; *Bhimbhat v. Yeshwantrao* (1901) ILR 25 Bom 126.

breach is repudiatory.[52] Hence, a mortgage, notwithstanding partial failure of consideration, may be enforced to the extent of money actually advanced by the mortgagee to the mortgagor.[53] The doctrine of frustration applies to executory contracts, and hence does not apply to a present transfer of property,[54] or even to leases.[55]

Thus, actionable claims[56] are related to contract.[57] A gift being made without consideration, cannot be based on a contract. But by express provision in the statute,[58] a gift can be revoked in any of the cases (except for want of consideration) in which, if it were a contract, it might be rescinded.

VI. Necessity of Registration

64. The system of registration of instruments of transfer enables notice of transactions. The Indian Registration Act 1908 provides for the procedure and mechanism of registration of instruments. Registration is not necessary for a valid contract unless any law requires it.

Transactions, or even decrees, affecting immovable property require registration. A sale, lease, mortgage, gift, exchange, or even a trust of immovable property require registration for effectively transferring the interest the document purports to transfer. This requirement affecting substantive validity is required by the Transfer of Property Act and the Indian Trusts Act. Therefore, a sale of immovable property is not valid and complete until it has been registered.

A transaction affecting movable property can be made by any act showing an intention to transfer the interest intended, like delivery of possession or mere writing. Registration can be done, but is not necessary for validating the transaction.

Registration does not guarantee the validity of the transfer or transaction, or the title of the transferor or parties to it. It is for the parties to assess and satisfy themselves about the title of any interest-holder in the property.

VII. Payment of Stamp Duty

65. Agreements and instruments and certain other documents require payment of stamp duty. This is a source of revenue for governments. Stamp laws differ from state to state, but some commercial documents[59] are governed by the central Indian

---

52. *Kandaswami Pillai v. Ramasami Mannadi* AIR 1919 Mad 168; *Rashik Laf v. Ram Narain* (1912) ILR 34 All 273.
53. *Motichand Jivraj Guzarathi v. Sagun Jethiram Guzarathi* (1905) ILR 29 Bom 46.
54. *H V Rajan v. C N Gopal* AIR 1975 SC 261.
55. *Raja Dhruv Dev Chand v. Raja Harmohinder Singh* AIR 1968 SC 1024.
56. This is a claim to any debt, other than a debt secured by mortgage of immovable property or by hypothecation or pledge of movable property, or to any beneficial interest in movable property not in the possession, either actual or constructive, of the claimant, which the civil courts recognize as affording grounds for relief.
57. *S Amarchand & Co v. Ramdas V Durbar* AIR 1914 Bom 290.
58. Section 126 of the Transfer of Property Act 1882.
59. Like negotiable instruments, receipts, insurance policies, etc.

Stamp Act. A document evidencing or affecting any interest or right in property requires stamp duty according to the enactment applicable to it. Non-payment of stamp duty, however, does not affect the validity of transaction. The deficit stamp duty is liable to be recovered with penalty. There may also be criminal liability for those evading duty.

§7. Contract and Trust

66. A trust might be created by contract or even by a mere declaration of intention. It involves appropriation of property by the owner for the benefit of another. A contract creates a personal obligation by the promisor to perform his promise, a promise to do or not to do an act. A trust creates a right in rem, a contract – a right in personam. A beneficiary of a trust can enforce a trust even though not party to its creation. The trustee and beneficiary are in fiduciary relationship with each other, which may not necessarily arise among the promisor and the promisee of a contract.

I. Trusts

67. The law relating to trusts in India derives from the common law. A trust is an equitable device, the origin which can be traced back to early 1800s. Trust was the exclusive product of the Courts of Chancery, but has been enforced in courts of law since the Judicature Acts of 1873 and 1875.

Unlike the civil law, in common law a trust is not created by a contract, but by a unilateral act. Common law provides for two types of trust, that is, charitable trusts and private trusts.

Trusts can be of two kinds – private and public. In private trusts, the beneficiaries are specific individuals capable of being ascertained, and the trust property can be exclusively enjoyed or used by such persons. In public trusts, the beneficiary is the general public or a class of persons incapable of ascertainment, and the property is intended for the benefit of the general public.

Trusts in India are governed by two different types of legislations. The Indian Trusts Act 1882 governs private trusts other than religious or charitable endowments. The Charitable and Religious Trusts Act 1920 has been made to provide for more effectual control over administrations of charitable and religious trusts. But the principles governing private trusts under the Indian Trusts Act have been held applicable to other cases also, wherever appropriate.[60]

Public and charitable trusts are also governed by state legislations, which would deal mainly with control, regulation, and supervision of administration of public trusts by government authorities.

60. *Som Giri v. Ram Ratangiri* AIR 1941 All 387.

II. Meaning

68. A trust is a confidence reposed in a person with respect to property of which he has possession or over which he can exercise a power to the intent that he may hold the property or exercise the power for the benefit of some other person or object.

The Indian Trust Act 1882 defines a trust as 'an obligation annexed to the ownership of property, and arising out of a confidence reposed in and accepted by the owner, or declared and accepted by him, for the benefit of another, or of another and the owner'. Courts generally take a view that the intention of the parties is decisive while determining whether a particular institution or instrument constitutes a relationship of trust between the parties.

III. Personality

69. A trust is not a legal person. Its property vests in the trustees. It cannot sue or be sued in its own name. Suits for enforcing rights by or against the trust are filed by or against the trustees.

IV. Creation and Extinction of a Trust

70. A trust is created when the author of that trust indicates with reasonable certainty his intention to create a trust, purpose of the trust, the beneficiary and the trust property, and transfers the trust property to the trustee. He may also declare himself a trustee or declare a trust by his will. The purpose of the trust must be lawful.

A trust in relation to immovable property can be created by will to take effect after the death of the author of the trust, else only by declaration in writing registered under the Indian Registration Act. A trust in relation to movable property can be created by a similar declaration or in any manner by transferring ownership of the property to the trustee. The author of the trust may constitute himself trustee of that property.

A trust may also be created by will. Such a trust can be revoked by the testator during his lifetime. A trust created otherwise than by a will can be revoked by the author only subject to certain statutory provisions. It is extinguished when the purpose for which it is formed is fulfilled or when fulfilment of its purpose becomes impossible as a result of destruction of trust property.

A trust is extinguished in the following ways: (i) the trust is revocable and is expressly revoked; (ii) its purpose is completely fulfilled; (iii) its purpose becomes unlawful; (iv) its purpose becomes impossible and hence cannot be fulfilled.

A trust may be revoked by consent of all beneficiaries or by revocation by the author if the power has been expressly reserved to him. A revocation will not prejudice what the trustees have duly done in the execution of the trust.

V. Trust Property

71. There cannot be a trust without property, whether movable or immovable. Property capable of being transferred to the beneficiary can be the subject matter of a trust. A trust cannot be created in respect to a beneficial interest under a subsisting trust.

Except in trusts created by will, transfer of the property to the trustee is essential. Where the author nominates himself as a trustee, the law assumes the transfer has taken place. In these cases, the author loses his beneficial ownership and transfers such beneficial ownership to the beneficiaries of the trust.

The trust property stands in the name of the trustee, but it is a separate fund and does not form part of the trustee's personal property. The interest of the trustee ceases on his death and cannot, therefore, be inherited by his heirs or legatees under his will. Nor is it liable to be attached by his creditors.

A trustee is entitled to reimbursement or payment from the trust property for expenses incurred by him in execution of the trust, or the realization, preservation or benefit of the trust property, or for the protection or support of the beneficiary.

Where trust property comes into the hands of a third person inconsistently with the trust, the beneficiary may require him to admit formally, or may institute a suit for a declaration, that the property is comprised in the trust.[61] He cannot trace property in the hands of a transferee in good faith for consideration without notice of trust.[62]

VI. Trustees

72. The trustee is the person in whom the author of the trust has reposed confidence and who has accepted such confidence. It also includes a manager of trust property. The trust property vests in him, either alone or along with other persons. More than one trustee acts as a body, and they are equally liable in law. Co-trustees cannot act singly, unless the instrument of trust provides.

A trustee may be an individual, a number of individuals, or even a corporate body. Any person capable of holding property can be a trustee, but he must be competent to contract if the trust involves exercise of discretion. His office ends by his death or discharge from office. His office is discharged (i) on completion of duties; or (ii) in the manner provided in the instrument; or (iii) on appointment of a new trustee in his place; or (iv) with the consent of all beneficiaries; or (v) with the order of a court. The trustee's interest in the property ceases on his death and cannot be inherited by his heirs on his death.

A person appointed as trustee is not bound to accept a trust. A trustee may accept by signing the deed creating the trust or by any other act or conduct showing acceptance. Once he has accepted the trust, he cannot renounce it unless he has the power

61. Section 63 of the Indian Trusts Act 1882.
62. Section 64 of the Indian Trusts Act 1882.

in the instrument of trust or else with the permission of the court or the beneficiaries. A trustee may disclaim the trust within reasonable time. If one of many trustees disclaims the trust, the trust property vests in other trustees.

VII. Powers, Duties, Functions, and Disabilities of Trustees

73. A trustee has all the powers given to him by the Indian Trusts Act 1882 and by the instrument creating the trust. In addition he has the power to do all acts that are reasonable and proper for the realization, protection, or benefit of the trust property and for the protection or support of a beneficiary who is not competent to contract. He has discretion as to time for effecting sale of trust property or investment of trust money.

The trustee is bound to fulfil the purpose of the trust, to obey the author's legal directions. All beneficiaries, if competent to contract, can modify directions.

A trustee must act in good faith and exercise reasonable standard of care while performing his functions as a trustee, the standard being that which a man of ordinary prudence would exercise while dealing with such property. If he does not do so, he will be personally responsible for loss, destruction, or deterioration of the trust property.

Along with his general duty he has certain mandatory statutory duties as provided in the Act, such as promptly invest money, collect debts as they fall due, maintain and defend all suits, and take steps for preservation of trust property and protection of title, and so on. He is required to invest trust money in specified safe securities and has power to vary the investments from time to time. He must keep clear and accurate accounts of the trust property. He must furnish full and accurate information about the trust property when requested by the beneficiary.

A trustee may exercise all powers and do all reasonable and proper acts for the realization or protection of the trust property and object of the trust. Though a trustee is not eligible for remuneration, he has a right to be reimbursed and indemnified for all expenses and liabilities that he may incur by bona fide acts carried out on behalf of the trust.

A trustee cannot use the trust property for his own benefit or for any purpose unconnected with the trust. He cannot buy trust property or the beneficiary's interest. He cannot mix trust funds with his own. He cannot set up any title adverse to the beneficiary. He cannot delegate his office or his duties to his co-trustee or to strangers, unless the instrument of trust provides or the beneficiaries consent. He can of course delegate in the regular course of business or appoint another person to do any act of a ministerial nature not involving discretion.

If the trustee commits breach of trust, he is liable to make good the loss sustained by the trust property or by the beneficiary. As a general rule, a trustee is liable only for breach of trust committed by him, and not for any committed by his co-trustee. But he is bound to take proper steps to protect the beneficiary's interest when he becomes aware of any breach of trust committed by any co-trustee.

VIII. Beneficiary

74. The person for whose benefit the confidence is reposed by the author and accepted by a trustee is called the beneficiary. Every person capable of holding property may be a beneficiary. A corporation or a juristic person can also be a beneficiary.

A beneficiary is free to renounce his interest in the benefit. The beneficiary has the right (i) to have the intention of the author of the trust specifically executed to the extent of the beneficiary's interest; (ii) to have the intention of the author of the trust specifically executed; (iii) to require the trustee to transfer the trust property to him or them, or to such person as he or they may direct, this right to be exercised by all beneficiaries together; (iv) to transfer the beneficial interest; (v) to take accounts of trust property; (vi) to compel the trustee to perform any act of duty.

IX. Relationships Resembling Trusts

75. Chapter IX of the Indian Trusts Act deals with certain obligations in the nature of trusts. These are what English law terms as constructive trusts. Relationships of this nature arise by operation of law. These are resulting and non-resulting trusts. Some of these are as follows:

(i) If the trust is incapable of being executed, or the trust is completely executed without exhausting the trust property, the trustee must hold the property for the benefit of the author or his legal representatives.

(ii) If the owner of a property transfers it for an illegal purpose to a purchaser who is not as guilty, such purchaser holds the property for the benefit of the transferor.

(iii) Where property is transferred under a contract liable to rescission or induced by fraud or mistake, the transferee must hold the property for the benefit of the transferor. A person who gains an advantage by exercising undue influence to the prejudice of a person must hold the advantage for the benefit of the person whose interests have been prejudiced.

(iv) If a transferee is aware that the property is affected by an existing contract of another person that can be specifically enforced, the former holds the property for the benefit of the latter.

(v) If a trustee uses his position to obtain a personal advantage by availing himself of his character, or makes dealings in situations in which his own interest are adverse to that of a beneficiary, he must hold the benefit in trust for the beneficiaries. The same principle applies to executors, agents, partners, directors of companies, legal advisers, or any person bound in a fiduciary character to protect interests of another person.

X. Trusts and Contracts

76. A trust is an exception to the settled principle of privity of contract. This exception of trust as a promise has been applied to a promise to pay money or to transfer property, but is confined within narrow limits.[63] Another exception to the privity principle is contracts for settlement or marriage and family arrangements. The Specific Relief Act 1963 enables specific performance of such contracts in a suit of any person, though not a party, who is beneficially entitled under such settlement or arrangement. Thus, a son of a married woman can enforce any property settlement that might have been made between his mother and father-in-law.

As a statutory rule, specific performance of a contract may be enforced when the interest in question is in the nature of a trust.[64]

§8. Good Faith and Fair Dealing

77. Indian law follows the common law and imposes no obligation of good faith in the negotiation process or during performance or enforcement of the contract.

It does not impose on parties the obligation to negotiate in good faith. The rules of formation gives parties ample freedom. Each party is free to withdraw before the final contract is concluded. The parties will make demands and counter-demands, withdraw demands, and have lengthy negotiations. The offeror is entitled to withdraw his offer at any time, even where he has promised to keep it open for some time or where he has promised not to revoke it.[65] He will be bound only where the promise to keep an offer open is supported by consideration. Each party also bears his own expenses for the process of preparing for the contract and for negotiations. It has not yet been decided whether an obligation will be enforced that binds its promisor to negotiate with other party only or not to negotiate with any other person. Parties can always agree that preparatory expenses incurred by the party for the purposes of making the contract or for negotiations shall be reimbursed by the party that withdraws from or fails to complete negotiations.

Nor does the law impose any obligation to disclose information had by a party that might affect negotiations or the decision to contract. Parties negotiating with each other are adversaries, and negotiate 'at an arms' length'. Each party acts at his own risk. Each is expected to seek his own advice and inform himself about facts affecting the contract and take care of his own interests. None is bound to disclose any facts to the other during negotiations, except in those situations in which there exists a duty to speak,[66] for example, where the parties stand in fiduciary relationship.

Parties must perform their contractual obligations strictly as agreed, unless performance is waived by the promisee. The right of a party not to consent to an

63. *Inuganti Kasturamma v. Chelikani Venkatasurayya Garu* AIR 1916 Mad 605.
64. Section 11 of the Specific Relief Act 1963.
65. See para. 119 *infra*.
66. See para. 244 *infra*.

assignment or give any approval under the contract is unrestricted. The right of terminating the contract is also unrestricted, so long as the termination is effected in the manner and according to the procedure provided in the contract.

Good faith and fairness in dealing can be a relevant factor in the exercise of discretion by courts while granting remedies in the nature of specific relief, such as specific performance,[67] injunction, rescission, rectification, or cancellation.

§9. Style of Drafting

78. The interpretation of documents follows the principles derived from the English law. They are close to the rules of interpretation of statutes. It is, therefore, obvious that the style of drafting, especially in English, closely follows the style of legislative drafting.

Contracts may be drafted in the local language known to both parties. Drafting in Indian languages would be informal. A term 'The Vendor hereby transfers to the Purchaser absolutely the said property, and has handed over possession of the said property to the Purchaser', might be written in local language (translated into English) as 'I have given to you my land, and you can enjoy it forever'. Where the parties intend to register the document, they will have to draft it in the language recognized for the purposes of registration in the state in which they register it.

Commercial contracts drafted with assistance of lawyers will be very comprehensive, dealing with every foreseeable point. It is not unusual to come across drafts dealing with essential points, leaving terms to be implied by law. Parties may not always seek advice of lawyers before making their contracts. Drafts made by contracting parties without a lawyer's assistance will cover essential points only.

The degree of formality with which the contract is drafted will affect the manner in which it is interpreted. This is also expressly recognized in section 92 of the Indian Evidence Act, which first states that no oral agreement can be admitted to contradict, vary, add to, or subtract from the terms of a written contract and then makes an exception allowing proof of any separate oral agreement as to any matter on which a document is silent and that is not inconsistent with its terms. In considering whether to allow such proof, the court will consider the degree of formality of the document.

With the growing number of contracts involving dealings with parties in foreign countries, the styles of drafting and of interpretation in other jurisdictions are bound to affect contracting.

67. See paras 491–493 *infra*.

§10. SOURCES OF THE LAW OF CONTRACTS

I. Main Divisions of Law in India: Main Codes and Enactments

A. *Constitution*

79. India has a written Constitution. Its Constitution establishes and describes the structure and composition of the basic organs of government and administration, their powers and function, their inter-relationship, the relationship of the organs and the people.

The three basic organs are the Legislature, the Executive, and the Judiciary. The Constitution guarantees to people certain Fundamental Rights, which the State cannot take away by legislation or by executive action. The judiciary protects these rights. Laws made by the Legislature are thus subject to judicial review.

The Constitution of India is the source of all laws. India has a federal structure with unitary features and is a Union of states. The Constitution specifies and delimits the legislative and executive powers of the Centre and the states.

B. *Legislation*

80. Legislation is the primary source of law. Much of English common law was codified during the British rule. The Indian Contract Act 1872, the Indian Evidence Act 1872, and the Indian Penal Code of 1860 are examples of legislation based on common law in force in England at that time. India has many statutes. Some critics say they are too many. A visit to the official website[68] discloses that more than 1,100 Acts are in force in India. Yet some areas of law are uncodified and follow common law principles adopted from time to time by Indian courts or principles developed by courts themselves. The law of torts, for example, remains primarily uncodified.

The Parliament for the whole of India, and the state legislatures for their respective territories, enact legislation called Acts. An Act is made when the Bill for its enactment is passed by simple majority in both Houses of Parliament, the *Lok Sabha*, or the House of the People, and the *Rajya Sabha*, the Council of states, and in case of disagreement between the two, in a joint sitting of both the Houses. Some laws, especially those amending the Constitution, require a special majority. Some laws affecting states falling within the legislative competence of Parliament might require consent of states. It is also possible for the Parliament to make a law falling exclusively within the domain of states, on request made by two or more states. Only the Parliament has the power to make laws with extraterritorial operation; for implementing any treaty, agreement, or convention with any other country; or for any decision made at any international conference. A list of all Acts in force in India is available at the site <http://indiacode.nic.in/>.

Some legislation is a comprehensive dealing about a subject, and is termed a Code. Examples are the Civil Procedure Code, the Indian Penal Code, and the

68. <http://indiacode.nic.in/> visited 15 Aug. 2015.

Criminal Procedure Code. States have Land Revenue Codes dealing with land revenue. Acts are amended by Amending Acts, which are made in the same manner as any Act.

Some states have two Houses of legislature. A state legislation must be passed by the Lower House (of directly elected representatives) only. The Upper House, if the state has one, has only a recommendatory role.

81. When neither of the Houses of the legislature is in session, the President of India and the Governor of the state, as the case may be, can make 'Ordinances', which have the same force as an Act. These must be ratified by the legislature within six months, else they lapse.

82. The law of any state will start with the name of the state, for example, the Maharashtra Rent Control Act in the state of Maharashtra. Laws made by Parliament do not have any such indication. The word 'Indian' associated with many enactments, including the Indian Contract Act, indicates that the law was made by the British for their Indian colony at that time. The subject matter of the Act is often found within its name. An Act is divided into sections and arranged in chapters.

83. An Act comes into force after notice has been published in the Official Gazette,[69] which happens after it is passed by the relevant Houses and signed by the President or the Governor. The Act itself may provide that it can come into force at a later date. There are instances of Acts for which notice has been published but that have not been brought into force for some time. An Act will extend to the whole territory of India or the state, but might be made applicable only to specified persons, areas, localities, and so on, as may be indicated in the Act.

C. *Subordinate Legislation*

84. Apart from Acts and Codes, a lawyer will have to refer to Rules, Regulations, or other subordinate legislation. There is a vast body of laws in the form of rules, regulations, and bye-laws made by Central or state governments and local governments and local authorities such as municipal corporations, municipalities, *gram panchayats* (local bodies at village level). This is made under authority conferred or delegated either by Parliament or state legislatures concerned in Acts made by them, hence the term 'delegated legislation', which is defined as 'that which proceeds from any authority other than the sovereign power and is, therefore, dependent for its continued existence and validity on some superior or supreme authority'.[70]

The Legislature determines and chooses the legislative policy and formally enacts that policy into a binding rule of conduct. In India, it enjoys a wide power of delegation. After laying down the legislative policy, it will confer on an administrative agency the execution of the policy and leave it to the agency to work out the details

69. < http://egazette.nic.in/> visited 15 Aug. 2015.

70. Salmond, *Jurisprudence* 116 (12th edn, Sweet & Maxwell 1996).

within the boundaries of the policy. The delegation is to 'fill up the details'. A statute can be struck down on the ground of 'excessive delegation'.

The Act of the Legislature will state the powers given to that agency, often the Central government or the state government or some officer of authority of the government, to make 'Rules' for purposes and topics enumerated in the Act. The Rules will give the details, such as the procedures, the fees, and so on.

Other subordinate legislations come under various names: order, regulation, directions, schemes, circulars, bye-laws, and so on. These will be subordinate to rules. Bye-laws are usually intended to govern the internal working of autonomous institutions. Corporate bodies such as a university are authorized to make statutes, ordinances, regulations; this classification arises because of the different authorities of the universities from which they originate.

The power to make subordinate legislation is derived from the enabling Act. The delegate on whom such a power is conferred has to act within the limits of authority conferred by the Act and within the policy of the Act. Subordinate legislation is open to scrutiny by the courts and can be invalidated on two grounds: (i) it violates the Constitution; (ii) it violates the enabling Act.

Subordinate legislation has come to stay for various reasons: (i) pressure on parliamentary time; (ii) fill details, especially requiring knowledge of matters of technical, local, or specialized nature; (iii) need for flexibility – rules can be amended easily; and (iv) growth of independent regulatory authorities and administrative agencies, which need to regulate and monitor their activities.[71]

D. Precedents

85. Judicial precedent is an important source of Indian law. A precedent means a previous instance or case that is or may be taken as an example or rule for subsequent cases. The doctrine of precedent was recognized in the ancient Hindu law. Precedent is a necessary source of law, especially in cases in which legislation needs interpretation or there is no statute dealing with the case before a court.

The doctrine of stare decisis applies in India. Therefore, judicial decisions have a binding force for the future.

When the High Court or the Supreme Court has decided a case, the decision has a two-fold effect. The order is binding on the parties. The principle of decision is binding as precedent and has the force of law. This principle of law formulated by the judge for deciding the problems before him is the *ratio decidendi*, and is binding on lower courts. If the court is divided, the majority judgment is the precedent. Other statements made by the judge 'by the way', which are not essential for the decision, are termed obiter dicta. They have persuasive value. But obiter dicta of the Supreme Court are binding.[72] Decisions essentially on questions of fact cannot be cited as precedent.[73]

71. S.P. Sathe, *Administrative Law* (7th edn, Lexis Nexis 2004), Chs 2 and 3.
72. *Commissioner of Income-Tax v. Vazir Sultan and Sons* AIR 1959 SC 814.
73. *Prakash Chandra Pathak v. State of UP* AIR 1960 SC 195.

Article 141 of the Constitution provides that the law declared by the Supreme Court shall be binding on all courts within the territory of India. The Supreme Court is free to depart from its own decision.[74]

The High Courts in India are bound by the law declared by the Supreme Court. The decisions of a High Court are binding on all the courts subordinate to it. Precedent value of judgments of High Courts is not derived from any enactment. Judgment of one High Court is not binding on other High Courts, but has persuasive value. Often, decisions of High Courts conflict with each other, until the Supreme Court has determined the question.

To promote certainty and consistency in development of law, a rule is followed that the statement of law by a division bench is considered binding on a division bench of equal or smaller number of judges. If a bench finds that a decision of a coordinate bench requires reconsideration, the case is referred to a larger bench for judgment. If judgments of a court cannot be reconciled, the one given by a larger bench is binding.

86. In 1958, the Law Commission of India considered whether the doctrine of precedent should continue in India and recommended that it should on the grounds that it makes for uniformity and certainty in administration of law, promotes convenience, and avoids delays.

The doctrine of precedent is closely linked with a sound reporting system.[75] Publication of decisions is necessary for the theory of precedent to operate.

E. Customs and Usages

87. Custom is any rule that, having been continuously and uniformly observed for a long time, has obtained the force of law in any local area, tribe, community, group, or family.

It may be general and, therefore, applicable to all. It may be special, that is, of a family, locality.

Custom having force of law is of two kinds – legal and conventional. The legal authority of a legal custom is absolute. The rule of pre-emption is a legal custom. It may be local – existing in a particular locality. It may be general – prevailing throughout the territory of the state.

Conventional custom is one whose authority is conditional on its acceptance and incorporation in agreements between parties to be bound by it. It is an established rule concerning trade, contract, and so on. Such incorporation may be express, but more often, customs will get incorporated as terms of a contract by implication.

88. A custom obtains the force of law when a particular class of people has been consistently adhering to it for a fairly long period of time. To have the force of law, it must (i) be ancient; (ii) be continuous; (iii) be reasonable; (iv) not be immoral or

---

74. *Bengal Immunity Co Ltd v. State of Bihar* AIR 1955 SC 661.

75. See para. 97 *infra*.

against public policy; (v) not be contrary to justice, equity, and good conscience; and (vi) not be contrary to express provision of law.

The English rule that a custom should be of immemorial usage, traced back to a period beyond the memory of man, is not applied in India. The Supreme Court of India has held that a custom derives its force from the fact that by long usage it has obtained the force of law. All that is necessary to prove is that the usage has been acted on in practice for such a long period and with such invariability as to show that it has, by common consent, become established governing rule of a particular locality.[76] Instances of exercise or recognition of custom within the previous twenty or forty years have been recognized for establishing custom.

89. A custom can be proved by (i) opinions of persons likely to know of its existence of having special means of knowledge; (ii) by a transaction by which it was claimed, modified, recognized, asserted, or denied; and (iii) by particular instances when it was claimed, recognized, or exercised.

Much of customary law has acquired the force of precedent by recognition in judgments of Courts.

90. Usage is a habitual practice, not yet a source of law. It can add terms to a contract. It can also be excluded by contract. A usage is a particular course of dealing or conduct generally adopted by persons engaged in a particular business. It is a particular course of dealing or conduct that is so well known that when persons make contracts, they must have intended to follow that course of dealing or conduct. When parties contract with reference to a usage, it must be proved, and then it is part of the contract. The usage adds to the express terms of the contract.

II. Sources of the Law of Contracts

A. Constitution

91. The Constitution recognizes powers of the Union and states to carry on trade and to contract. The Union and the states can carry on any trade or business and can acquire, hold, and dispose of property and can make contracts for any purpose. Article 299 provides for the form in which contracts can be made by Union and state governments.[77]

B. Acts

92. The law of contract is mainly governed by the provisions of the Indian Contract Act 1872. Sections 1–75 of this Act state the general principles applicable to all contracts. The Act also deals in separate chapters about special contracts of indemnity and guarantee, bailment, pledge, and agency.

---

76. *Gokal Chand v. Parvin Kumari* AIR 1952 SC 231.

77. See paras 169, 770–773 *infra*.

Separate laws have been enacted from time to time concerning special contracts. Some of these are as follows:

(i) Carriage by Air Act 1972.
(ii) Indian Carriage of Goods by Sea Act 1925.
(iii) Carriage by Road Act 2007.
(iv) Consumer Protection Act 1986.
(v) Forward Contracts (Regulation) Act 1952.
(vi) Indian Partnership Act 1932.
(vii) Information Technology Act 2000.
(viii) Marine Insurance Act 1963.
(ix) Negotiable Instruments Act 1882.
(x) Powers-of-Attorney Act 1882.
(xi) Public Liability Insurance Act 1991.
(xii) Sale of Goods Act 1930.
(xiii) Transfer of Property Act 1882.

Many other laws also deal with contractual aspects of transactions of their subject matter. For example, Insurance Act 1938 and Banking Regulation Act 1949 contain some provisions affecting insurance and banking contracts, respectively.

C. *Judgments*

93. Principles of contract law have developed from judgments of the High Courts, the Supreme Court, and the Privy Council, when it heard appeals from India.

English common law as expounded in judgments of English courts is the primary source of the principles enunciated in the Indian Contract Act and other special laws relating to contracts. It might seem natural that Indian courts take guidance from English Law where no statutory provision to the contrary is in existence. However, principles of English Law will not be called to aid when the statutory provision is clear, unless the statute is such that it cannot be understood without the aid of English Law; or where any matter cannot be brought within the provisions of the Contract Act, in which case the courts may look at the English law for the purposes of interpretation.

Although the provisions of the Indian Contract Act are exhaustive, if there are cases it does not provide for, they will be decided on the principles of justice, equity, and good conscience. The Indian legal system has derived its own jurisprudence and the large part of its law. English judgments or any foreign judgment will have persuasive value.

A lawyer will naturally refer to principles of English law where there is no provision in an Indian statute or case law in respect of the case in hand.

94. The Supreme Court of India[78] and the High Courts have been required to decide cases on matters not dealt with by express provisions of statutes relating to contracts. They have been required to interpret provisions of these statutes and derive a new principle to decide a case when the situation is not covered by the statute. In such events, courts have reviewed doctrines of common law and often modified them for the Indian situation, for example, the non-application to postal rule in contracts made over the telephone, effect of a minor's agreement, the doctrine of privity, maintenance and champerty, enforcement of unlawful agreement, validity of restraint on trade during subsistence of the contract, circumstances in which time is of the essence of contract, and applicability of the doctrine of frustration in India.

Often, courts will also consider judgments in foreign jurisdiction for guidance, even in cases not involving foreign law.

D. Customs and Usages

95. The provisions of the Indian Contract Act do not affect customs and usages.[79] Hence, a trade usage in conflict with the Act can be pleaded. Where a contract is in writing, oral evidence can be given to prove any usage or custom by which incidents not expressly mentioned in the contract are usually annexed to contracts of that description, provided that the annexing of such incident would not be repugnant to, or inconsistent with, the express terms of the contract.[80]

E. Justice, Equity, and Good Conscience

96. Courts must observe at trial the law contained in Acts of Parliament and Rules and in the absence of such Acts and Rules, usage, and in the absence of specific law and usage, according to principles of justice, equity, and good conscience.[81] Earlier, this meant applying English law, but such narrow view is no longer taken.

III. Finding the Law

97. Acts and Rules are published in the *Official Gazette*,[82] which is also available on subscription. These are also available on the official website, and many other websites. Some manuals give all Acts with commentary according to sections. The *All India Reporter* (AIR) *Manual* and the *Madras Law Journal* (MLJ) *Manual* are examples. The commentary consists of principles and interpretation of the text of

78. Earlier, the Privy Council, then the Federal Court.
79. As s. 1 of the Act is interpreted by the Privy Council in *Irrawaddy Flotilla Company v. Bugwandas* (1891) 18 IA 121.
80. Indian Evidence Act, s. 92(5).
81. *Gurunath v. Kamalabai* AIR 1955 SC 206; *Harinagar Sugar Mills Ltd v. Shyam Sundar Jhunjhunwala* AIR 1961 SC 1669.
82. <http://egazette.nic.in/> visited 15 Aug. 2015.

the Act and citation of case law. Text of Acts and Rules are also available in books dealing with the subject.

Judgments of Supreme Court and High Courts are published under authority of these Courts themselves as, respectively, the Supreme Court Reports (SCR)[83] and the Indian Law Reports (ILR). These are the official reports. Private reports are abundantly available. Judgments of Privy Council in cases from India have been reported in series called Moore's Indian Appeals (MIA), and Indian Appeals (IA). The latter is often referred to in this monograph.

The Law Reports Act 1875 provides that no court shall be bound to hear cited or receive as authority any report of any case other than a report published under the authority of the government. This leaves it to the option of the courts to hear cited any unofficial report.

The one used most commonly – AIR – cited in this monograph, publishes judgments of all High Courts and the Supreme Court (earlier the Privy Council) since 1914. The MLJ, *Allahabad Law Journal*, *Maharashtra Law Journal*, and other similar reports publish the judgments of the Madras, Allahabad, Bombay, or other High Courts, respectively, and appeals to the Supreme from these courts. Some journals are specialized and restricted to a particular area of law, for example, *Corporate Law Reports*, *Banking Law Journal*, *Accident Claims Journal*, *Divorce and Matrimonial Cases*, *Patent and Trade Mark Cases*, *Labour Law Journal*, and *Taxation Law Reports*. Each law report has its own style of citation. Many reports are now available in electronic form or off the Internet.

Private law reports are too many and compete with each other. The quantity of cases reported in these is much in excess of requirements. Often cases are reported despite there being no principle involved, for example, those restricted to facts and those in interlocutory matters. They provide quick reporting. Official reports are very expensive and very slow.

Fortunately with the advent of the Internet, recent judgments are also available on official websites of the courts at <http://judis.nic.in>.

One reaches the appropriate report or case from its citation given in books. More often, general digests and manuals or those compiled for particular subjects are useful in locating cases. AIR's digests and manuals, annual and quinquennial digests published by Supreme Court Cases (SCC) and so on, are useful. Some websites, particularly of report publishers, also facilitate searching.

98. Unlike many continental legal systems, articles in journals and juristic writings are rarely referred in argument or in decisions of courts. Reference to books or treatises is more common.

---

83. <http://supremecourtofindia.nic.in/scr.htm> Supreme Court Reports visited 15 Aug. 2015.

Part I. General Principles of the Law of Contract

Chapter 1. Formation

§1. Agreement and Quid Pro Quo (Reciprocity)

I. Offer and Acceptance

99. The Indian Contract Act 1872 analyses a contract as an agreement enforceable by law; an agreement as a promise or set of reciprocal promises, and a promise as an accepted proposal.[84] This traditional analysis of the agreement process in two distinct steps of offer (referred to in the Indian Contract Act as a proposal) and acceptance may not be appropriate in all situations, but it is a useful method to ascertain whether a contract has in fact been concluded.

The Act provides that proposal and acceptance must be communicated.[85] Because contractual liability requires proof of assent of parties, such a rule ensures that assent is manifested in some way expressly – by words or by conduct. However, the offeror may waive communication of acceptance.[86]

In Indian law, a mere proposal does not entail legal consequences, and the offeror is not bound to keep his proposal open,[87] unless the promise to keep his proposal open is supported by consideration.

A. *The Objective Test of Intention*

100. Proposal or acceptance or its revocation is made by any act or omission of the party proposing, accepting, or revoking, by which he intends to communicate it, or which has the effect of communicating it.[88] The test of the person's intention in

84. Section 2 of the Indian Contract Act.
85. See paras 102–103 *infra* – communication of offer; paras 108–113 *infra* – communication of acceptance.
86. See para. 112 *infra*.
87. *Visweswaradas Gokuldas v. B K Narayan Singh* AIR 1969 SC 1157.
88. Section 3 of the Indian Contract Act.

making a proposal or an acceptance is an objective one, that is, as it would be reasonably construed by a person in the position of the person to whom it is addressed.

In an electronic transaction, it becomes necessary to attribute to a person the data messages expressing proposal and acceptances generated solely by computers without human intervention. An electronic message sent by an information system programmed by or on behalf of the originator (one who sends, generates, stores, or transmits any electronic message) to operate automatically shall be attributed to the originator.[89] Such attribution procedures also give to a receiving party the benefit of presumption that the message came from the sender.

B. The Offer or Proposal

101. A person is said to have made a proposal (as an offer is called under the Indian Contract Act) when he signifies to another his willingness to do or to abstain from doing anything, with a view to obtaining the assent of that other to such act or abstinence.[90] Thus, a proposal is an offer to be bound by a promise on receiving the assent from the offeree. It must, therefore, be sufficiently definite to conclude the contract by mere acceptance. For the same reason, the terms of the intended or proposed agreement must be indicated with sufficient certainty in the proposal itself.

It may be express or implied.[91] A proposal made 'subject to contract' indicates not to be bound in contract unless a formal document has been executed. Such a proposal might not create a contract on mere acceptance.

1. Communication of Offer

102. A proposal and acceptance, like any other expression of will or intention, may be communicated by any means, including by data messages in electronic form. The Information Technology Act now makes express provision that proposals, acceptances and their revocation can be expressed by means of electronic record.[92] Its communication is complete when it comes to the knowledge of the offeree.[93]

An acceptance without knowledge of the proposal does not result into a contract. Consequently, cross-offers do not make a contract, even though their terms are identical.

A proposal may be addressed to an individual, to a specified group of persons, or to the world at large. The person to whom the proposal has been made can accept it.

---

89. The Information Technology Act 2000, s. 11(c).
90. Section 2 cl(a) of the Indian Contract Act.
91. Section 9 of the Indian Contract Act.
92. Section 10A inserted in the Information Technology Act 2000 by the Information Technology (Amendment) Act 2008.
93. Section 4 of the Indian Contract Act.

2. Communication of Electronic Messages

103. The Information Technology Act 2000 provides that unless otherwise agreed, the despatch of an electronic record occurs when it enters a computer resource outside the control of the originator.[94]

If the addressee has designated a computer resource for receiving an electronic record (for instance, in the case in which the proposal expressly specifies the address to which acceptance should be sent), and it is sent to such resource, it will be considered as received when the electronic record enters the designated computer resource.[95] If instead, it is sent to a computer resource that is not the designated computer resource, the record is considered as received when it is retrieved by the addressee.[96] If the addressee has not designated a computer resource along with specified timings, the record is received when it enters the computer resource of the addressee.[97]

The sender of the electronic record is entitled to stipulate that the record sent shall be binding only on receipt of acknowledgment.[98]

3. Exclusion Clauses and Special Terms

104. Special terms in the proposal that seek to exclude or restrict liability or impose other onerous obligations on the other party must be communicated effectively. Whether this is done would depend on (i) nature of the document; that is, is it known or expected to contain contractual conditions; (ii) adequate notice of such terms to the other party; and (iii) time at which such terms are brought to his notice, that is, before or at the time the contract is made. Conditions of carriage placed on a website and referred in an e-ticket will bind passengers.[99] If special terms were incorporated during the previous course of dealings between the parties, it would be relevant.

4. Invitation to Offer, Statements of Intention, and Invitations to Treat

105. A proposal differs from statements of intention, invitations to make offers, or invitations to do business, for example, stating price in response to requests or enquiries, quotations of price, advertisement of goods in newspapers, or displays at shop windows.

The distinction between proposal and such a statement depends on the intention of the person making it; it is a proposal if he intends that he would be bound no

94. The Information Technology Act 2000, s. 13(1).
95. *Ibid.*, s. 13(2)(a)(i).
96. *Ibid.*, s. 13(2)(a)(ii).
97. *Ibid.*, s. 13(2)(b).
98. *Ibid.*, s. 12.
99. *InterGlobe Aviation Ltd v. N Satchinand* (2011) 7 SCC 463.

sooner than the offeree signifies his assent to it and nothing more. Similarly, an auctioneer's request for bids is not a proposal, but an invitation to the customers to bid. An invitation for tenders for the supply of goods or for execution of works is also not a proposal.

C. The Acceptance

106. When the person to whom the proposal is made signifies his assent thereto, the proposal is said to be accepted.[100] The assent may be by express words or by positive conduct. It may also be implied. The offeree cannot be said to have accepted where he seeks clarifications about the proposal or merely acknowledges receipt of the proposal.

There cannot be an acceptance of a proposal that has not come to the knowledge of the offeree.

A proposal may be accepted by the person to whom it is made. Where a person accepts on behalf of a legal person, he must have authority for the purpose.

1. Absolute and Unqualified

107. The acceptance must be absolute, unqualified, and without conditions. It must extend to all the terms of a proposal. This does not mean that the proposal and acceptance must match completely. Where the acceptor accepts the proposal unconditionally, the contract is made even if some directions or requests accompany it.[101] In order to decide whether there is an absolute and unqualified agreement between the parties to a contract, the entire negotiations and correspondence will be considered.[102]

An acceptance with a condition or qualification is a counter-proposal,[103] which when accepted would create a binding contract.

A conditional or qualified acceptance revokes the original proposal, and withdrawing the conditional acceptance cannot revive the contract on the terms originally proposed.

2. Communication of Acceptance

108. An acceptance must be communicated to the offeror. Mere mental resolve, writing acceptance on a piece of paper and keeping it, interdepartmental communication proposing acceptance, or resolution of acceptance by a company, would not result into a contract until these are communicated to the offeror.

---

100. Section 2 cl(b) of the Indian Contract Act.
101. *D Wren International Ltd v. Engineers India Ltd* AIR 1996 Cal 424.
102. *Dhulipudi Namayya v. Union of India* AIR 1958 AP 533.
103. See para. 120(v) *infra*.

An acceptance may be communicated by any act or omission by which the offeree intends to communicate or has the effect of communicating it. It may be express or implied.

109. Where the acceptor uses an instantaneous mode of communication, such as telephone or telex, the contract is made as in the case of parties in the presence of each other, when the acceptance reaches the offeror.[104]

Where the acceptance is sent by post or telegraph, its communication is complete as against the offeror when it is put into a course of transmission to him so as to be out of the reach of the acceptor, and as against the acceptor, when it reaches the offeror.[105] Where the acceptance is sent by post, the acceptance binds the offeror even though it never reaches him.

There is, therefore, a certain time, while the acceptance is on its way, when the offeree is bound while the sender is not. This rule is justified on the ground that the offeror can avoid this risk and protect himself by requiring that the acceptance must reach him.

110. To the extent the provision that the acceptance is complete when the letter is posted, this follows the rule of English law. However, it departs from the English law to the extent that the acceptance is binding only on the offeror when the letter is posted and on the acceptor only after the letter has reached the offeror. During the time it is in transit, it is binding only on one of the parties, that is, the offeror, and the acceptor is able to revoke it by a faster means of communication.[106] The postal rule has not been applied to communication by e-mail or fax.[107]

111. The postal rule can be excluded by the terms of the proposal. If the offeror requires that the acceptance shall be notified to him, the acceptance will be effective only when it reaches the offeror.

3. Communication of Acceptance Not Necessary

112. Because the general rule that acceptance must be communicated to the offeror is for the benefit of the offeror, the offeror may waive this requirement, expressly or impliedly. In such cases, acceptance may be effective even before it comes to the notice of the offeror.

Performance of a condition of the proposal would also amount to acceptance.[108] If a proposal takes the form of a promise in return for an act, the performance of that act is in itself an assent.

---

104. *Bhagwandas Goverdhandas Kedia v. Girdharlal Parshottamdas* AIR 1966 SC 543 (telephone); *Triveni Oil Field Service Ltd v. Oil and Natural Gas Commission* AIR 2006 Del 331 (telex).
105. Section 4 of the Indian Contract Act.
106. Section 5 of the Indian Contract Act.
107. *Triveni Oil Field Service Ltd v. Oil and Natural Gas Commission* AIR 2006 Del 331 (fax); *P R Transport Agency v. Union of India,* AIR 2006 All 23 (e-mail).
108. Section 8 of the Indian Contract Act.

4. Silence as Acceptance

113. An offeree is under no duty to reply to the proposal, and hence acceptance cannot be inferred from inaction of the offeree. As a general rule, a proposal is not accepted by mere silence of the offeree.

Acceptance can be inferred from silence only under exceptional circumstances. Mere silence is not acceptance, but when taken together with certain facts, may constitute acceptance. There is acceptance if there has been a course of dealings between the parties, for example, where previous offers to buy goods have been accepted as a matter of course by despatch of the goods. The conduct of using a vessel even after its charter party was over, indicated acceptance of the arbitration clause in the charter party.[109] A debtor's proposal to give additional security was held accepted by the creditor's forbearance to sue for that debt. Silence may also constitute acceptance by custom of trade or business in question.

5. Manner of Acceptance

114. The offeror may prescribe the manner of acceptance,[110] that is, that the acceptance must be sent to a particular place or by post or any particular mode.

If the acceptor does not send the acceptance in the manner prescribed by the offeror, the acceptance is nevertheless valid unless the offeror intimates to the acceptor that he does not 'accept the acceptance'. The burden then lies on the offeror to notify the acceptor that such an acceptance in insufficient; if he fails to insist on an acceptance such as he required, he is bound by the acceptance.

115. A person sending a message by electronic record may require the addressee that its receipt be acknowledged in a particular form or by a particular method, else the acknowledgment may be given by any communication or by conduct.[111]

Such sender (originator) of the electronic record can exclude liability for the message by stipulating that this record will not be binding on him unless acknowledgment is received. Then, if acknowledgment is not received, the 'electronic record shall be deemed to have never been sent by the originator'.[112]

If the originator stipulated for an acknowledgment, but has not stipulated that the electronic record shall be binding only on receipt of acknowledgment, and acknowledgment has not been received within time specified or agreed, or within reasonable time (if no time is specified), and the addressee has not sent any acknowledgment, the originator must give notice to the addressee specifying a time for receipt of acknowledgment, and if it is still not received, 'treat the electronic record as though it has never been sent'.[113]

109. *Bharat Petroleum Corpn Ltd v. Great Eastern Shipping Co Ltd* AIR 2008 SC 357.
110. Section 7 of the Indian Contract Act.
111. The Information Technology Act 2000, s. 12(1).
112. *Ibid.*, s. 12(2).
113. *Ibid.*, s. 12(3).

Therefore, where the sender (originator) of electronic record has stipulated for an acknowledgment, failure to give acknowledgment by the addressee may absolve the sender (originator) of liability for the electronic record sent. Whether or not sending that acknowledgement amounted to accepting the proposal is not dealt with by these provisions, but by the substantive law of contract; and matters of establishing despatch, receipt, and acknowledgments by the law of evidence.

D. Place of Contract

116. In any proceedings involving a contract, it may become necessary to locate a contract for the purposes of determining a court's jurisdiction or for application of laws such as those relating to taxes or duties.

The Indian Contract Act does not make any provision for determining such place; it is determined by the same rules of communication of acceptance. A contract made by parties in the presence of each other is made at that place. If made on the telephone and telex, and it is suggested even where made by fax or e-mail, it is made at the place where the offeror hears the acceptance.[114] But where the postal rule, as stated above applies, the contract is made at the place where the acceptance is posted and not where it is received by the offeror. This is so even if the acceptance is lost or misplaced and may never reach the offeror.

117. In regard to communication by electronic mode, between the originator, that is, the person sending the electronic record or causing it to be sent, and the addressee, the record is deemed to be despatched at the place where the originator has his place of business, and deemed to have received where the addressee has his place of business.[115] This rule applies wheresoever the computer resource of the party for conducting such transactions is located.[116] If the party has more than one place of business, the principal place of business will be taken into account.[117] If the party does not have a place of business, the usual place of residence of such party will be considered (which for a body corporate shall mean the place where it is registered).[118] These provisions provide a location for the despatch and receipt of the offers or acceptances in the form of electronic record.

E. Revocation of Proposal and Acceptance

118. Both proposal and acceptance can be revoked. Revocation must be communicated. It may be express or implied.

---

114. *Bhagwandas Goverdhandas Kedia v. Girdharlal Parshottamdas* AIR 1966 SC 543 (telephone); *Triveni Oil Field Service Ltd v. Oil and Natural Gas Commission*, AIR 2006 Del 331 (telex); *Quadricon Pvt Ltd v. Bajarang Alloys Ltd*, AIR 2008 Bom 88 (fax); *P R Transport Agency v. Union of India*, AIR 2006 All 23 (e-mail).
115. The Information Technology Act 2000, s. 13(3).
116. *Ibid.*, s. 13(4).
117. *Ibid.*, s. 13(5)(a).
118. *Ibid.*, s. 13(5)(b) and (c).

1. Revocation of Proposal

119. A proposal may be revoked at any time before acceptance, even though the offeror has promised to keep the proposal open for a specified time, unless such promise is supported with consideration.

This rule is peculiar to the legal systems following English common law, and has been strongly criticized. It does not protect an offeree who may have undertaken other engagements or incurred expenditure relying on the continuance of the proposal. This is so even if the offeror should reasonably have expected that the proposal might induce action or forbearance of a substantial character on the part of the offeree; such withdrawal of a proposal before the period has expired does not render the offeror liable in damages.

Hence, a tender submitted in response to an invitation to tender can be withdrawn at any time before its acceptance, and if accepted by post or telegram, till such time the acceptance is posted or handed over for delivery. It can be withdrawn even if the tenderer has agreed to keep it open until a specified date. If the acceptance of a bid or tender is subject to confirmation or approval of a higher officer or authority, the bid or tender can be revoked at any time before the condition is fulfilled, that is, before the confirmation or approval.[119]

120. A proposal is revoked in the following cases:[120]

(i) if the offeror gives such notice, which may be express or implied, that is, by varying the terms of the proposal;
(ii) death or insanity of offeror, if the acceptor has notice of the death or insanity before acceptance;
(iii) if the acceptor fails to accept any condition prescribed in the proposal as precedent to acceptance; or
(iv) if the proposal is not accepted within the time prescribed for its acceptance, or within reasonable time (what is reasonable time being a question of fact and depending on the purpose of the proposal, its subject matter, the method by which the proposal is communicated, or the subsequent conduct of the parties, such as renewals of the offer);
(v) if the offeree seeks to vary the terms of the proposal, when he actually makes a counter-proposal, and cannot later accept change his mind and insist on accepting the original proposal;
(vi) if the offeree clearly and expressly rejects the proposal, indicating his refusal to accept, after which he may not change his mind and accept again, unless the proposal is revived by the offeror.

121. A proposal stands rejected only if the offeree shows a definite indication of an intention to reject. There is no rejection if the offeree merely makes further enquiries about the proposal, or accepts the proposal but offers to enter into further

119. *Haridwar Singh v. Bagun Sumbrui* AIR 1972 SC 1242.
120. Section 6 of the Indian Contract Act.

contract. Seeking clarifications about the proposal is neither acceptance nor a counter-proposal and does not amount to rejection.

122. In order to be effective, the revocation must reach the offeree before he accepts or posts the acceptance, as the case may be.[121] Where a proposal is made to the general public, it is sufficient if the offeror has taken sufficient steps to bring the revocation to the attention of such persons.

2. Revocation of Acceptance

123. Unlike English law, an acceptance can be revoked. It is effective if it reaches the offeror before the acceptance.

F. Implied Terms

124. The parties to a contract may not always state the terms in express words, out of forgetfulness, or because of bad drafting, or they thought the obligation too obvious as to 'go without saying'. They may also do so deliberately, being content to state only the most important terms, at times with an understanding that custom or trade usage, or the practices already established between them would be applicable in any case.

After disputes arise, it may become necessary to imply terms to give business efficacy to contracts and so that the rights under the contract may not be rendered useless. What matters are to be implied is determined with reference to the surrounding circumstances and the parties who made them, or may be imported under trade, mercantile, or local usage.

G. Agreement Subject to Formal Document

125. Sometimes parties may expressly stipulate that their agreement shall not be complete or operative until its terms are reduced into writing or they have executed a formal document.

Whether the terms agreed are then binding without such writing or formal document is a question of interpretation and depends on whether:

(i) the parties regard the proposal and acceptance as sufficient to conclude the contract and intend the document to be a record of this contract; or
(ii) they regard it as incomplete and do not intend it to be legally binding until the terms of the formal document are agreed and the document is duly executed in accordance of the terms of the agreement.

121. Section 5 of the Indian Contract Act.

It must then be found whether the formal document is of such a nature that it was the very condition of the contract or whether it was intended merely to provide evidence of its terms.[122]

II. Intention to Create Legal Relations

126. A proposal binds by mere acceptance, that is, assent of the offeree. It must, therefore, have been made in contemplation of producing legal consequences. This intention may be negatived, expressly, or impliedly by the nature of the agreed promise. Such intention is presumed to exist in commercial transaction and not to exist in agreements to give hospitality or made in the course of family life between members of a family. The test of intention to create legal relations is an objective one, and the promisor who has no intention to create legal relations will be bound if a reasonable person would consider that there was an intention to contract.[123]

III. Consideration

127. The requirement of consideration is not an aspect of formation of contract under the Indian law, but of substantive validity. An agreement without consideration is void, unless it falls within exceptions. In case of such exceptions, it is a valid contract.

A. Consideration Essential under Indian Law

128. Existence of consideration is necessary to render a contract enforceable. The consideration must be lawful.

Existence of consideration is an essential requirement of a valid and enforceable contract.[124] An agreement without consideration, with few exceptions, is void.[125] The person who alleges lack of consideration must prove it.[126] Such consideration, or every part of consideration of a contract must also be lawful.[127]

Consideration does not, however, require an exact element of quid pro quo between the parties. First, because it is immaterial who is benefited by the act done or not done or the promise of the promisee; and more particularly, under the Indian law, consideration need not have moved from the promisee.

---

122. *Harichand Mancharam v. Govind Luxman Gokhale* AIR 1923 PC 47.
123. *Carlill v. Carbolic Smoke Ball Co* [1893] 1 QB 256, [1891–1894] All ER Rep 127.
124. Section 10 of the Indian Contract Act.
125. Section 25 of the Indian Contract Act.
126. *Food Corpn of India v. Surana Commercial Co* (2003) 8 SCC 636; *Ranganayakamma v. K S Prakash* AIR 2009 SC (Supp) 1218.
127. Sections 23 and 24 of the Indian Contract Act.

B. What Is Consideration?

129. When, at the desire of the promisor, the promisee or any other person has done or abstained from doing, or does or abstains from doing, or promises to do or to abstain from doing, something, such act or abstinence or promise is called a consideration for the promise.[128]

A valid consideration for a promise is, therefore: (i) something in the nature of; (ii) an act, an abstinence or promise; (iii) of the promisee or any other person; (iv) done in the past or present or promised for the future; (v) at the desire of the promisor.

1. Benefit or Detriment

130. Consideration for a promise may be a benefit conferred on the promisor, or detriment suffered by the promisee, or both. The benefit may be any right, interest, profit, or benefit given to the promisor at his request; and the detriment suffered by the promisee may be any forbearance, detriment, loss, or responsibility suffered or undertaken by the promisee or any other person at the request of the promisor.[129] The Supreme Court has accepted this benefit-detriment analysis.[130]

Any detriment suffered by the promisee is enough, even where there is no benefit to the promisor. It may benefit the promisor or a third party, or may be of no apparent benefit to anybody and a detriment to a third party.[131]

2. Act, Forbearance, or Promise

131. Giving up, or forbearing to exercise, an actually existing and enforceable right is good consideration, for example, forbearance to sue or compromise of doubtful claims.

3. Past Consideration Is Good

132. The words '*has* done or abstained from doing' in the definition given in the Act provide that an act done by X at Y's request, without any contemporaneous promise from Y, may be a consideration for a subsequent promise from Y to X, for example, services previously rendered at the desire of a promisor, a promissory note executed as security for repayment of a loan already received by the debtor. Old debts form good consideration for mortgage or transfer of property. This is also a departure from the English law.

128. Section 2(d) of the Indian Contract Act.
129. *Currie v. Misa* (1875) LR 10 Ex 153.
130. *Chidambara Iyer v. Renga Iyer* AIR 1966 SC 193.
131. *Keshub Mohindra v. Commissioner of Gift Tax* (1968) 70 ITR 1.

C. *Consideration Is for the Promise, Not the Contract*

133. As the definition indicates, one reckons consideration for a *promise*, and not for the *contract*. The benefit or detriment relates to each promise looked at separately, and the promisee who seeks to enforce the promise or some other person must have given something (act or abstinence or promise) at the request of the promisor.

D. *May Move from the Promisee or Any Other Person*

134. Under the Act, consideration may proceed from the promisee *or any other person*. This is a departure from the English law, under which consideration must move from the promisee.

E. *Consideration Must Be 'Valuable' and 'Real'*

135. Consideration must be 'something', that is, have some value in the eyes of law. A meritorious or gratuitous consideration such as love and affection, or obedience and submission by way of respect,[132] or an expectation of spiritual and moral benefit,[133] or a mere moral duty to perform a promise, is not good consideration.

The performance of what one is already bound to do, either by general law or by a specific obligation to the other party, or any promise to do so, is not a good consideration;[134] because such performance is no legal burden to the promisee; it rather relieves him of a duty.

136. The courts are not concerned with adequacy of consideration, or whether the act done by the promisee is equivalent to what the promisor has done or promised as his part of the bargain. Adequacy is for the parties to decide. The smallest of benefit or detriment is enough.

Although inadequacy of consideration does not affect the validity of contract if the consent of the parties to it is free; it is a relevant factor for deciding whether consent of the promisor was freely given.[135]

F. *Act Done or Not Done at the Desire of the Promisor*

137. The act constituting the consideration must have been done *at the desire or request of the promisor*, and not any third party, though it may benefit any third party.

---

132. *Shakuntala v. State of Haryana* AIR 1979 SC 843.
133. *Debi Saran Koiri v. Nandalal Choubey* AIR 1929 Pat 591.
134. *Muthukaruppa Mudali v. Pi Mu Kathappudayan* AIR 1915 Mad 528.
135. Explanation 2 to s. 25 of the Indian Contract Act.

This is the 'return' element of consideration. Thus, where a person promises to pay a subscription for a particular object, and steps have been taken in furtherance of the object on the faith of the promised subscription, the subscriber is liable on the promise.[136] A promise to compensate for a past voluntary act is also enforceable as an exception under section 25(2) of the act, if the voluntary act is done 'for the promisor'.

G. Gratuitous Agreements

138. A gratuitous promise is one for which there has been no exchange at all. One party confers advantage on another without the intention of obtaining any reciprocal advantage for himself.

Unlike civil law systems, promises under Indian law are not categorized as gratuitous. Like in English law, they are seen as agreements lacking consideration.

They are ordinarily not enforceable, unless accompanied by some formality that (i) provides proof of the intention to make a gift, and (ii) provides solemnity to the transaction and cautions the promisor about the significance of his act.

1. Contracts without Consideration are Enforceable in Certain Cases

139. An agreement without consideration is void.[137] But the following agreements are valid contracts even though not supported by consideration as defined above:

(i) A registered agreement, made between near relations, made on account of natural love and affection.
(ii) A promise to compensate a person who has voluntarily done something for the promisor, or that which the promisor was legally compellable to do.
(iii) A promise in writing and signed by the debtor to pay wholly or in part a time-barred debt.

The validity of a gift actually made cannot be challenged on the ground of lack of consideration.

The English doctrine that the 'solemnity of a deed' is of itself sufficient to make a promise expressed in a sealed writing valid has never been received in India.

2. Promise to Subscribe

140. Subscription agreements serve a purpose. They foster and encourage public enterprises and charitable causes. Such contributions facilitate their growth.

---

136. *Kedar Nath Bhattacharji v. Gorie Mahomed* (1887) ILR 14 Cal 64; *District Board of Ramnad v. Mahomed Ibrahim* AIR 1933 Mad 524.
137. Section 25 of the Indian Contract Act 1872.

Where an institution undertakes activities or works on faith of promises to subscribe to their funds, such promises ought to be enforced. A promise to subscribe to a charitable cause has received a treatment different than under English law.

A municipality invited and collected subscriptions for the purpose of building a town hall. The defendant signed his name in the subscription book for an amount. As soon as sufficient amount was ensured, the municipality engaged a contractor for construction of the town hall. The defendant refused to pay as promised. In the suit for its recovery it was held that the promise was with consideration because the subscriber knew the purposes to which the subscriptions were to be applied and also that a contractor would be engaged for the work. The promise was: 'In consideration of your agreeing to enter into contract to erect, I undertake to supply money for it'.[138] In later cases it was held that a promise to pay a subscription becomes enforceable as soon as any definite steps have been taken in furtherance of the object, and on the faith of the promised subscription,[139] but not where the payment is to be applied to a liability already incurred.

H. Natural Obligations

141. The concept of natural obligations as found in Belgian law, is not a part of Indian law.

I. Promissory Estoppel

142. The doctrine of promissory estoppel is used for enforcing a promise in favour of a promisee who has relied and acted on the promise. It belongs neither to the realm of contract nor of estoppel and is evolved to avoid injustice. It gives a cause of action in situations in which the promisee may not find consideration for enforcement. To this extent it dilutes the principle of consideration. In order to apply this doctrine, parties need not have any pre-existing contractual or any other legal relationship.

In a case recognizing this doctrine as applicable in India,[140] the Supreme Court stated the principle thus:

> Where one party has by his words or conduct made to the other a clear and unequivocal promise which is intended to create legal relations or affect a legal relationship to arise in the future, knowing or intending that it would be acted upon by the other party to whom the promise is made and it is in fact so acted upon by the other party, the promise would be binding on the party making it and he would not be entitled to go back upon it, if it would be inequitable to

138. *Kedar Nath Bhattacharji v. Gorie Mahomed* (1887) ILR 14 Cal 64.
139. *Perumal Mudaliar v. Sendanatha Mudaliar* AIR 1918 Mad 311.
140. *Motilal Padampat Sugar Mills Co Ltd v. State of Uttar Pradesh* AIR 1979 SC 621.

> allow him to do so having regard to the dealings which have taken place between the parties, and this would be so irrespective of whether there is any pre-existing relationship between the parties or not.

Such promise would be enforced where it is clear and unequivocal, and the promisee has relied on it and changed his position; he need not show any more detriment.[141]

143. Developed by case law, the doctrine has been invoked invariably in administrative law, to enforce representations constituting promises made by or on behalf of the State or public bodies.[142] Remedies are limited to specific enforcement or preventive relief.

The doctrine has not yet been applied between private parties, though such possibility has been indicated by the Supreme Court in the above case. The questions whether compensation granted for breach of such promise should put the plaintiff into a position before the promise was made, or a position as if the promise were performed (as applied under section 73 of the Indian Contract Act) remains to be seen. The doctrine cannot be invoked when the parties have a contract.[143] It was not applied to prevent the termination of a contract.[144]

Limits on its operation are recognized. For example, such promise may not be enforced against the government if public interest would suffer thereby.

IV. Modifications of the Contract

A. Modification by Both Parties

144. Parties to a contract are free (i) to substitute the entire contract; (ii) to rescind (cancel) the contract entirely; (iii) to alter, modify, or vary it; or (iv) rescind only some of its terms, and in such an event, the original contract need not be performed.[145]

Novation or modification of a contract is effected in the same manner as any contract, for example, by proposal and acceptance of the proposed new contract or of its modification. Therefore, if one party proposes new terms, and the other gives a *qualified* acceptance, an existing contract is not affected. Such substituted or altered contract may be oral or in writing, or may also be implied from conduct of parties, even where the original contract is in writing, unless original contract was compulsorily registrable.

---

141. *Ibid.*
142. See S.P. Sathe, *Administrative Law* 620 (7th edn, 2004).
143. *C V Enterprises v. Braithwaite & Co Ltd* AIR 1984 Cal 306.
144. *Ashok Kumar v. Union Territory Chandigarh* AIR 1995 SC 461.
145. Section 62 of the Indian Contract Act.

B. Novation

145. Novation is a term used to describe a new contract between the same parties, or between different parties. It has two elements – discharge of one contract and substitution of a new one. Thus, where A owes money to B under a contract, and later A, B and C agree that B shall thereafter accept C as his debtor instead of A, the old debt of A to B is at an end, and a new debt from C to B has been contracted.

The consideration for such novation is the mutual discharge of the old contract. Whether there is a new contract depends on the intention of the parties to end the earlier contract and to substitute the new one, as seen from the substance of the agreement. This is a question of fact in each case to be clearly proved. Thus, material changes in the terms of the original contract would indicate substitution.[146] There is no novation if the nature of rights and liabilities parties has not changed.[147] Parties may choose expressly not to end the old contract, for example, by making the operation of the new one conditional.

Mere non-performance of the new contract would not itself revive the earlier contract. A negotiable instrument (bill of exchange, promissory note, or cheque) given for discharging a debt does not operate as a novation, but is presumed to be a conditional payment; it does not extinguish the debt, but only suspends the payment.[148] If the instrument is dishonoured, or fails for any reason, the creditor can sue for the payment under the original contract.

146. All parties must agree to the new contract. It cannot be forced on an existing party, or any person sought to be substituted. Thus, where A owes B an amount under a contract, B owing C a similar amount, and B orders A to credit C with that amount in his books, but C does not assent to the arrangement, there is no new contract, and B still owes C the amount.

For the same reason, a person who becomes a partner in an existing firm does not become liable for any act of the firm done before he became a partner;[149] unless the new firm has assumed the liability and the creditor has agreed to accept the new firm as debtor, discharging the old firm from liability.

147. The new contract gives a new cause of action, ending the earlier one, and the period of limitation for commencing action will be reckoned based on the new contract. An arbitration clause in the earlier contract will also lose its force.[150]

146. *Andheri Bridge View Co-op Hsg Society Ltd v. Krishnakant Anandrao Deo* AIR 1991 Bom 129.
147. *Chatterjee Petrochem Co v. Haldia Petrochemicals Ltd* AIR 2014 SC (Supp) 699, 2014 AIR SCW 237.
148. *Dargavarapu Sarrapu v. Rampratapu* (1902) ILR 25 Mad 580; *Ananda Namdeo Kharde v. Pundalik Tukaram Chaudhury* AIR 1936 Nag 225.
149. Section 31(2) of the Indian Partnership Act 1932.
150. *Union of India v. Kishori Lal Gupta & Bros* AIR 1959 SC 1362; *Larsen and Toubro Ltd v. Mohan Lal Harbans Lal Bhayana* AIR 2014 SC (Supp) 1366.

1. Novation after Breach

148. As to whether parties can make a new contract to replace an old one after breach, the opinions of High Courts differ; but parties may settle the amount of damages.[151]

2. Novation and Assignment

149. An assignment by a promisee of rights under a contract differs from novation. Assignment is done without consent of the promisor. Assignment of liabilities under a contract can be made only with the consent of the promisee, making it a novation.

C. Alteration

150. Parties to an agreement may vary some of its terms by a subsequent agreement. The terms of the original contract continue to be binding, except to the extent superseded by such variation.

The consideration for the variation lies in mutual abandonment of existing rights or in conferring new benefits by each party on the other, or in assuming additional obligations or incurring additional liabilities.

1. Modification of Contracts by Statutes

151. Statutes, especially those effecting acquisition or transfer of undertakings, may substitute or vary, or empower to substitute or vary, contracts made by the acquired or transferred undertakings. Statutes may also provide for termination of contracts, or may empower a court or any authority to terminate a contract, or may restrict the power of termination.

2. Unilateral Variation

152. Unless the contract gives such power to a party, a contract or any of its terms cannot be rescinded[152] or varied unilaterally. Such powers might, for example, enable price variation or enable ordering changes in the works or extra works in works contracts.

Any such unilateral rescission or variation without power under the contract, would amount to repudiatory breach, and entitle the other party to damages or to rescind the contract as the case may be.

---

151. *Ram Nath v. Mannu Lal* AIR 1923 All 518; *Kamal Narayan Shopowner Sitaram v. Baniram Shopowner Sheonarayan* AIR 1923 Nag 332.
152. *Jainarayan Ram Lundia v. Surajmull Sagarmull* AIR 1949 FC 211.

The power of variation or rescission is strictly construed, and will not entitle a party to vary matters other than those provided in the contract. Such powers must be exercised according to the terms, as to mode of their exercise and circumstances in which they may be exercised.

D. Rescission

153. Parties may rescind, that is, cancel, all or some only of the terms of their contract, expressly or impliedly. Total rescission of an entire contract ends the contractual relationship. Partial rescission merely modifies the relation by changing rights and obligations of the original contract.

Consideration for the promise of releasing the other party from obligations is the abandonment of one's own rights under the contract.

1. Rescission or Variation by a Court

154. Apart from agreement by parties, or exercise of powers by any party under terms of a contract, the terms of a contract cannot be varied even by a court, unless it has powers under statutes.

A court can revise the transaction of loan between parties, to reopen accounts, or set aside or alter any security for a loan, if the interest on the loan is found excessive, and the transaction is substantially unfair.[153]

§2. Formal and Evidential Requirements

155. The Indian Contract Act does not require any writing or form for making an agreement. Formal requirements of writing, witnesses, or registration may be required by other statutes. Such statutes will also provide for the effect of not complying with required formalities.

A law requiring form seeks to protect parties from being legally bound for hastily drawn transactions. Formality arouses awareness of transaction, causes the parties to reflect on it and seek advice if required, and ensure familiarity with the text of the matter transacted. Formalities enable proof of a contract and its terms.

Where it is registered, there is an institutional safeguard against haste because the registering officer enquires about the contents and the signatures on documents. He verifies that proper persons seek registration, and they are competent to act. He requires their identification to his satisfaction. Documents registered are also preserved, and its copies are available.

In any case, a contract in writing has evidentiary advantages over a parol contract.[154]

---

153. Usurious Loans Act, 1918.
154. See paras 186–194 *infra.*

I. Formal Requirements

A. *General Principle of Informality*

156. The Indian Contract Act follows the general principle of informality, providing that a contract is concluded in the manner set out in the Act, that is, by mode of proposal and acceptance. It allows other laws to require any particular contract to be made in writing or in the presence of witnesses. Nor do the provisions of the Act affect any law relating to registration of documents.

Therefore, an oral contract by which the parties intend to be bound is valid and enforceable, unless required by any other law to be in writing or to comply with any other formality.

157. The formalities prescribed by various statutes for particular contracts may vary – writing, signatures, seal, witnesses, form, prescribed contents, and registration. Non-compliance with such requirements produces different consequences. It may render the agreement invalid, that is, of no effect, in which case the formalities must be complied with to create liability, or merely unenforceable. Much depends on whether the provision prescribing formalities, unless it so expressly provides, is interpreted as mandatory or directory. Such a law may prohibit proof of the document, yet in some cases allowing collateral use in evidence. Not complying with the forms may also attract criminal liability under some statutes.

B. *Writing and Signature*

158. A contract is in writing, not only where it is made in the form of a document by the parties to it and signed, but also where it is formed by a written proposal and acceptance, perhaps also where either the proposal or the acceptance only is in writing. It may also be in the form of an accepted application, for example, for membership or admission to an institution. Minutes of meetings recorded after the meeting incorporating terms agreed between parties would also satisfy this formality.

Written contracts would include handwritten or printed documents or those made by any mechanical mode. Documents in electronic form are treated as equivalent of writing under the Information Technology Act 2000, except powers-of-attorney, negotiable instruments, wills, conveyances of immovable property, or other documents notified by the government.[155]

159. An arbitration agreement must be in writing. The Arbitration and Conciliation Act 1996 specifically provides that it can either be a document signed by the parties or an exchange of letters, telex, telegram, or other means of telecommunication that provide a record of the agreement.

155. Section 1(4) of the Information Technology Act 2000.

Some transactions, particularly those recording transfer or assignment of rights or property, require a more formal document – an instrument.[156]

A claim to an unsecured debt or beneficial interest in movable property not in possession that can be enforced by commencing an action, that is, a suit, is an actionable claim,[157] for example, a creditor's claim for money owed by his debtor or a purchaser's claim for goods to be delivered by the seller. Actionable claims can be transferred by an instrument in writing signed by the transferor. Upon such transfer, all rights and remedies of the transferor vest in the transferee, who can claim the debt or the property from the promisor.

160. A written agreement need not be signed. Statutes do, however, require signature, that is, execution, as a formality. This involves not only signing, but all other acts necessary to bind the party to the contract. The intention to be bound by the contract must accompany the act of signing. An electronic document can be signed with a digital signature.

C. Attestation

161. Some documents are valid transactions only if executed in the presence of witnesses, usually two. A mortgage and gift of immovable property require attestation, without which the title to property will not be affected. Where attestation is compulsory, the attesting witness, if alive, must be called in any trial for proving the document.[158]

D. Registration

162. Registration as a formality is typical of contracts effecting transfer of property or interest in property. Under the general law of registration, that is, the Indian Registration Act 1908, or under the law affecting the particular contract or transfer, it may be required, as follows:

(i) to validate the transaction, that is, sale, mortgage, some leases, gift, or exchange of immovable property.[159] The general law of registration also requires that certain transactions affecting immovable property must be compulsorily registered.[160] In such cases, the transaction does not affect the property at all unless duly registered;

156. See for example, the Transfer of Property Act 1882, s. 54 (Sale of immovable property), s. 59 (mortgages), s. 107 (lease) and s. 123 (gifts); the Companies Act, 2013 s. 56 (transfer of securities of a company).
157. See ss 3 and 130 of the Transfer of Property Act 1882.
158. Section 68 of the Indian Evidence Act 1872.
159. Under the Transfer of Property Act 1882.
160. Section 17 of the Indian Registration Act 1908.

(ii) to record the transaction in a public record – the Register, enabling notice of such transaction to the public; and
(iii) to give priority to a transaction made by a written registered document over any oral agreement or unregistered documents in certain cases.[161]

The process of registration under these laws requires the public officer to enquire about the identity of parties, their consent to the transaction, and compliance of other provisions of law under which the document is registered. The public officer registering the document is not concerned with the validity of the transaction or with any prior claims or transactions. In the event of any dispute, these would be decided by courts on the basis of priorities as reflected by the effect of transactions.

163. The effect of non-registration varies and is found in the relevant statute covering registration of the transaction.

It may render the transaction void or invalid and, therefore, the document ineffective. It may simply render the document unenforceable, thus striking only at the document and not the transaction. It may prohibit use of the document in evidence, but allow its use in evidence for collateral purposes, for example, to prove possession, termination of possession, payment of money, acknowledgment of liability, or even the state of mind of one party who has alleged that his consent is not free. Thus, if a deed selling immovable property is not registered, the deed does not transfer ownership, but it can still be admitted in evidence to protect possession of the transferee acquired under the terms of such deed.

E. Notarization

164. There is no requirement of law that any contract shall be executed by or before a notary. Some laws or rules of procedure might require applicants for benefits or claims under them to support their applications with affidavits or declarations made before notaries.

F. No Contracts under Seal under Indian Law

165. A 'contract under seal', a feature of English law, referred to an obligation undertaken by a person expressing his intentions on paper or parchment, attaching his seal and delivering it 'as his deed'. The requirement of seal was removed under the English law in 1989[162] for all deeds executed by an individual and later also for those executed by companies.[163] Earlier, this mode enabled enforcement of executory contracts and gratuitous promises. The requirement of sealing has now been replaced under English law by that of execution of a deed, that is, in a manner indicating clear intention of making a deed, a signature, attestation, and delivery.

161. Sections 48 and 50 of the Indian Registration Act 1908.
162. The (English) Law of Property (Miscellaneous Provisions) Act 1989.
163. (English) Companies Act 1985 amended in 1989.

This is thus not a contract, the bargain element being absent. It is a formula lending the promise enforceability.

Despite being based on the English law in 1872, the Indian Contract Act 1872 never required sealing. Even a company is not required to put its seal on its contracts, except on a power-of-attorney or any other document mentioned in the articles of association of that company. Nor does the contract law require that any contract be executed in the form of a deed. Nor are there any formalities for execution of deeds, except those the law requires to be in the form of instruments or in writing.[164]

G. Payment of Stamp Duty

166. Some instruments[165] are liable to stamp duty. Stamp duty is a source of revenue for the government. It is paid by affixing an adhesive stamp or by recording the instrument on a stamp paper (called impressed stamp). The duty can also be paid in cash in certain cases. An unstamped document must be stamped before it is acted on in India.

167. Stamp duty is levied on an instrument, and not on the transaction. An instrument is chargeable with duty. Therefore, where the transaction is oral, no stamp is required, because there is nothing to which a stamp can be affixed.

The charging provisions of stamp law enumerate the instruments by their types and indicate the duty payable for them. Therefore, if the charging provision is not applicable to a particular instrument, no stamp duty is payable. Parties to transactions, therefore, attempt to design their transactions in such a manner that they pay no duty or less duty. Some exemptions are given in the statutes, and the governments remit from time to time the duty payable on some instruments.

Stamp duty is levied under various laws that give charging provisions and set up machinery for recovery. Legislative power in India is divided between the Centre and the states. The Parliament can prescribe stamp duty[166] in respect of bills of exchange, cheques, promissory notes, bills of lading, letters of credit, policies of insurance, transfer of shares, debentures, proxies, and receipts. Duty payable on these instruments is found in the Indian Stamp Act. Stamp laws of states prescribe rates of stamp duty on other documents, particularly those affecting immovable properties.

168. Non-payment of stamp duty does not affect the validity of a transaction in the instrument, but the instrument is not admissible in evidence in proceedings (barring few exceptions, such as matrimonial or criminal proceedings). Nor can secondary evidence be given of its contents. It is possible to pay the stamp duty and penalty applicable under the stamp law, and admit the instrument in evidence. The stamp

---

164. See paras 156 onwards.
165. An instrument is a document which creates or affects any right or liability.
166. Entry 91 in the Union List of Schedule VII of the Constitution of India.

laws provide for penalties for non-payment of duty and punishment where such non-payment is wilful.

H. Contracts with Government

169. To bind the government, at the Centre or of any state, the contract must be in writing, executed by a person duly authorized by the President of India or a Governor of the state, and expressed to be made by the President or Governor.[167] Otherwise, it is cannot be enforced against the government, but it will be binding personally on the officer who actually made it.

I. No 'Solemn' Contracts under Indian Law

170. Under the Indian Law, a contract can be oral, unless any provision of law requires formalities. These are discussed earlier.[168]

II. Evidential Requirement: Proof

A. The Law of Evidence

171. The Indian Evidence Act 1872 is a comprehensive code stating provisions relating to relevancy, proof, admissibility of oral and documentary evidence and primacy of the latter, burden of proof and presumptions, and competency of witnesses and rules of examining them. But it is not a complete code. Judges enjoy considerable freedom in assessing the truthfulness of evidence led by the parties, its appreciation, and its effect on the case. The Act does not prescribe any standard of proof to be met in cases before the court. The judge will decide on his own judgment whether any fact has been sufficiently proved and whether a party in a civil case has established his case on balance of probabilities.

The law of evidence restricts the scope of enquiry in a case. It gives rules for efficient and impartial determination and proof of facts in an enquiry. It also restricts the investigation within the bounds required by general convenience.

Evidence can be given only of facts that are expressly declared as relevant under sections 5–55 of the Indian Evidence Act. Evidence given must also be admissible under the provisions of the Indian Evidence Act.

172. Proof is the effect of evidence. Facts may be proved by oral or documentary evidence. The latter includes electronic record. However, every fact need not be proved. Facts need not be proved where they are admitted by the other party in civil proceedings, or are 'judicially noticed', that is, sufficiently known or obvious.

---

167. Article 299 of the Constitution of India; see paras 770–773 *infra*.
168. See paras 156 onwards.

Facts may also be presumed, when they are considered as sufficiently proved if certain other facts or propositions are established.

173. The Evidence Act does not contain all rules of evidence. The Civil Procedure Code and Criminal Procedure Code contain rules of particular matters. The Bankers Books Evidence Act states rules regarding proof and presumptions relating to bankers' books. Many special or local laws, mainly dealing with substantive laws, incidentally also provide rules of evidence, especially presumptions.

B. *Oral and Documentary Evidence*

174. Any fact may be proved by oral or documentary evidence, or both.

C. *Oral Evidence and Affidavits*

175. Oral evidence refers to depositions given by witnesses on oath before the court and under the amended Civil Procedure Code, also before a commissioner appointed by the court for taking evidence. The test of competency is of understanding. A witness is competent to testify if he can understand questions put to him and is able to give rational answers to them. No particular number of witnesses is required to prove any particular fact. Traditionally affidavits, that is, statements made by persons on oath, are not considered evidence. However, the Civil Procedure Code was amended in 2000 with a view to speed procedures, enabling filing of affidavits of parties and witnesses in civil proceedings instead of their examinations in chief.

D. *Documentary Evidence*

176. A document is not merely any matter in writing (including electronic record), but matter expressed on any substance by letters, figures, or marks intended to be used for recording that matter. Documents, therefore, include maps, plans, and charts.

In relation to documents, the following three things must be proved: (i) its existence; (ii) its genuineness; and (iii) its contents. Oral evidence can be given of the existence and genuineness of a document, but not its contents.

1. Documentary Evidence Superior

177. The law of evidence favours documentary evidence. Oral evidence cannot be given of contents of documents, which can be proved by primary evidence (the original document). If the original is lost or in custody of the opposite party or similar circumstances, copies or oral 'account' of contents (secondary evidence) can be given.

Oral evidence can, however, be given to prove the existence or genuineness of a document. Oral evidence of contents of electronic record cannot be given unless its genuineness is in question.

2. Production of Documents

178. The original document must be produced in evidence to prove contents of documents. Its copy can be produced only if a cause is shown for not producing the original, because the original is with the other party or because it is lost or destroyed.

3. Proof of Documents

179. A document will be evidence in the proceeding if it is proved. This applies to every document, including that which is registered or notarized.

Document need not be proved if (i) it is admitted by the other party or (ii) there is a legal presumption of due execution.

Presumptions of due execution are available in respect of public documents, depositions, or statements recorded by judicial officers, gazettes, maps, and plans made by government. An important presumption relates to ancient documents. If a document of more than thirty years is produced from proper custody, the court may presume that it has been duly executed and attested.

180. The mere fact that an instrument is signed has not special probative effect. Signature must be proved. This is done by showing that the document is signed or is in the handwriting of the author. The author of the document will state so. Otherwise it may be proved by calling a witness, especially an attesting witness, who has either seen the author sign it or is familiar with the signature or handwriting of the author. The document may also be referred to a handwriting expert to compare signature or handwriting with an admitted signature or handwriting of the author.

Gifts and most mortgages of immovable property are required by law to be attested by two witnesses. If such a document is registered, it may be proved in the manner set out previously. The attesting witness must be called to prove the signature only if its execution (signature) is denied by the executant.

4. Probative Value of Certain Commercial Documents

181. The Commercial Documents Evidence Act 1939 makes special provisions about certain commercial documents, most of which relate to shipping or carriage by air. It gives a list of commercial documents relating to which the court shall presume genuineness and also that contents are correct, for example, Lloyd's Register of Shipping and Loading List, certain documents relating to marine insurance, certificates of registration of aircrafts, consular certificates of goods shipped and of origin, receipts for payment of customs duty.

In regard to other documents, the court may draw such presumption. Some of these are certificates issued by a port, dock, and so on, relating to date or time of shipment or arrival of goods, passenger list and ticket of an aircraft, air consignment note and baggage check, force majeure certificate issued by recognized Chamber of Commerce, receipt granted by the post, copy certified by the Registrar of Companies of balance sheet, profit and loss account, and audit report of a company filed with the Registrar of Companies.

5. Probative Effect of Registration

182. Mere registration of an instrument in the offices of registration[169] under various laws relating to registration is not in itself proof of execution of the document. It does not give a presumption of validity. Particulars of registered instruments are entered in registers and indexes, which are public documents. Entries in these registers can, therefore, be proved by producing certified copies of registers and indexes. The instrument itself is a private document and must be proved like any other document.

A statute requiring registration[170] of any transaction may provide for the consequences of non-registration, often that such instrument cannot be used as evidence of transaction unless registered. For example, the Indian Registration Act compels registration of certain instruments, mainly those affecting immovable property.[171] It provides that if such instrument is not registered, it cannot be used as evidence of any transaction affecting such property, though it may be received in evidence to prove collateral transactions.[172] Therefore, if a sale deed requiring registration is not registered, it cannot be used in evidence to show the transfer of title, but can be used to show who is in possession of the property or that the price has been paid, or as evidence of the transaction to support a suit for specific performance.

6. Probative Effect of Notarization

183. There is no other express statutory provision giving any higher probative effect to any notarial act other than a power-of-attorney.[173] Therefore, mere production of a notary's certificate of execution or authentication of a document in India is not by itself evidence of such execution or authentication. Such document will have to be proved like any ordinary document. But observations in some cases suggest a presumption of due execution and authentication, that is, the fact that the document is duly done and in order.[174] This is an initial presumption of genuineness of the document (authorship only and not contents) courts have drawn on the general

169. Under the Registration Act 1908, which is the general law relating to registration.
170. See paras 162–163 *supra*.
171. Section 17 of the Indian Registration Act 1908.
172. Section 49 of the Indian Registration Act 1908.
173. For function of notaries, see paras 204–208 *infra*.
174. *In the goods of Mulne* (1906) 33 ILR Cal 625; *Gaganmoyi Debi v. Troilucka Nath Chowdhry* (1906) 8 Bom LR 375 (PC); *Pratima Chowdhury v. Kalpana Mukherjee* AIR 2014 SC 1304.

principle that a court can presume the existence of any facts it thinks likely to have happened, with regard to the common course of public and private business.[175] Certificates of notaries in civil law countries might enjoy a presumption of due execution and authentication if the law of those countries provide for such presumption.

Contents of documents made before a notary must be proved like any other fact, by documentary or oral evidence.

184. A power-of-attorney executed before and authenticated by a notary public or any court, judge or magistrate, or the representative abroad of the Central government, is presumed to have been so executed or authenticated.[176] This presumption may extend also the competency of the person executing it, especially of his authority as representative of a corporation. It does not, however, extend to contents of the power-of-attorney. This is proof of its signature and its authentication, not of its contents. The effect is that the authority of the attorney will be recognized by the court and the agent allowed to act without calling the principal or notary for its proof. The presumption is not conclusive; it means that the party challenging execution or attestation may prove that it has not been executed by the principal or that it was not properly authenticated.

A power-of-attorney need not be executed before a notary. But if so executed and authenticated, it has the benefit of the above presumption.

184.1. Since 2005, India is a member of the Hague Convention of 5 October 1961 that abolished the requirement of legalization of foreign public documents. Apostille (certificates) can be issued from India and are accepted in India.[177]

7. Effect of Non-payment of Stamp Duty

185. Parties to a transaction are liable to pay prescribed stamp duty on the contracts or transactions,[178] else that instrument is inadmissible in evidence in any court or in arbitration proceedings and it cannot be acted on or authenticated by any public officer. This defect can be cured by paying the amount of duty and penalty.

E. The Parol Evidence Rule

186. The rules relating to parol evidence are found in sections 91–100 of the Indian Evidence Act 1872. Extrinsic evidence is not admissible to supersede the terms of a document, or to control it, that is, to contradict, vary, add to, or subtract from the terms of the document. It is admissible in aid of and to explain that document.

175. Section 114 of the Indian Evidence Act 1872.
176. Section 85 of the Indian Evidence Act 1872.
177. <http://mea.gov.in/apostille.htm>, Ministry of External Affairs.
178. See paras 166–168 *supra*.

1. Exclusive and Conclusive Character

187. The contents of a document can be proved only by producing the document – its original, or by secondary evidence (its copy) where permissible. Contents cannot be orally narrated. Even oral admissions of contents are not admissible.

Where the question is about the matter contained in the document, two questions arise: (i) does the fact that the document forms its record *exclude other* evidence of that matter; (ii) to what extent such matter recorded can be affected by *other evidence*. The law prefers documentary evidence in both cases.

The document is the exclusive evidence of terms and matters contained in it in the following cases: (i) of the *terms* of a contract, grant, or other disposition of property reduced to the form of a document; or (ii) in all cases in which any *matter* is required by law to be reduced to the form of a document. The writing itself, or secondary evidence of its contents, is not only the best but is the only admissible evidence of such terms or matter which it contains.

188. This restriction applies only to the: (i) *terms* of a contract, grant, or any other disposition of property made in writing; or (ii) any *matter* required by law to be in writing. Oral evidence can, therefore, be given to prove a receipt for payment of money or of the existence of the contract or grant.[179]

The word 'terms' refers to statements, representations, and assertions contained in a written contract that relate to the subject matter of the contract and to something to be done or not to be done under it. It refers to the undertakings and promises made.[180] Oral evidence can also be given to prove all statements except the terms, such as (i) defect in title of a vendor; (ii) consideration; (iii) that consideration stated as paid in the document was never actually paid;[181] (iv) that a document was never intended to operate as an agreement;[182] (v) that the true nature of document was different, for example, that a contract of hire-purchase was truly one of security for advance given;[183] (vi) statements relating to who is a party, or his capacity; (vii) recitals. Such statements can also be contradicted.[184]

189. The rule that document is exclusive evidence would apply only if the document is intended to be the whole contract. Before evidence is excluded under sections 91 and 92, it must be proved that the document in question records or purports to record all the terms of the contract between the parties.[185] Therefore, where parties intend to make a contract partly oral and partly in writing, parol evidence is admissible to prove the oral terms.

---

179. *P B Bhatt v. V R Thakkar* AIR 1972 Bom 365.
180. *Venkatasubbiah Chetty v. Govindarajulu Naidu* (1907) 31 ILR Mad 45; *P B Bhatt v. V R Thakkar* AIR 1972 Bom 365.
181. *Sah Lal Chand v. Indrajit* (1899) 27 IA 93.
182. *Tyagaraja Mudaliyar v. Vedathanni* AIR 1936 PC 70.
183. *Sukumar Bysack v. Sushil Kanta Banerjee* AIR 1972 Cal 207.
184. *Sah Lal Chand v. Indrajit* (1899) 27 IA 93; *P B Bhatt v. V R Thakkar* AIR 1972 Bom 365; *Radhamohan Thakur v. Bipin Behari Mitra* AIR 1938 Pat 505; *Md Murtaza Hussain v. Abdul Rahman* AIR 1949 Pat 364.
185. *Mohammed Akbar Khan v. Attar Singh* AIR 1936 PC 171.

190. Once such document is proved, oral agreement or statement cannot be proved as between parties to that contract, to contradict, vary, add to, or subtract from its terms, subject to exceptions discussed later. A third party can, however, lead oral evidence to contradict, vary, add to, or subtract from its terms.

191. The rule, though criticized, is useful. This rule throws the burden on the opposite party to show that the document did not record all the terms, and many a times the argument that the document did not record all the terms will fail.

2. Exceptions to Parol Evidence Rule

192. The exceptions referred to previously are as follows:

(i) facts that invalidate the document, such as fraud, intimidation, illegality, want of due execution, want of capacity, mistake, want of consideration, and so on;
(ii) a separate oral agreement on which the document is silent, provided it is not inconsistent with its terms;
(iii) a separate oral agreement constituting a condition precedent to attaching of any obligation under that contract;
(iv) a subsequent oral agreement to rescind or modify any such contract, except in those cases in which such contract is required by law to be in writing;
(v) any usage or custom may be proved if it is not inconsistent with the express terms of the contract;
(vi) any fact may be proved that shows in what manner the language of a document is related to existing facts, for example, to identify parties or subject matter of the contract.

193. Oral evidence can also be led to prove facts necessary for interpreting the documents.[186]

Oral evidence cannot be given (i) where the document is on its face ambiguous or defective – to supply the defects and (ii) where the language in a document is plain in itself and applies to existing facts – to show that it was not meant to apply to such facts. But when language used in a document is plain in itself, but is unmeaning in reference to existing facts, evidence may be given to show that it was used in a peculiar sense. When the facts are such that the language used might have been meant to apply to any one, and could not have been meant to apply to more than one, of several persons or things, evidence may be given of facts that show which of those persons or things it was intended to apply to. When the language used applies partly to one set of existing facts, and partly to another set of existing facts, but the whole of it does not apply correctly to either, evidence may be given to show to which of the two it was meant to apply. Evidence may be given to show

186. *Tulsi v. Chandrika Prasad* AIR 2006 SC 3359.

the meaning of illegible or not commonly intelligible characters, of foreign, obsolete, technical, local, and provincial expressions, of abbreviations and of words used in a peculiar sense.

194. There is a distinction between dispositive and non-dispositive documents. The former are made for disposing rights and will describe contractual incidents. These are made deliberately, with selected words having settled legal or business meaning. Non-dispositive documents, on the contrary, are casual and describe non-contractual incidents, are dependent on extraneous circumstances, and cannot be explained unless those circumstances are also put into evidence.

F. Proof and Presumptions

195. Presumptions, which allow the court to dispense with requiring production of evidence, are of three kinds – mandatory and rebuttable (*shall presume*), discretionary and rebuttable (*may presume*), and those which are conclusive proof, that is, mandatory and irrebuttable. Where a court can presume a fact, it infers fact 'A' when fact 'B' is established.

Where the court *may* presume a fact 'A' on fact 'B' being established, it may either regard fact 'A' as proved unless it is disproved or may call for proof of it. This presumption is directory.

If the court *shall* presume fact 'A', it is bound to regard it as proved after fact 'B' is established, unless it is disproved. This is a mandatory presumption.

If the presumption amounts to conclusive proof, it must infer fact 'A' and no evidence can be led to disprove fact 'A'.

196. Most presumptions relating to documents are based on the principle that solemn and official acts were done in the ordinary manner. Certificates or certified copies certified in the manner prescribed by law by authorized government officials, maps and plans made under the authority of government, books published by the government containing laws or reports of judgments, are presumed to be genuine.

Every electronic record purporting to be an agreement containing the digital signature of the parties is presumed to be so concluded by affixing the digital signature of the parties.

1. Proof

197. Proof of a fact is neither suspicion nor demanding of absolute certainty, but such conviction of the mind of a prudent person. A prudent person would be certain of a fact when he believes it to exist, or he may think it very extremely probable and act on assumption of its existence. The test of whether a fact is proved or not is whether a prudent man after considering the matters before him, deemed it proved or not.

The law of evidence quite obviously does not state any test for standard of proof, the amount of evidence necessary for proving a particular fact, or the case. The courts are to use their common sense and experience in judging the effect of particular facts without being subject to technical rules. The effect of evidence in civil and criminal proceedings differs, though there is no absolute standard of proof. In the former case, the case is decided on balance of probabilities and in the criminal case after the charges are proved beyond reasonable doubt.

198. A fact is proved when, after considering the matters before it, the court either believes it to exist, or considers its existence so probable that a prudent man ought, under the circumstances of the particular case, to act on the supposition that it exists.

A fact is disproved when, after considering the matters before it, the court either believes it does not exist, or considers its non-existence so probable that a prudent man ought, under the circumstances of the particular case, to act on the supposition that it does not exist.

A fact is said not to be proved when it is neither proved nor disproved.

2. Admissions

199. Admissions may be made in two situations: admissions made in the course of proceedings and other statements.

200. Admissions made in proceedings are deliberate, and have high probative value. Facts admitted in this manner need not be proved.

Admissions also can be derived from pleadings of parties. The Civil Procedure Code requires that the defendant must specifically deny every allegation made in the plaint. If he does not so deny, or fails to deny, he is considered to have admitted such fact.

Admissions in proceedings may be derived from contents of other applications or documents filed during the course of proceedings. The Civil Procedure Code allows either party to call on the other to admit facts or documents. The other party can respond and can admit facts or documents. Admissions relating to documents may be restricted to genuineness only, leaving the contents in dispute. To the extent facts are admitted, they need not be proved.

Admissions might be given by parties in their depositions and can also be drawn from witnesses during cross-examination.

201. An admission made otherwise than in the course of proceedings is an oral or documentary statement suggesting an inference of a fact. Such statement can generally be proved if it is against the interest of the maker.

Thus, a statement by A: ‘B owes me money’ cannot be proved by A in his suit for recovery from B, but a statement ‘B does not owe me any money’ may be proved in such suit. A statement made in one’s own favour may be proved by way of exceptions.[187]

---

187. Section 21 of the Indian Evidence Act.

An admission carries a special probative value. When the admission is clear and unequivocal, it is strong evidence. An admission, even if it is writing, is not conclusive proof of the fact stated, but may amount to estoppel.

Such admission may not, however, be relevant if it is made 'without prejudice', that is, on an express condition that evidence of it is not to be given, or it can be inferred that parties had agreed that its evidence would not be given. This enables parties to negotiate compromises freely, without fear of their statements being used against them.

3. Experts

202. In matters of foreign law, science, art, identity of handwriting, or finger impressions, evidence of opinion of experts is admissible, and can be offered by parties in support of their case. An expert is a person specially skilled in the subject by special study or special experience.

An expert has to state his opinion about such matter, not his opinion on the facts in issue in the case. When calling an expert as a witness, his expertise will first be established. He will also state the grounds for his opinion. An expert's evidence is special because he can speak of his opinion on facts, which is not allowed of other witnesses. His testimony may also cover citations from authoritative texts on his subject and other cases bearing similarity to cases in hand. Moreover, he can be asked hypothetical questions.

4. Entries in Business Books

203. Entries in books kept in the ordinary course of business or in the discharge of professional duty have an inherent circumstantial guarantee of trustworthiness. Such entries are relevant, whether made by a party to the suit or by any servant or clerk. Evidence of such entries can be given even where the maker of entries is dead or not available. They can be proved even by persons who have not made those entries.

When the entry is against the interest of the person keeping the books of accounts, it would be relevant as admission and can be proved against the person making it.

An entry in books of account can be proved in one's favour also and can be used to show that the debtor owes an amount. But such an entry is not itself sufficient evidence to charge the debtor. Corroborative evidence will be required.

G. The Notary in India

204. An Indian notary is closer to his British counterpart, and does not have as many responsibilities as a notary under the civil systems. He does not perform judicial functions. Notaries are appointed to afford to the public the facility for securing authenticity for acts performed by them.

1. Compared with Notaries in the Civil Law

205. While the main role of a notary in the civil law is drafting agreements and notarizing declarations lending them validity, the Indian notary's role is mainly of authenticating documents. Notarization is not an essential form for any transaction.

A notary in the civil law will also receive and preserve documents. An Indian notary is required to keep a register recording notarial acts, with signatures of executants and persons identifying them. The Indian Registration Act enables registration of any instrument. Copies of registered instruments are preserved and are available for inspection by anyone.

Unlike his civil counterpart, documents executed before a notary have a presumption about execution, but notarizing does not create any presumption about contents of the document. The evidentiary value of a notarial certificate was discussed earlier.[188]

2. Appointment

206. A notary is appointed by the Central or state government.[189] He will either be an advocate[190] or any other person possessing experience in the legal field, such as a judge or law officer of the government. He is not a public officer. His is not a full-time occupation.

A person requires a certificate authorizing him to practice the profession of a notary. The certificate is for five years at a time and needs to be renewed.

He is appointed for a local area within which he can practice. Appointments depend on the need for notaries in any local area. The law also states the maximum number of notaries that may be appointed by the Central and various state governments.[191]

3. Notarial Acts

207. Under the Notaries Act, a notary can by virtue of his office under his signature and official seal[192] do the following:

(i) verify, authenticate, certify, or attest to the execution of any instrument;
(ii) present any promissory note, *hundi* or bill of exchange for acceptance or payment, or demand better security;
(iii) note or protest the dishonour by non-acceptance or non-payment of any promissory note, *hundi* or bill of exchange, protest for better security, or prepare acts of honour under the Negotiable Instruments Act, 1881;

188. See para. 183 *supra*.
189. Under the Notaries Act 1952.
190. Legal practitioner enrolled as Advocate under the Advocates Act 1961.
191. The Schedule to the Notaries Rules 1956.
192. Section 8 of the Notaries Act 1952 and Rule 11 of the Notaries Rules 1956.

(iv) note and draw up ship's protest, boat's protest, or protest relating to demurrage and other commercial matters;
(v) administer oath to, or take affidavit from, any person;
(vi) prepare bottomry and respondentia bonds, charter parties, and other mercantile documents;
(vii) prepare, attest, or authenticate any instrument intended to take effect in any country or place outside India in such form and language as may conform to the law of the place where such deed is entitled to operate;
(viii) translate and verify the translation of, any document from one language into another;
(ix) act as a Commissioner to record evidence in any civil or criminal trial if so directed by any court or authority;
(x) act as an arbitrator, mediator, or conciliator, if so required.

The Notaries Rules enable him also to do the following:

(i) draw documents, including conveyance of properties;
(ii) note and certify the general transactions relating to negotiable instruments;
(iii) prepare a will or other testamentary documents; and
(iv) prepare and take affidavits for various purposes for his notarial acts.

Under the laws of civil and criminal procedure, whenever any affidavit is required in any proceeding, it may be made before a notary.[193]

4. Procedure

208. A notary is bound to make entry of any notarial act. He has to exercise care about identifying the person executing any document and must seek identification unless the person is personally known to him. He must examine personally the parties and ascertain that they are fit and able to give consent to the transaction. Notaries will usually ask for identification by an advocate. The executant and the advocate must sign his register.

III. Burden of Proof

209. The Indian Evidence Act also deals with the question as to which of the parties before a court is bound to supply evidence, that is, on whom the burden of proof lies. The term 'burden of proof' has two meanings. It refers to (i) the duty of producing evidence to prove particular facts as the case progresses and (ii) the duty to establish the truth of the claim by preponderance of evidence.

193. Section 139 of the Code of Civil Procedure 1908, and s. 297 of the Code of Criminal Procedure 1976.

The general burden of proof is on the party who would fail, if no evidence at all were given. The burden of proving any particular fact is on the party who affirms it. The Act also enumerates the presumptions that determine the burden of proof of particular facts in particular cases. After enumerating particular presumptions, it also gives to the court the discretion to draw inferences from particular facts, where the court will be guided by its own experience and knowledge of the common course of natural events and public and private affairs. The court may thus presume, for example, that judicial and official acts have been regularly performed or that the common course of business has been followed in particular cases, or that evidence that could be and is not produced would, if produced, be unfavourable to the person who withholds it; that when a document creating an obligation is in the hands of the obligor, the obligation has been discharged. As indicated, the court is free not to draw any such presumption.

A. *Is There a Distinction Made between 'Obligation of Means' and 'Obligation of Result'?*

210. This distinction is not found in Indian law. Questions of burden of proof are resolved according to the general rules of burden of proof discussed previously.

Therefore, where the promisor is under an obligation to take reasonable care, the burden of proving the care he took lies on him, the fact being within his special knowledge.

A bailee is responsible for proper care of goods entrusted to him. The loss or damage of goods entrusted to a bailee is prima facie evidence of negligence, and the burden of proof, therefore, to disprove negligence lies on the bailee.[194] This is because the bailee being in possession of the goods, he only would know how the loss was caused. The bailee has to show that loss arose because of events and causes over which he had no control.[195] The bailee must call all material and witnesses to show that he took care or that the events went beyond his control, but it remains for the plaintiffs to satisfy the court that the true inference from those materials is that the servants of the defendant company have not shown due care, skill, and nerve.[196]

§3. Liability and Negotiations

I. Negotiations

211. It is usual for parties to discuss and negotiate terms and conditions of their transaction before finalizing their contract. They may carry on prolonged negotiations anticipating an agreement, make demands and counter-demands, and

194. *N R Srinivasa Iyer v. New India Assurance Co Ltd* AIR 1983 SC 899; *Economic Transport Organisation v. Dharwad Dist Khadi Gramudyog Sangh*, AIR 2000 SC 1635; *Central Bank of India v. Grains and Gunny Agencies* AIR 1989 MP 28; *Cochin Port Trust v. Associated Cotton Traders Limited* AIR 1983 Ker 154.
195. *Rivers Steam Navigation Company v. Choutmull Doogar* (1899) 26 IA 1.
196. *Dwarka Nath Pai Mohan Chaudhuri v. Rivers Steam Navigation Co Ltd* AIR 1917 PC 173.

propose, change, or withdraw terms. Because there is no contract unless a proposal is accepted, parties are still under negotiations and under no obligation or liability to each other.[197]

A court may be required to decide whether, and at what stage, negotiations have resulted in a contract. When there is a lengthy course of negotiations between parties, it may be difficult to decide when they have reached an agreement and have made a binding contract.[198] If one party has acted on the basis that a contract existed or performance has been rendered, a court is more likely to hold that there is a contract.[199] In ultimate analysis, a court would consider steps in negotiations as offer-acceptance-counter-offer-acceptance.

212. Parties may, however, make an agreement governing the scope and duration of negotiations. They may impose obligations of good faith, sharing private information, confidentiality, not withdrawing their offers before a stated period, or not negotiating with any third party for a stated period of time or until the negotiations in hand are complete.

They may also provide for consequences of breaking these obligations or breakdown in negotiations. For example, A may agree with B that if B withdraws from negotiations, he shall pay the preparatory or pre-contractual expenses or a stated amount to A. Agreements of confidentiality will survive breakdown of negotiations.

II. Pre-contractual Liability

213. There is no obligation to observe good faith during negotiations, unless the negotiating parties have bound themselves to do so under an agreement supported by consideration. Similarly, an agreement not to negotiate with any third party for a specified period of time would be enforceable.

A party is also not bound to inform to another any private information received related to the subject matter of the contract, even though such information would affect the decision of the other to make that contract, unless the contract is of the nature *uberrima fides*, in which one party is bound to observe good faith toward another. Even in such cases, failure to give information, or non-disclosure, would make a contract voidable at the option of the other party for misrepresentation or fraud, as the case may be.

III. Breakdown of Negotiations

214. It is already seen that the offeror is not bound to keep his proposal open and may withdraw it at any time before its acceptance, even if he has promised to keep the proposal open for a specified time, unless the promise to keep the proposal open is supported by consideration.

---

197. *Haji Mohamed Haji Jiva v. E Spinner* (1900) ILR 24 Bom 510.
198. *RickmersVerwaltung GmbH v. Indian Oil Corporation Ltd* AIR 1999 SC 504.
199. *Geo-Group Communications INC v. IOL Broadband Ltd*, AIR 2010 SC (Supp) 271.

Any party negotiating a contract is free to call off negotiations without any liability. The reason or motive for withdrawing from a proposal or negotiations is immaterial. However, a 'lock-out' agreement under which one party agrees for good consideration not to negotiate except with the other party for a specified time is enforceable. Such a negative agreement enables parties time to consider proposals and incur expenditure to consider whether the proposed contract is a worthwhile project.

Chapter 2. Conditions of Substantive Validity

§1. Capacity of the Parties

I. Competency

215. The competency[200] to make a contract or to enter into legal transactions does not arise merely because a person has rights. A person having rights or property may be incompetent by law to deal with them. Competency to contract refers to the capacity of a person to bind himself by promise. A person competent to contract is competent to transfer property.[201] Therefore, a person may be a transferee of property, may enforce a contract as promisee, or may take benefit under a contract, even if incompetent.

Indian law does not recognize limited capacity to contract, and a person who is incompetent to contract as above, is wholly incompetent to contract. Any transaction imposing liability on such person is void. The issue of comparative advantage or economic disadvantage or *le'sion* is, therefore, of no consequence.

A statutory person can exercise power of contracting subject to the restrictions and formalities imposed by statute governing it. The governments of the Union and the states can make contracts in the manner provided by the Constitution of India.[202]

216. Every person is competent to contract if he (i) is of the age of majority according to the law to which he is subject; (ii) is of sound mind; and (iii) not disqualified from contracting by any law to which he is subject.[203]

Contracts may be made by guardians for minors and by guardians or managers of persons suffering from mental illness. Their respective powers and the effect of such contracts are discussed later.

II. Protection of Incompetent Persons

217. The purpose of provisions of competency is to protect persons whose mental faculties are undeveloped, from doing injury to themselves and from exploitation by others. Any agreement made by such persons is, therefore, *void ab initio.*[204]

There is a presumption in favour of competency to contract. The burden of proving incompetency, which is a strict one, lies on the party alleging incompetency.

The aim of protecting incompetent persons takes precedence over the needs of business. Thus, a person dealing with a minor cannot show that he reasonably

200. Sections 10 and 11 of the Indian Contract Act use the term 'competency' to contract.
201. Section 7 the Transfer of Property Act 1882.
202. See paras 769–773 *infra*.
203. Section 11 of the Indian Contract Act.
204. *Mohori Bibee v. Dhurmodas Ghose* (1903) 30 IA 114.

believed the minor to be of age or that the minor induced him to contract by fraudulently misrepresenting age. A minor is not estopped from pleading minority and can always set up his own incompetency.

218. However, if a person incapable of entering a contract, or any one whom he is legally bound to support, is supplied by another person with necessaries suited to his condition in life, the person who has furnished such supplies is entitled to be reimbursed from the property of such incapable person.[205] This is a liability in *quasi-contract.*[206]

III. Minors

A. *Who Is a Minor?*

219. Every person is competent to contract who is of the age of majority according to the law to which he is subject.[207] Every person *domiciled in India* shall be deemed to have attained his majority when he shall have completed his age of 18 years.[208] Ordinarily, the age of majority will be determined by the law of minor's domicile; but despite such express statutory provision, competency might be determined in case of mercantile contracts by the law of the place where the contract was made.[209]

B. *Effect of Agreement*

220. Under the Indian law, an agreement with a minor is *void ab initio,*[210] unlike English law, which considers a minor's contract voidable in certain cases. A minor need not repudiate it.

C. *Cancellation*

221. A minor may, if he so wishes, sue to set aside the agreement. If any such agreement is in writing, he can sue to have the instrument cancelled.[211] However, his agreement being *void ab initio*, the minor can directly seek the true relief he seeks, viz. possession, without seeking cancellation.[212]

---

205. Section 68 Indian Contract Act.
206. See paras 805–807 *infra*.
207. Section 11 of the Indian Contract Act.
208. Section 3 of the Indian Majority Act 1875.
209. *T N S Firm v. V P S Muhammad Hussain* AIR 1933 Mad 756.
210. *Mohori Bibee v. Dhurmodas Ghose* (1903) 30 IA 114.
211. Section 33 of the Specific Relief Act 1963 provides for the relief of cancellation.
212. *Prem Singh v. Birbal,* (2006) 5 SCC 353.

On cancellation of an instrument at the instance of a minor, the court can require the minor to restore the benefit received under the agreement or to compensate the other party.

Where a minor defendant resists any suit against him on the ground of his own incompetency, he may be required to restore to the plaintiff the benefit he received under the agreement, for example, to repay the money received.[213]

The remedy of cancellation is discretionary and is exercised equitably. The court might even refuse to order return of benefit or compensation. Return of benefit or compensation might be more readily ordered where the minor has misrepresented his age.

D. Minor Can Take Benefits

222. A minor will not be liable, but can enforce a contract made in his favour. Thus, a sale in favour of minor who has paid the price is valid. A minor mortgagee can sue to recover the principal and the interest of the amount advanced by him. He can sue for possession of the property he has purchased and for the price of goods sold by him. He can sue on a promissory note or a bond executed in his favour.

A minor cannot be a partner, but can be admitted into the benefits of partnership.[214] As between the principal and third persons, even a minor may become an agent; but he will not be responsible to the principal.[215] A minor may draw, endorse, deliver, and negotiate any negotiable instrument so as to bind all parties except himself.[216]

Because a lease imposes obligations on a lessee, a minor's lease is void.[217] A minor might not be a member of a company, but if shares of a company are owned by a minor, his guardian may be shown as member in the register of members. However, the minor's name can be entered in the register if he has received shares by succession.[218] A minor may be admitted to membership of certain societies.[219] A person who has attained 15 years of age can become a member of a Trade Union.[220]

E. Guardians and Their Powers

223. Natural guardians and guardians appointed by a court, as legal guardians, can contract on behalf of minors. Personal law determines the natural guardian of

213. *Mohori Bibee v. Dhurmodas Ghose* (1903) 30 IA 114.
214. Section 30 of the Indian Partnership Act 1930.
215. Section 184 of the Indian Contract Act.
216. Section 26 of the Negotiable Instruments Act 1882.
217. Section 107 of the Transfer of Property Act 1882.
218. A. Ramaiya, *Guide to the Companies Act* 382–384 (14th edn); Datta on the Company Law, 166–68 (5th edn).
219. See for example s. 22 of the Maharashtra Cooperative Societies Act 1960, which provides that a person competent to contract can become a member of a Cooperative Society, but allows minors to be admitted to a society exclusively formed for benefit of students of a school or a college.
220. Section 21 of the Trade Unions Act 1926.

the minor. A minor's father is his natural guardian under all personal laws. The guardian in the absence of the father is different under various laws. A court can appoint in guardianship proceedings, a guardian for the person or property (or both) of a minor.[221]

224. A natural guardian of a minor can do all acts necessary or reasonable and proper for the minor's benefit or for realization, protection, or benefit of the minor's estate. Such a contract binds the minor even after he becomes a major.

A guardian cannot bind a minor by personal covenant, including a contract for purchase or sale of immovable property. He cannot without permission of the court mortgage, charge, or transfer by way of sale, gift, exchange, or lease any immovable property for more than a prescribed number of years.[222] If he does so, the minor can avoid the transaction on becoming major. Any transaction made on behalf of a minor by a self-appointed guardian not otherwise having any authority, or by a de facto guardian, is void and does not bind the minor at all.[223]

IV. Unsoundness of Mind

225. A person is incompetent to contract if he is of unsound mind at the time of making it.

A. Mental Incompetency to Contract

226. Mental incompetency to contract is quite distinct from being illiterate or unfamiliar with language, which also prevent a person's understanding of how a contract affects his interests.

Mental incompetency involves not only a lack of understanding about the transaction, but also an awareness that one does not understand it. It may arise because of mental disease or disorder, lack of mental development, illness, old age, bodily illness or distress, drunkenness, or influence of drugs. A person is not incompetent merely because he is mentally weak, has lost memory, or is illiterate or unexposed to urban life.

B. Sound Mind

227. A person is of sound mind for the purpose of contracting if, at the time when he makes it, he is capable of understanding it and of forming a rational judgment as to its effect on his interests.[224] There is no fixed standard of soundness of mind for all transactions.

221. The Hindu Maintenance and Guardianship Act 1956; The Guardian and Wards Act 1890.
222. Section 29 of the Guardians and Wards Act, 1890.
223. *Madhegowda v. Ankegowda* AIR 2002 SC 215.
224. Section 12 of the Indian Contract Act.

This test must be satisfied at the time the contract is made. A person who is usually of unsound mind, but occasionally of sound mind, may make a contract when he is of sound mind. A mentally ill person in a psychiatric hospital or nursing home, who is at the intervals of sound mind, may contract during those intervals. A person who is usually of sound mind, but occasionally of unsound mind, may not make a contract when he is of unsound mind. A sane person, who is delirious from fever, or who is so drunk that he cannot understand the terms of a contract, or from a rational judgment as to its effect on his interests, cannot contract while such delirium or drunkenness lasts.

C. Burden of Proof

228. There is a presumption in favour of sanity. The person who alleges unsoundness must prove it. If a person has been adjudged lunatic or mentally ill person under the Mental Health Act 1987, it would only shift the burden of proof on the person who alleges sanity.

D. Effect

229. An agreement or transfer of property is void if made by a person of unsound mind at the time of making it. It has the same effect as in case of minority. A contract made with sound mind will not be affected if a party subsequently becomes of unsound mind.

The property of a person of unsound mind will be liable for necessaries supplied to him or to those dependant on him.

E. Guardian's Powers

230. When a person is adjudged under the Mental Health Act 1987 as mentally ill or incapable of taking care of himself or his property, the district court can appoint a guardian to take care of his person, or a manager to take care of his property. Such a manager can exercise all powers for management of the property. If he has to mortgage, charge, sell, gift or exchange, or lease for more than five years, immovable property of the mentally ill person, he must seek permission of the district court; else the transfer is void.[225]

V. Persons Disqualified by Law

231. Certain classes of persons may be disqualified by statute from making contracts, specifically or generally, for example, persons whose properties are under superintendence or management under laws made to protect encumbered estates.

225. Sections 51 and 59 of the Mental Health Act 1987.

Yet other classes of persons may be disqualified by statutes from making contracts where their connection with the business involved in the transaction is likely to enable them to use influence or information acquired. Thus, a judge, legal practitioner, or office of the court cannot deal in actionable claims. Officers in patent offices cannot take any interest in any patent. A forest officer cannot have interest in any lease of contract for working any forest.

VI. Married Women

232. A married woman in India has always had contracting competency. Her competency is not affected by marriage, nor is her right to own or dispose of property.

VII. Aliens

233. An alien can contract if he is competent according to the law to which he is subject. This matter properly belongs to another branch of law – private international law.

VIII. Legal Persons

234. A legal person like a company or corporation does not have inherent incapacity to contract like minors do. It can exercise its power subject to the formalities imposed by statute.

A company cannot contract before its incorporation.[226] If a contract is made by the promoters for the benefit of a proposed company under formation, it can be enforced after its incorporation by or against the company, if the contract is warranted by the terms of incorporation and the company has accepted the contract and communicated such acceptance to the other party.[227]

IX. Insolvent Persons

235. An insolvent person[228] is not incompetent to make contracts after insolvency proceedings have commenced and before adjudication. Any debts or liabilities contracted by him after presenting petition and before adjudication can be proved by his creditor only if the creditor can prove that he had no notice of the insolvency petition. If he has notice, he is under a personal disability to prove it. He cannot, therefore, recover it at all.

226. *Andhra Pradesh Tourism Development Corporation v. Pampa Hotels Ltd* AIR 2010 SC 1806.
227. Sections 15(h) and 19(e) of the Specific Relief Act 1963.
228. The law of insolvency is contained in two laws: (i) The Presidency-Towns Insolvency Act 1900 and (ii) The Provincial Insolvency Act 1920.

After adjudication, the debtor applies for a discharge. He is discharged after a hearing. An absolute order of discharge brings him to his original status. It releases him from all provable debts (except those due to the government, maintenance of wife, debts of liabilities incurred by him by fraud), whether they were actually proved at insolvency or not. After discharge, the insolvent is a free man and can make new contracts and incur fresh debts and liabilities.

§2. Defects of Consent

I. Consent and Free Consent

236. Parties to contract must have consented to its terms, and such consent must be free.[229]

Two or more persons are said to consent when they agree on the same thing in the same sense.[230]

Consent is free when not caused by coercion, undue influence, fraud, misrepresentation, or mistake.[231] Thus, where despite the existence of such factors, consent has been given with full information of facts and after complete thought or deliberation, the contract cannot be attacked.

Where consent is caused by coercion, undue influence, fraud, or misrepresentation, the contract is voidable; mistake renders the agreement void.

II. Mistake

A. Mutual Mistake

237. A mistake might prevent parties from reaching an agreement at all. This can occur, for example, if one party intended to contract about one thing and the other about another, or where one party was mistaken about the identity of the person he wishes to contract with, or where the terms accepted by one party are different from those offered. Here there is no consent at all and no agreement to be enforced.

B. Common Mistake

238. When parties agree about the same thing, but their agreement is based on a fundamental mistaken assumption, the mistake affects contractual consent. An agreement exists, but is void. An agreement is void where both or all parties are under a mistake as to a matter of fact essential to the agreement,[232] as follows:

229. Section 10 of the Indian Contract Act.
230. Section 13 of the Indian Contract Act.
231. Section 14 of the Indian Contract Act.
232. Section 20 of the Indian Contract Act.

(i) there is a mistake as to fact, not one of unrealized erroneous expectations, or error of judgment about prospects under the contract. An erroneous opinion as to the value of the subject matter is not a mistake of fact. The mistake is not of Indian law, but mistake of foreign law is considered as one of fact.
(ii) all parties entertain the same mistake of fact. A unilateral mistake does not avoid the contract, nor a situation in which one party knows the facts but does not make them known to the other party.
(iii) the mistake is of a matter of fact *essential* to the agreement – that is, such that had the party realized the mistake, he would not have made that agreement. The mistake must be as to the substance of the subject matter – as opposed to its qualities; or as to the nature of the transaction – as opposed to its terms. Mistake vitiates the agreement if it relates to the existence of the subject matter, or the existence of state of things fundamental to the contract; or title or rights of parties to the subject matter of the contract; or quantity of subject matter, and if it is fundamental going to the root of the matter.

C. Doctrine of Narrow Limits

239. A party cannot invoke mistake to avoid his agreement if he has no reasonable grounds for his belief or where it was his duty to know or he had the means of knowledge about the fact essential to the agreement, or he could have easily verified the facts. Stupidity, ignorance or carelessness cannot affect contract.

In practice, courts would be reluctant to strike out a contract on the ground of mistake, because a number of situations not contemplated by the parties are at the risk of one or other of the parties. No party should be tempted to set up a mistake to get out of a bad bargain. The rule of mistake as invalidating a contract is, therefore, confined within very narrow limits.

D. Payment Made under Mistake

240. The grounds on which a *payment* made under mistake can be recovered under the principles of *quasi-contract* are much wider than mistakes invalidating consent and nullifying contract.[233]

III. Misrepresentation

241. A misrepresentation is a false representation. If made innocently, it does not affect the contract.

233. Section 72 of the Indian Contract Act.

A. *What Is Misrepresentation?*

242. There are three categories of misrepresentation entitling the misled party to avoid the contract:

(i) *False assertion:* A statement of fact that is false, if the maker believes it to be true, but which is not justified by the information he possesses. If made without honest belief in its truth, it amounts to fraud.
(ii) *Active concealment:* Any breach of duty that gains an advantage to the person committing it by misleading another to his prejudice, there being no intention to deceive. Where the facts are specially within one party's knowledge, a positive duty of disclosure is added, and the contract is made voidable by mere passive failure to communicate a material fact, such as contracts of insurance.
(iii) *Inducing a mistake:* Causing a party to an agreement to make a mistake as to the substance of the thing that is the subject of the agreement, even though done innocently.

B. *Representation and Term of Contract*

243. A statement is a representation that is intended to induce the other party, but the party making it does not undertake to make it good. If such a representation is false, the contract is voidable.

It is a term of the contract in which the party stating undertakes to make it good. Then the aggrieved party can claim damages for breach. Even where the parties do not make such express provision, if they represent or warrants the accuracy of the representation, that is, promises to make it good, it would be construed a term of the contract. The primary test is of the contractual intention, an intention of both the parties that contractual liability would attach in respect of inaccuracy of the statement.

IV. Fraud

A. *What Is Fraud?*

244. 'Fraud' means and includes[234] any of the following acts committed by a party to a contract, or with his connivance, or by his agent, with intent to deceive another party thereto or his agent or to induce him to enter into the contract:

(i) *False suggestion:* the suggestion, as to a fact, of that which is not true by one who does not believe it to be true. A positive knowledge of its falsehood is not necessary; it is fraud where the statement is made without belief in its

234. Section 17 of the Indian Contract Act.

truth. Thus, there is no fraud if the false statement is made through want of care or is honestly believed even on insufficient grounds.

(ii) *Active concealment:* the active concealment of a fact by one having knowledge or belief of the fact. The Indian law does not impose duty of disclosure on grounds of good faith. Thus, between traders, it is not a fraud for one party to withhold private information of change in prices that would affect the willingness of the other to make the contract. Each party is expected to obtain himself the necessary information and cannot expect it from the other, even when that other is aware of his ignorance. It is fraud where a party to the contract knows or believes a fact to be true, but conceals it *actively* from the other party with a view to induce that person to enter into a contract. Mere silence as to facts likely to affect the willingness of a person to enter into a contract is not fraud, unless the circumstances of the case are such it is the duty of the person keeping silence to speak or unless his silence is in itself equivalent to speech. Such duty of disclosure may arise in particular classes of contracts, for example, in insurance contracts between an insurer and insured[235] or where one party stands in fiduciary relationship with the other.

(iii) *A false promise:* a promise made without any intention of performing it. To bring the case within this clause, it must be shown that the promisor had no intention of performing the promise at the time of making it, for example, buying goods with the intention of not paying the price.

(iv) *Any other act fitted to deceive:* a provision inserted merely for the sake of abundant caution.

(v) *Other fraudulent acts:* any such act or omission as the law specially declares to be fraudulent.

Thus, under the Transfer of Property Act 1882,[236] a seller of immovable property is required to disclose to the buyer any material defect in the property or in the seller's title. The buyer is required to disclose to the seller any fact as to the nature or extent of the seller's interest in the property that materially increases the value of such interest. Any such 'omission to make such disclosures … is fraudulent'.

B. State of Mind

245. A mere false statement is not fraud. It is fraud where a person causes another to act on a false belief by a representation he does not himself believe to be true. Under the Indian Contract Act, certain forms of fraud can vitiate a contract, though there may not be any misrepresentation of fact. Where a false statement is knowingly made it is unnecessary to probe into the motive.

235. See for example the Marine Insurance Act, 1963, ss 19–20; *Krishnawanti Puri v. Life Insurance corporation of India* AIR 1975 Del 19.

236. Section 55 of the Transfer of Property Act 1882.

There is no fraud if the party alleging fraud had the facts before it or had the means to know them, even if a false statement has been made.[237]

C. *Effect of Fraud*

246. A contract consent to which is caused by fraud, is voidable. The party deceived has an option. He can affirm the contract and insist that he be put in the position in which he would have been if the representations were true.

Or he can rescind the contract to the extent it is not performed. If he affirms the contract, he may require performance of the whole and every part of it, or in default, damages for non-performance. Compensation can be awarded in lieu of completion or enforcement.[238]

V. Coercion

A. *What Is Coercion*

247. 'Coercion' is the committing, or threatening to commit, any act forbidden by the Indian Penal Code, or the unlawful detaining, or threatening to detain, any property, to the prejudice of any person whatever, with the intention of causing any person to enter into an agreement.[239] Coercion may have been used at any place. It need not have proceeded from a party to the contract, nor directed against a party.

The words 'act forbidden by the Indian Penal Code' make it necessary for the court to decide in a civil action, whether the alleged act of coercion is such as to amount to an offence. The language of the statute as it stands does not cover a threat to commit an offence punishable under any other criminal law, and a change in the law toward that end has been recommended.

Refusal to withdraw a prosecution unless a bond was executed for the amount due, or a threat of proceeding on strike, do not amount to coercion. Mere threat of bringing a criminal charge does not amount to coercion, as it is not per se forbidden by the Penal Code. But threat of bringing a false charge with the object of making another do a thing is coercion, the latter being forbidden by the Indian Penal Code. Where an agent whose services were terminated detained accounts to obtain his release, the release was induced by coercion.

B. *Economic Duress*

248. Compulsion of law is not coercion under this section. Although economic duress is recognized under English law as a factor vitiating a contract, the Indian

237. *Kamal Kant Paliwal v. Prakash Devi Paliwal* AIR 1976 Raj 79.
238. *Sorabshah Pestonji v. Secretary of State for India* AIR 1928 Bom 17.
239. Section 15 of the Indian Contract Act.

Contract Act does not recognize it as a factor entitling the aggrieved person to avoid the contract.

C. *Effect*

249. A contract induced by coercion is voidable at the option of the party whose consent is so caused.

D. *Claim in Quasi-Contract*

250. Although the definition of coercion for avoiding the transaction is narrow, if money is paid under any type of compulsion, it is recoverable as *quasi-contract.*[240]

VI. Undue Influence

A. *What Is Undue Influence*

251. A contract is induced by 'undue influence' where the relations subsisting between the parties are such that one of the parties is in a position to dominate the will of the other and uses that position to obtain an unfair advantage over the other.[241]

It requires the court trying a case to consider two things:[242] (i) are the relations between the parties such that one is in a position to dominate the will of the other; and (ii) has such position been used to obtain an unfair advantage over the other? Unlike in English law, which requires that the person influenced must show manifest disadvantage to him, Indian law requires an unfair advantage to the person exercising undue influence.

B. *Dominating Position*

252. The relationships in which such dominating influence exist are many. Parties need not be related by blood, marriage, or adoption.

A person is deemed to be in a position to dominate the will of another (i) where he holds a real or apparent authority over the other (employer and employee, an officer and his subordinate, an income-tax officer and an assesse, a police officer and an accused) or where he stand in a fiduciary relation to the other (parent and child, solicitor and client, trustee and *cestui que* trust, doctor and patient); or (ii) where he

---

240. Section 72 of the Indian Contract Act; see paras 818–819 *infra*.
241. Section 16 of the Indian Contract Act.
242. *Ladli Parshad Jaiswal v. Karnal Distillery Co Ltd* AIR 1963 SC 1279.

makes a contract with a person whose mental capacity is temporarily or permanently affected by the reason of age, illness, or mental or bodily distress.

The doctrine of undue influence would not arise between banker and customer, husband and wife, creditor and debtor, landlord and tenant, or because the parties stand on unequal footing in terms of their bargaining power.

C. Influence Must Be Undue

253. It is not enough to show exercise of influence; influence must be 'undue'. Advice, persuasion, appeal to the affections or ties of kindred, to a gratitude of sentiment for past services, or pity for future destitution – are legitimate and do not amount to undue influence.

When such influence is exercised, the acts of a person under influence are not his free and voluntary acts. Undue influence is such influence, which having regard to the age and capacity of the party, the nature of the transaction and all the circumstances of the case appear to hinder exercise of free and deliberate judgment.

D. Unconscionability

254. Undue influence must be proved, mere unconscionability cannot avoid a contract.[243]

The fact that the transaction is unconscionable shifts the burden of proof in a case in which undue influence has been alleged. Thus, where a person is in a position to dominate the will of another, enters into a contract with him, and the transaction appears on the face of it or on the evidence adduced to be unconscionable, the burden of proving that such contract was not induced by undue influence lies on the person in the dominating position.

The reason for this rule is that a person who has dominated the will of another and obtained an advantage can suppress evidence supporting the plea of undue influence. This presumption can be rebutted by showing that the person alleging undue influence had independent advice from a disinterested person.

VII. Gross Disparity

A. Inadequate Consideration

255. Disparity between the benefit or performance required by the parties does not affect the contract. If consent of the promisor is free, an agreement is not affected merely because the consideration is inadequate. Where a party alleges that his consent is not free on account of coercion, undue influence, misrepresentation, or fraud, the fact that consideration is inadequate will be considered relevant.

243. *Kesavulu Naidu v. Arithulai Ammal* (1912) 36 ILR Mad 533.

B. Unequal Bargaining Powers

256. A contract cannot be avoided by one party merely by reason that it arose out of inequality of bargaining powers under the Indian Contract Act, unless it was induced by undue influence.

The Supreme Court was required to invoke the doctrine of public policy to strike down an unfair and unreasonable clause in a contract made between parties not equal in bargaining powers.[244]

It also prescribed limits of this principle. It would apply where the inequality of bargaining power is the result of the great disparity in the economic strength of the contracting parties in situations in which the weaker party is in a position in which he can obtain goods or services or means of livelihood only on the terms imposed by the stronger party or go without them. It will also apply where a person has no meaningful choice, but to give his assent to a contract or to sign on the dotted line in a prescribed or standard form or to accept a set of rules as part of the contract. Unconscionability in such circumstances is grounds for invalidating the contract by the court, which considers it void as opposed to public policy.

This principle will not apply to a commercial contract between businessmen.[245]

C. Unfair Advantage and Hardship

257. Where the terms of the contract, the conduct of the parties at the time of making it, or the circumstances under which it was made are such that the contract, though not voidable, gives the plaintiff an unfair advantage over the defendant, the court may refuse specific performance. Mere inadequacy of consideration or the mere fact that the contract is onerous to the defendant or improvident in its nature do not constitute an unfair advantage.

A court cannot control performance or relieve parties of their obligations under a contract on the grounds that its performance is onerous or causes hardship to any party. But unforeseen hardship suffered by the defendant can be grounds to refuse the discretionary relief of specific performance.[246] Subsequent rise in price does not warrant refusal of specific performance. Hardship is to be reckoned at the time of the contract.

D. Unfairness

257.1. In its 199th Report of 2006, the Law Commission of India makes recommendations that courts shall give remedies if a contract is affected by procedural or substantive unfairness.

A term shall be procedurally unfair if it has resulted in an unjust advantage or unjust disadvantage to one party on account of the conduct of the other party, or the

244. *Central Inland Water Transport Corporation Ltd v. Brojo Nath Ganguly* AIR 1986 SC 1571.
245. *S K Jain v. State of Haryana* 2009 AIR SCW 1934.
246. Section 20 of the Specific Relief Act 1963.

manner in which or the circumstances under which the contract has been entered into or the term thereof has been arrived at by the parties. In deciding this question, a court may take into account various enumerated factors, such as knowledge and understanding of the promisee, relative bargaining strength of parties, standards of fair dealing, one party suffering disadvantage, and so on.

A term shall be substantively unfair if such contract or the term thereof is in itself harsh, oppressive, or unconscionable to one of the parties. Factors that courts can take into account are whether the term is unreasonably difficult to comply with, whether contract is in standard form, disproportion of benefits, and disproportionate penalty. A clause allowing unilateral power of termination will also be affected if it can be exercised without good reason.

A court shall have power to raise the issue of unfairness, even if no party has raised it in pleadings. If it finds that any term is procedurally or substantively unfair, it can refuse to enforce the entire contract of the term, declare the term void, or vary the contract to remove the unfairness, apart from usual reliefs of refund of price, compensation, injunction, and so on.

E. Usury

258. The Usurious Loans Act 1918 empowers a court to reopen transactions of loans in cases in which it is satisfied: (1) that interest or other return is excessive and (2) that the transaction is substantially unfair and to revise the transaction between the parties. The court can also reduce the amount payable to a reasonable amount, having regard to the risk and all circumstances of the case.

§3. Other Conditions of Validity

259. The Indian Contract law makes a distinction between agreements that are void being unlawful and other void agreements.[247] A void agreement is not enforceable. It need not be forbidden by law.

The difference between the two can best be seen with reference to effect on collateral transactions. A loan given with the purpose of financing a simply void agreement is recoverable. But a loan given for financing an unlawful agreement is unlawful because it has an unlawful object.

I. Void Agreements

260. An agreement is not enforceable if it is declared void by the Indian Contract Act or by any other law in force. The Indian Contract Act declares the following agreements void.

247. *Gherulal Parakh v. Mahadeodas Maiya* AIR 1959 SC 781.

A. *Agreement without Consideration*

261. An agreement without consideration is void, unless it is (i) a registered agreement made out of natural love and affection between parties standing in near relation to each other, (ii) a promise to pay a time-barred debt, or (iii) a promise to pay for past voluntary act.[248]

B. *Agreement in Restraint of Marriage*

262. An agreement in restraint of marriage of any person is void.[249] It is in restraint of marriage if its object or effect is to restrain or prevent a party from marrying any person or that deters a person from marriage as to render uncertain the prospect of his marriage, for example, an agreement not to marry any person other than the other party to the agreement, or that has the effect of preventing a party from marrying within a certain time. A contract to pay a widow or woman an allowance until her death or marriage or remarriage is valid.

Unlike English law, Indian law bars even partial restraints, for example, a prohibition against marrying a named person or class of persons.

C. *Agreement in Restraint of Trade*

263. An agreement restraining a person from carrying on a lawful profession, trade, or business is void to that extent.[250] This is an absolute provision and invalidates all restraints, whether general or partial, whether reasonable or not. The only exception is in favour of purchaser of goodwill of a business, restricted to narrow local limits. Such rigid provision is severely criticized. This provision was made at a time when trade was undeveloped and required protection from restraints. The Law Commission has already recommended that reasonable partial restraints be permitted.[251]

1. Restraint of Trade

264. An agreement in restraint of trade is one in which one party agrees to restrict his liberty in the future in such a manner as he chooses to carry on trade with other persons not parties to the contract.[252] Such a term is common in contracts for sale of business and employment. It is also found in contracts of exclusive dealership, franchise, professional engagements of sportsmen and performers, and so on.

---

248. Section 25 of the Indian Contract Act; see para. 139 *supra*.
249. Section 26 of the Indian Contract Act.
250. Section 27 of the Indian Contract Act.
251. Thirteenth Report of the Law Commission of India, 1958.
252. *Petrofina (Great Britain) Ltd v. Martin* [1966] Ch. 146.

This provision strikes only those agreements that impose a total bar to the exercise of a lawful business, howsoever short the period or limited the area. It does not affect agreements that restrain any aspect of conduct of business. An agreement not to sell for less than the rate fixed by contract is valid, so is a seller's agreement not to sell goods to others so long as he is to sell to the defendant. But an agreement is in restraint of trade if it binds a manufacturer not to sell goods to any person other than the other party, but does not bind the other party to buy all the produce or any definite quantity.

2. Restraint during Contract

265. The Indian courts have consistently held that any restriction operating during the subsistence of a contract is not one in restraint of trade unless the contract is one-sided.

A promise by an employee to serve the employer and no one else during the continuance of employment can be enforced. A restriction in a franchise agreement not to sell products or services of any other person also can be enforced during the subsistence of the agreement. Such a restraint can be enforced by injunction where it contains a negative clause, express or implied.[253]

Restrictions operating after termination of the contract are void as in restraint of trade.[254]

Unlike in English law, such restraint extending beyond the term of the employment or the main contract is void, even in circumstances in which the restraint would stand the test of reasonableness.

3. Effect of Restraint

266. The restraint only is invalid, and if severable, does not affect the validity of the main contract.

4. Exceptions

267. An agreement not to carry on within specified local limits a business similar to the business of which goodwill is sold can be enforced, provided the limits of the restraint are reasonable.

The Indian Partnership Act 1932 enables certain restraints on the rights of partners to carry on competing business or trade.[255] A partner can restrain himself from carrying on any business other than that of the firm while he is a partner or from

253. Section 42 of the Specific Relief Act 1963.

254. *Niranjan Shankar Golikari v. Century Spinning and Manufacturing Co Ltd* AIR 1967 SC 1098 (employment); *Gujarat Bottling Co Ltd v. Coca Cola Co* AIR 1995 SC 2372; *Percept D'Mark (India) Pvt Ltd v. Zaheer Khan* AIR 2006 SC 3426 (sportsman).

255. Sections 11(2), 36(2), 54 and 55(3) of the Indian Partnership Act 1932.

carrying on a similar business on ceasing to be a partner within a specified period or local limits. Partners may, on or in anticipation of the dissolution of the firm, agree that some or all of them will not carry on a business similar to that of the firm within a specified period or local limits. Any partner may, on sale after dissolution of the goodwill of the firm, agree with the buyer that such partner will not carry on any business similar to that of the firm within a specified period and within specified local limits. In the last three cases, the agreement would be valid if the restrictions imposed are reasonable.

D. Agreement in Restraint of Legal Proceedings

1. Restraint of Legal Proceedings

268. An agreement is void to the extent it restricts *absolutely* a party from enforcing his contractual rights by usual proceedings in ordinary courts or if it limits the time within which he may enforce his rights.[256] Thus, an agreement by an employee not to sue for wrongful dismissal is void, or a condition restraining a transferee from enforcing in any way his rights under the transfer. But an agreement not to file appeal is valid.[257]

2. Restricting Limitation Period

269. An agreement is also void if it provides that a suit should be brought for the breach of any terms of the agreement within a time shorter than the period of limitation prescribed by law.

3. Extinctive Clauses

270. The Indian Contract Act was amended in 1997 to prohibit clauses seeking to extinguish rights of any party thereto, or discharge any party thereto from any liability, under or in respect of any contract on the expiry of a specified period so as to restrict any party from enforcing his rights.

Such clauses usually found in insurance contracts had been upheld before the amendment. They ensured that claims under insurance policies were made early and facilitated prompt investigation. This prohibition will not, however, affect a term requiring notice of claim to the insurer, which is a condition precedent to the liability of an insurer. An amendment of 2012 excepts guarantees given by banks from this provision.

256. Section 28 of the Indian Contract Act.

257. *Anant Das v. Ashburner & Co* (1876) ILR 1 All 267, FB.

4. Effect of Restraint

271. Where an agreement contains a clause void under these provisions, only that clause is void and unenforceable and not the whole agreement.

5. Arbitration

272. This provision does not affect contracts (i) with a stipulation than an arbitration award shall precede a cause of action and (ii) to refer existing disputes to arbitration.

6. Choice of Jurisdiction

273. Parties often agree that any dispute shall be filed only in a specified court. Such a stipulation is valid.

Jurisdiction of a court to try a dispute is determined with reference to provisions of the Code of Civil Procedure. Under its provisions, a plaintiff can file his suit in the court within whose territorial jurisdiction (i) the defendant or any of them resides or (ii) where the cause of action arose, that is, where the contract was made, or was broken.

Where more than one court has jurisdiction, parties can make a valid agreement that their dispute shall be tried by only one of these courts.[258] This is not an *absolute* restriction, but merely a selection of forum. Such an agreement will oust jurisdiction of other courts only if it is clear, unambiguous, and explicit.

Parties cannot by agreement confer jurisdiction on a court that it does not possess, nor can they divest a court of jurisdiction it possesses under the ordinary law. The chosen court, therefore, must have jurisdiction under the provisions of the Civil Procedure Code. If chosen court has jurisdiction, jurisdiction of all other courts will be excluded.[259] If the court mentioned in the contract has no jurisdiction at all, the jurisdiction of other courts is not barred. However, in a contract involving an international element, parties can choose to submit their dispute to the exclusive jurisdiction of a foreign court as a neutral court, although it has otherwise no jurisdiction.[260]

E. Uncertain Agreement

1. Uncertain Terms

274. An agreement is void if its meaning is not certain or not capable of being made certain.[261]

---

258. *A B C Laminart Pvt Ltd v. A P Agencies, Salem* AIR 1989 SC 1239.
259. *2. Hanil Era Textiles Ltd v. Puromatic Filters (P) Ltd* AIR 2004 SC 2432.
260. *3. Modi Entertainment Network v. WSG Cricket Pte Ltd* AIR 2003 SC 1177.
261. Section 29 of the Indian Contract Act.

An agreement might be uncertain either because its terms are ambiguous or vague, because it is incomplete or vague, or because it is incomplete.

A party must be able to identify with sufficient precision that obligation which he seeks to enforce. A contract is enforceable if its meaning is clear on the face of it. But it also can be enforced if its meaning can be found. If this is not possible, the contract cannot be enforced.

2. Removing Uncertainty

275. Something intended to have effect should not be struck down so easily. A contract is not void if its terms can be made certain. Vagueness or uncertainty can be removed by proper interpretation. The court will attempt to give meaning to the terms and uphold the contract; and for that purpose apply the objective test, imply terms, consider the words used, their context, and so on.

In commercial and business contracts, the contracts will be struck down for uncertainty only in extreme cases. Courts may be more willing to find a binding contract where the contract has been partly performed or where significant reliance has taken place. Moreover, a contract will be void for uncertainty only if its essential terms are uncertain or incomplete.

3. Court Cannot Make New Contract

276. A court will attempt to give meaning only to terms agreed. It cannot supply defects or clear ambiguity occurring in language of the document.[262] When the language in the document is plain and applies accurately to existing facts, extrinsic evidence cannot be given to show that the language was not meant to apply to such facts.[263]

If the language in a document is clear but unmeaning to existing facts, evidence can be given to show that the language was used in a peculiar sense, that it applies to one of several persons or things, or to give meaning to illegible characters.[264]

F. Wagering Agreements

277. A wagering agreement is a promise to give money or money's worth on the determination or ascertainment of an uncertain event.[265] Agreements by way of wager are void; and no suit can be brought for recovering anything alleged to be won on any wager or entrusted to any person to abide the result of any game or other

262. Section 93 of the Indian Evidence Act 1872.
263. Section 94 of the Indian Evidence Act 1872.
264. Sections 95–98 of the Indian Evidence Act 1972.
265. Sir William Anson, *On Law of Contracts*, quoted with approval by the Supreme Court in *Gherulal Parakh v. Mahadeodas Maiya* AIR 1959 SC 781.

uncertain event on which any wager is made.[266] The nature of such agreements and their enforceability is discussed later in Chapter 3 of Part II.

G. *Initial Impossibility*

278. An agreement to do an act impossible in itself is void.[267] But if one party person has promised to do something that he knew, or, with reasonable diligence might have known, and that the promisee did not know to be impossible or unlawful, such promisor must make compensation to such promisee for any loss that such promisee sustains through the non-performance of the promise.[268]

II. Unlawful Agreements (Existing and Licit Cause)

279. Cause and consideration have the same role to play in the law of contracts. They make it enforceable. Unlike the requirement of a cause in the French family of legal system for the validity of contract, the Indian law requires consideration. In a legal system that does not recognize or require consideration or price for the bargain, the existence of a lawful and moral cause becomes necessary to bind the promisor to his promise. Cause and consideration are two different issues.

III. Lawful Consideration and Object

A. *Unlawful Consideration and Object*

280. In regard to legality or lawfulness, the Act provides that an agreement would be enforceable if it is made for a lawful consideration and lawful object. Consideration or object of an agreement is lawful[269] unless it is:

(i) forbidden by law;
(ii) is of such nature that, if permitted, it would defeat the provisions of any law or is fraudulent; or
(iii) involves or implies, injury to the person or property of another; or
(iv) the court regards it as immoral or opposed to public policy.

Further, even if any part of a single consideration for one or more objects, or any one or any part of any one of several considerations for a single object, is unlawful, the agreement is void.[270]

266. Section 30 of the Indian Contract Act.
267. Section 56 of the Indian Contract Act.
268. Section 56 of the Indian Contract Act.
269. Section 23 of the Indian Contract Act.
270. Section 24 of the Indian Contract Act.

The seriousness and culpability of illegality varies from case to case. An otherwise valid contract may be refused because a provision of statute makes it unlawful in express terms, else because it defeats the provisions of law, or on other grounds like immorality or public policy.

The effect of illegality on a contract also varies. Some agreements may be refused enforcement altogether, whereas in the case of others, the contract may be enforced at the instance of that party which is not guilty, although the Indian Contract Act does not provide so. The law relating to illegality affecting contracts is complex and has grown in an unsystematic manner.

B. Lawful Object

281. The word 'object' means the purpose or design. Thus, where A agrees to sell goods to B, and B while in insolvent circumstances has assigned the benefit of this contract to C for a *consideration* of INR 100, the *object* both of B and C is to defraud B's creditors. The consideration for the assignment of INR 100 is lawful, but the object unlawful because it defeats the provisions of the insolvency law.[271] Where A promises B to drop a prosecution that he has instituted against B for robbery and B promises to restore the value of the things taken, the agreement is void because its object is unlawful.

1. Forbidden by Law

282. Something is forbidden by law if:

(i) it violates an enactment prohibiting that act;
(ii) it is punishable under any enactment;
(iii) it violates any principle of unwritten law, such as personal laws;
(iv) it violates any other rule or regulation;
(v) it is forbidden by an order of a competent authority that has the force of law.[272]

283. To find whether a statute forbids an act one has to see whether its provision intends to prevent the doing of that act or merely to lay down the terms and conditions in which it might be done. It may prohibit in public interest the doing of an act, yet provide no penalty. Another statute may provide a penalty for a seemingly harmless act. It may affect not the contract, but manner of its performance.

If the statute prohibits the agreement itself, it is *void ab initio* and cannot be enforced at all.[273] But where it provides a penalty for making it or for its performance, an innocent party can sue. This would depend on the gravity of the offence or illegality and purpose of the statute. If the purpose of a prohibition in the statute

271. *Jaffer Meher Ali v. Budge Jute Mills Co* (1907) ILR 34 Cal 289.
272. *Abdul Hameed v. Mohd Ishaq* AIR 1975 All 166, FB.
273. *Gulabchand v. Kudilal* AIR 1966 SC 1734.

is merely protection or revenue, the agreement will not be void where the prohibition makes contravention expensive,[274] or is made for administrative purposes, such as for convenient collection of revenue.[275]

284. Examples of agreement prohibited by statute are:

(i) agreements to transfer licenses granted under enactments by the government, such as license to vend liquor or manufacture salt, and so on, or agreements to conduct such business in partnership when prohibited by terms of the license;
(ii) agreements to transfer land prohibited by land reform legislations;
(iii) forward contracts are in contravention of statute regulating them;
(iv) agreement to give or take dowry;
(v) any borrowing of money upon or charge of funds by a local authority made otherwise that for the purposes given under statute;
(vi) any contract limiting or restricting rights in certain statutes declaring such contract void – for example, laws relating to employers' liability, minimum wages, workmen's compensation, payment of wages.

2. Agreements That Defeat the Provisions of Law

285. An agreement reducing or restricting protection given by a statute to a class of persons, or an agreement that enables evading payment of taxes would be unlawful as defeating the purpose of the statute.

3. Agreement Involving Injury to the Person or Property of Another

286. The consideration or object of an agreement is unlawful when it involves or implies injury to the person or property of another. Thus, an agreement between competing bidders at an auction sale to form a ring, peg down the price, purchase the property at the knockout price and share the property is unlawful as implies injury to the debtor.[276]

4. Fraudulent Agreement

287. An agreement to defraud revenue is illegal; for example, an agreement to conceal the actual income so as to reduce the assessment of land revenue is fraudulent.

---

274. *Pamulapati Bhushayya v. Kommareddy Chinnapareddi* AIR 1960 AP 39.
275. *Teegula Babiah v. Mohammed Abuds Subhan Khan* AIR 1954 Hyd 156 FB; *Janki Bai Chunnilal v. Ratan Melu* AIR 1962 MP 117, FB.
276. *Gurmukh Singh v. Amar Singh* (1991) 3 SCC 79.

5. Immoral Agreement

288. Although the word immoral has a wide meaning to include anything that is corrupt or dishonest, for the purposes of provisions in contract law, it has been confined by the Supreme Court to concepts of sexual immorality.[277] An agreement will be declared void if the court considers it as immoral. The concept of immorality changes with time and place.

6. Agreement Opposed to Public Policy

289. The principle of public policy is that law cannot recognize acts tending to injure public welfare. This principle subordinates freedom of parties to contract to the need of public welfare. Public policy requires the court to take into account the interest of persons (the public) other than parties to the contract.

The Indian Contract Act does not define the term 'public policy'. It is not possible to define the expression. It is not the policy of the government, but refers to public good and public interest.[278] It changes with the times. But the court should be cautious and extremely reserved in holding a contract void on this ground.

The Supreme Court has observed:[279]

> the primary duty of a Court of Law is to enforce a promise which the parties have made and to uphold the sanctity of contracts ..., but in certain cases, the Court may relieve them of their duty on a rule founded on what is called the public policy. The doctrine of public policy is extended not only to harmful cases but also to harmful tendencies; ... the principles have been crystallized under different heads and though it is permissible for Courts to expound and apply them to different situations, it should only be invoked in clear and incontestable cases of harm to the public; though heads [of public policy] are not closed and though theoretically it may be permissible to evolve a new head under exceptional circumstances of a changing world, it is advisable in the interest of stability of society not to make any attempt to discover new heads in these days.

290. The courts in India have held following types of contracts as opposed to public policy:

(i) *Maintenance and champertous agreements*: A maintenance agreement is one in which a person, without cause, supports litigation in which he has no legitimate interest. Champertous agreement is where the maintainer stipulates for a share of proceeds of action or property involved in the dispute, it is in essence speculative. Unlike in English law, champertous agreements have never been void per se under the Indian law. The court can hold it opposed to

277. *Gherulal Parakh v. Mahadeodas Maiya* AIR 1959 SC 781.
278. *Central Inland Water Transport Corporation Ltd v. Brojo Nath Ganguly* AIR 1986 SC 1571.
279. *Gherulal Parakh v. Mahadeodas Maiya* AIR 1959 SC 781.

public policy, if it is extortionate and unconscionable so as to be inequitable against the party or has been made for the purpose of gambling in litigation rather than with the bona fide intention of assisting the claim.[280] The court might also award compensation for legitimate expenses incurred by the lender or order recovery of money advanced.[281]

(ii) *Unconscionable agreements*: There being no statutory provision allowing intervention in unconscionable or unfair transactions that fall short of undue influence or coercion, the Supreme Court has struck down such terms on the ground of public policy,[282] where the parties stand in a relationship of disproportionate and unequal bargaining power, leaving no meaningful choice for the disadvantaged party but to agree to the terms offered. This does not apply where the bargaining power of the contracting parties is equal or almost equal, or where both parties are businessmen and the contract is a commercial transaction.

(iii) *Agreements tending to injure good government*, for example, sale or dealings in public offices and appointments that injure public services or that involve bribery.

(iv) *Agreements interfering in the course of justice* or tending to abuse legal process, for example, agreements to conceal crime or to stifle prosecution, compromises of criminal proceedings involving non-compoundable offences, promises to pay money as incentive to give evidence, promise to indemnify a person standing surety for appearance in court of an accused.

(v) *Agreements affecting personal liberty*, for example, a promise compelling the promisor to daily attendance and manual labour until a certain sum was repaid.

(vi) *Agreements affecting freedom or security of marriage*, for example, a promise to enable a married woman to obtain divorce.

(vii) *Marriage brokerage agreements*, for example, agreements to procure marriages of others for payment.

(viii) *Agreements affecting parental authority*.

(ix) *Agreements tending to create monopolies* or that tend to prevent competitive bidding.

C. *Effect of Unlawfulness*

291. If the object or consideration is unlawful, the agreement is void and hence unenforceable.

However, relief may be given if and to the extent provided by the statute that makes the agreement unlawful.

A court can order rescission of a contract where it is unlawful (i) for causes not apparent on its face and (ii) if the defendant is more to blame than the plaintiff.[283]

280. *Ram Coomar Coondoo v. Chunder Canto Mookerjee* (1876) 4 IA 23.
281. *Ratanchand Hirachand v. Askar Nawaz Jung* AIR 1976 AP 112.
282. *Central Inland Water Transport Corporation Ltd v. Brojo Nath Ganguly* AIR 1986 SC 1571.
283. Section 27 of the Specific Relief Act 1963.

This is a discretionary remedy and can be refused if the plaintiff has ratified the contract, where parties cannot be restored to a position before they made the contract, or where third parties have acquired rights in good faith without notice and for value.

D. Unlawful Agreements Enforceable

292. A strict view to refuse enforcement to all agreements tainted with illegality may cause injustice, particularly in cases in which the illegality is not severe or where the plaintiff has not participated in the illegality. Indian courts enforce unlawful agreements.

1. Agreement When Enforceable

293. A contract that is made with an object of committing an illegal act is absolutely unenforceable, especially at the instance of that party who is guilty of that act. A contract expressly or impliedly prohibited by statute also cannot be enforced.

When a contract is prohibited by statute, the court has the power to work out equities and place the parties on terms.[284]

In the case of other unlawful agreements, the intention of parties at the time of making the contract is material, as to whether they knew of the illegality, or participated in it. Unless the intention of the legislature is clear or public policy demands that the contract be prohibited altogether, an innocent party can sue on the contract.

2. Prohibiting Statute Allows Enforcement

294. A prohibiting statute might enable enforcement by only one of the parties. It is then unenforceable by the party whose duty is to observe statutory requirements. Thus, a landlord cannot enforce a term by which a tenant agrees not to claim the benefit of provisions made in rent control legislation.

3. Plaintiff Less Guilty

295. Relief is available to a plaintiff who has retracted from a contract before it is completed.[285] He need not show any reason for retracting.[286] Therefore, money may be recovered before the fraud or illegal purpose is carried out from a person to whom it has been advanced. If the fraudulent purpose is not carried into execution,

---

284. *Asaram v. Ludheshwar* AIR 1938 Nag 335, FB.
285. *Kedar Nath Motani v. Prahlad Rai* AIR 1960 SC 213.
286. *T P Petherpermal Chetty v. R Muniadi Servai* (1908) 35 IA 98.

a transferee of property will be deemed to hold the property for benefit of the transferor.[287]

Where parties are not *in pari delicto*, the less guilty party may be able to recover money paid or property transferred under the contract. This possibility may arise in three situations:[288] (i) the contract may be of a kind made illegal by statute in the interests of a particular class of persons of whom the plaintiff is one; (ii) the plaintiff has been induced to enter into the contract by fraud or strong pressure; or (iii) the defendant is under a fiduciary duty toward the plaintiff and hence cannot retain property or refuse to account for money received.

4. Claims in Property

296. A plaintiff can always found his claim on his right to possess or own, without founding his claim on an unlawful agreement.[289] Any amount deposited in connection with such a contract can also be recovered.[290] Such claim is recognized to prevent unjust enrichment.

297. In regard to transfers of property, a transfer for an unlawful object or consideration is prohibited.[291] Such a transfer is void, and the transferee cannot recover property on the strength of such a transfer.

But a transferor may recover property on the strength of his original title in the cases given below. Even in these cases relief will be given on terms as justice of the case may require, if:

(i) the illegal purpose is not carried out;
(ii) the transferor is not as guilty as the transferee;
(iii) the effect of permitting the transferee to retain the property might defeat the provisions of any law; (In the above three cases, the transferee must hold the property for the benefit of the transferor[292]);
(iv) where public interest or the interest of third parties requires that the relief should be given;
(v) where denial of the relief may defeat a legal prohibition;
(vi) where the transaction ought to be allowed to stand on the ground of public policy.

5. Unlawful in Part

298. If only a part of the agreement is unlawful, and it can be severed from the remainder, the lawful part can enforced.

287. Section 84 of the Indian Trusts Act 1882.
288. *Sita Ram v. Radha Bai* AIR 1968 SC 534.
289. *Surasaibalini Debi v. Phanindra Mohan Majumdar* AIR 1965 SC 1364; *T P Petherpermal Chetty v. R Muniadi Servai* (1908) 35 IA 98.
290. *Liladhar v. R S Sunderlal* AIR 1932 Nag 32.
291. Section 6(h) clause 2 of the Transfer of Property Act 1882.
292. The first three exceptions given by s. 84 of the Indian Trusts Act.

E. Subsequent Illegality

299. Performance of a contract can become unlawful because of subsequent change in law. The contract then becomes void.

The promisor, however, would be discharged only if it has become unlawful by reason of some event that he could not prevent.[293] In such an event the parties are liable to restore the advantage received by them under the contract or to compensate for it. Thus, a contract for cutting trees would end when a later law prohibits cutting of trees; so would a contract to supply sugar after a control order under a statute restricted release of sugar for domestic purposes. Orders made by the government restricting or prohibiting export or import would affect contracts in a similar manner.

IV. Unenforceable Contracts

300. 'Unenforceable' is a term used for contracts that are valid in all respects satisfying requirements of substantive law, but parties cannot sue upon it by reason of an impediment of some other law.

Such disability may arise because the contract is not registered,[294] a document containing the contract does not bear proper stamp duty,[295] the time for filing suit has expired,[296] a plaintiff partnership firm seeking to enforce it has not been registered,[297] or a lender seeking to recover money lent does not have a license under various state money-lending laws.

§4. The Consequences of a Defect of Consent or a Lack of Substantive Validity

301. The Indian Contract Act distinguishes between voidable contracts,[298] void agreements[299] and contracts that 'become void'.[300] Consequences of vitiating factors differ in their effect on the contract and rights and remedies.

293. Paragraph 2 of s. 56 of the Indian Contract Act.
294. Under the Indian Registration Act 1882; see paras 162–163 *supra*.
295. Under the Indian Stamp Act 1899 or other State stamp laws; see 166–168 *supra*.
296. Under the Limitation Act 1963; see paras 574 onwards.
297. As required by the Indian Partnership Act 1932.
298. Under s. 2(i) of the Indian Contract Act, an agreement which is enforceable by law at the option of one or more of the parties thereto, but not at the option of the other or others, is a voidable contract.
299. Under s. 2(g) of the Indian Contract Act, an agreement not enforceable by law is said to be void.
300. Under s. 2(j) of the Indian Contract Act, a contract which ceases to be enforceable by law becomes void when it ceases to be enforceable.

I. Avoidance of the Contract and Nullity

A. *Voidable Contract*

302. A contract is voidable at the option of that party whose consent to it is caused by coercion, undue influence, misrepresentation, or fraud. It is also voidable at the option of an aggrieved party in cases of certain types of breach.[301] Such party has an option to rescind the contract; the contract is valid until rescinded. Rescission is effective after it is communicated to the other party. There is no time limit for exercising this right of rescission, but it may be lost by delay, or if the aggrieved party affirms or ratifies the contract, or where third parties acquire rights bona fide without notice and for value.

303. When a person at whose option a contract is voidable rescinds it, the other party need not perform any of his promise under that contract. The party rescinding a voidable contract is liable to restore any benefit received under the contract from the other party.[302] In case of fraud or misrepresentation, such party may insist that the contract shall be performed and that he shall be put in the position in which he would have been if the representations made been true.[303] The contract is valid until voided, and a third party who takes under it without notice of the vitiating factors takes a good title.

B. *Void Agreement*

304. A void agreement[304] cannot be enforced at all, but restitution may be possible in some cases. The extent of enforcement would depend on whether the entire agreement is void or only the offending term. Enforcement may be objected to by any party. It is the duty of the court to give effect to such objection thus brought to its notice, although it is not raised in pleadings,[305] or where such a plea has been taken by either party.[306] Where an agreement is void being unlawful, the extent and conditions for enforcement are complex, and have been discussed earlier.[307] Remedy of cancellation is also available.[308]

C. *Agreement 'Discovered to Be Void' and a Contract That 'Becomes Void'*

305. A void agreement may *void ab initio* but was not known to be so by the parties. It is 'discovered to be void' where, for example, both parties work under a

301. See paras 435–436, 517–519 *infra*.
302. Section 64 of the Indian Contract Act.
303. See para. 246 *supra*.
304. See paras 43, 260 *supra*.
305. *Surasaibalini Debi v. Phanindra Mohan Majumdar* AIR 1965 SC 1364 (Illegality); *Nair Service Society Ltd v. K C Alexander* AIR 1968 SC 1165.
306. *Lakshmiayya v. Murahari* AIR 1930 Mad 547 (Immorality).
307. See paras 292–298 *supra*.
308. See para. 364 *infra*.

mutual mistake about an essential fact where the meaning of the agreement is not capable of being made certain, or where the court has declared the agreement to be champertous.

A contract 'becomes void' where it is a valid contract, but it ceases to be enforceable (i) because of a supervening impossibility or (ii) the condition subject to which the contract is to be performed does not occur. The contract is valid and binding until such a contingency occurs.

When an agreement is discovered to be void, or when a contract becomes void, any person who has received any advantage under such agreement or contract is bound to restore it or to make compensation for it to the person from whom he received it.[309]

II. Effect of Avoidance or Nullity

A. *Effect between Parties*

306. A party opting to rescind a voidable agreement is entitled to be restored as far as possible to his former position.[310] When a court grants relief of rescission in a suit for the purpose, it may require the party to whom such relief is granted to restore any benefit that he may have received from the other party and to make any compensation to him that justice may require.[311]

A void agreement is *void ab initio* and, therefore, unenforceable from the time it is made. An agreement that is 'discovered to be void' is also so unenforceable, but there is a liability of restitution, and any party receiving benefit is liable to return it.

When a contract 'becomes void', all acts done and liabilities incurred are valid. The contract, to the extent it is outstanding, is discharged. However, parties become liable only to restore or compensate for any advantage received. There is no liability for damages for breach. In all these cases, there is no further liability to perform because the obligations are discharged.

B. *Effect in Regard to Third Parties*

307. A void agreement is without effect. Any transfer of property to third party under a void agreement is ineffective. Because property is not transferred, any third party in possession of it will be liable to return it to the owner (usually transferor), else be liable for conversion.

A plaintiff can seek rescission of an unlawful agreement where a contract is unlawful for causes not apparent on its face and the defendant is more to blame than the plaintiff. In such a case a court may refuse to rescind the contract where third

309. Section 65 of the Indian Contract Act.
310. *Satgur Prasad v. Har Narain Das* AIR 1932 PC 89.
311. Section 30 of the Specific Relief Act 1963.

parties have, during subsistence of the contract, acquired rights in good faith without notice and for value.[312]

When a seller of goods has obtained possession thereof under a contract voidable for lack of free consent, but the contract has not been rescinded at the time of sale, the buyer acquires a good title to goods, provided he buys them in good faith and without notice of the seller's defect of title.[313]

III. Damages

308. Whether the contract is voidable for lack of free consent, or the agreement is void, and where the contract becomes void, there is no liability to pay damages. The parties may be required to do restitution as discussed above; however expenditure wasted or spent by the innocent party relying on a misrepresentation can be ordered to be paid.[314] A court granting the relief of rescission in cases of voidable contract or an unlawful contract not unlawful on the face of it, exercises discretion in doing so and can in appropriate cases order the party to whom the relief is granted to make any compensation to the other party that justice may require.

If the contract is voidable for breach, the injured party will be entitled to damages.

312. Section 27 of the Specific Relief Act 1963.
313. Section 29 of the Sale of Goods Act 1930.
314. *Chhanga Lal v. M C D* AIR 2008 Del 146.

Chapter 3. The Contents of a Contract

§1. The Different Clauses

I. The Terms of a Contract

309. A promise made in words is express, and that made otherwise than in words is implied.[315] The nature and extent of obligations under a contract will be determined by terms agreed between parties.

A. *Express Terms*

310. Terms are express when they are made in words. Despite express words, parties often hold different views about their meaning. The court is then required to construe the terms, that is, find meaning of words used, and determine legal effect to be given to them.

A written contract may not always contain all terms agreed, in which case, oral evidence can be given to supplement written terms.[316]

B. *Essential and Collateral Terms*

311. Terms of a contract may vary in importance, some being essential and others subsidiary or collateral. The distinction made by English law between conditions and warranties is not found in the Indian Contract Act, but these terms are used in other laws and in contract practice. Under the Act, parties are bound to perform their obligations, otherwise they are liable to pay damages for breach.

Where the breach indicates a repudiation of obligations under the contract in its entirety, it gives to the promisee a right to terminate the contract.[317] Where a term is vital or important and is broken, it may be construed as a refusal entitling the other party to terminate the contract. Parties may validly provide for an option to one or both of them to terminate the contract on breach of any specified term of the contract.[318]

C. *Term and Representation*

312. A term differs from a representation. The latter induces consent. It is not enforceable, but if false, may give the representee a right to avoid the contract in certain cases.[319]

315. Section 9 of the Indian Contract Act.
316. Proviso (2) of s. 92 of the Indian Evidence Act.
317. Section 39 of the Indian Contract Act.
318. *Central Bank of India Ltd v. Hartford Fire Insurance Co Ltd* AIR 1965 SC 1288; *Chotelal Lallubhai v. Champsey Umersey & Sons* AIR 1923 Bom 75.
319. See paras 242–246 *supra*.

A statement would be a condition or a warranty, enforceable as a term, if the person stating warrants accuracy of the statement, promises it to be good, and undertakes liability for its inaccuracy. Breach of such term gives the promisee a right to repudiate or to claim damages as the case may be. Where parties have not expressly stated so, the question of whether a statement is a representation or a warranty is a matter of intention to be gathered from facts of each case.

II. Implied Terms

A. *Implying Terms*

313. Under the Indian Contract Act a proposal or acceptance is implied if it is signified otherwise than by words. It may be necessary to imply terms into an express contract when the parties have not expressly stated all their obligations, possibly because they had thought about the terms but considered them so obvious as not deserving a mention. Possibly they have understood their obligations according to practices peculiar to their trade or already established practices in earlier dealings between them.

In the event of a dispute between them about their understanding of terms, the court would imply a term, mainly with a view to give efficacy to the contract. This exercise becomes necessary whether the parties had the terms in their mind or not at the time of making the contract.

314. Terms may be implied by law into certain classes or types of contracts. Thus, certain conditions and warranties are implied by statute into a contract of sale of goods.[320]

The court may also imply terms that do not contradict or that are subject to the express terms, unless a contrary intention appears from the agreement. These terms may not necessarily express the true intention or presumed intention of the parties but are imposed into the contract by law (unless contrary intention is expressed in the contract). There cannot be an implied contract with the government, because this would nullify the constitutional requirements as to formality.[321]

Terms may be implied into contracts by the custom of that trade, because the parties are presumed to have contracted with reference to some custom or usage well known in their locality or trade.

315. A term will be implied in fact by the court, first to give business efficacy to the contract and second to reveal the unexpressed intention of the parties. But no term will be implied inconsistent with or contradicting any express term. A court cannot make a new contract for the parties.

---

320. See paras 666–669 *infra*.
321. Article 299(1) of the Constitution of India; see paras 770–773 *infra*.

The implication of term depends on the intention of parties to be gathered from words used in the agreement and surrounding circumstances. The court would consider, for example, relationship between the parties, their previous course of dealings, and the nature of their contract.

III. Standard Terms and Exemption Clauses

316. Exemption clauses are valid under Indian law. These may be clauses excluding or limiting liability. They might limit rights relating to remedies or enforcement, for example, limiting damages payable on breach, limiting the right to rescind the contract, or limiting the right to file suit or proceedings in a particular court only.[322]

A. Is There a Contract on Those Terms?

317. In the first instance, it is important to find whether such a term has been agreed, that is, whether the party against whom such clause is invoked has accepted it, making it part of the contract. The court would consider the following various factors to determine this:

(i) Was the document containing such clause of a type that the party receiving would know or would expect to contain contractual conditions?
(ii) Were these conditions brought to the notice of the party before or at the time the contract was made?[323]
(iii) Moreover, did the party seeking to enforce the clause bring the clause to the notice of other party?

Such conditions might be incorporated by reference. Thus, conditions of carriage bound the carrier when these were incorporated into an e-ticket with a reference that these were available on the carrier's website.[324] However, such conditions incorporated into a receipt issued after the contract was made, would not be binding on the party seeking to avoid liability.

B. Strict Interpretation

318. An exemption clause is subject to strict interpretation, especially in consumer contracts. It can be invoked only exactly to the liability provided in it. In case of ambiguity, it will be interpreted against the party invoking it.

322. For clauses restricting choice of jurisdiction, see para. 273 *supra*.
323. *Mukul Dutta Gupta v. Indian Airlines Corporation* AIR 1962 Cal 311.
324. *InterGlobe Aviation Ltd v. N Satchinand* (2011) 7 SCC 463 (exclusive jurisdiction clause).

C. Unfair Terms

319. A clause exempting liability of a party from liability for wilful breach of contract or consequences of negligence has not come for decision before higher courts in India. The Law Commission of India recommended in 1984[325] that such terms shall be deemed unconscionable and the court may refuse its enforcement.

In 2006, the Law Commission of India gave a detailed report classifying terms as procedurally or substantively unfair, and giving to courts powers to give various appropriate reliefs.[326] Recommendation of neither of these reports has become law.

In the absence of any provision in the Indian Contract Act enabling a court to interfere in an unreasonable bargain, the Supreme Court in 1986[327] held that unfair and unreasonable clauses in contracts could be declared as void, being against public policy where these were made between parties not equal in bargaining power arising out of disparity in their economic strength and terms have been imposed by one party on the other who has no choice but to assent. The contract is not affected where parties were of equal bargaining power, or where the transaction was a commercial one.[328]

D. Certain Void Agreements

320. An agreement (or a clause in any agreement) is void if it restricts a party *absolutely* from enforcing his rights under or in respect of any contract, by the usual legal proceedings in the ordinary tribunals or that limits the time within which he may thus enforce his rights. An agreement (or clause in an agreement) is also void if it seeks to extinguish the rights of any party thereto, or discharges any party thereto from any liability, under or in respect of any contract on the expiry of a specified period so as to restrict any party from enforcing his rights.[329]

IV. Provisions in Statutes

A. Contracting Out of Provisions of Statutes

321. A number of statutes, especially laws relating to labour-welfare, expressly prohibit any party from contracting out of his provisions. But even where there is no such express provision, if the object of any statute is the protection of a class of persons, an agreement reducing or restricting this protection would be unlawful as defeating the purpose of the statute and hence unenforceable.[330] Such would be the

325. The 103rd Report of the Law Commission of India, 1984.
326. The 199th Report of the Law Commission of India, 2006, See para. 257.1 *supra*.
327. *Central Inland Water Transport Corporation Ltd v. Brojo Nath Ganguly* AIR 1986 SC 1571.
328. *S K Jain v. State of Haryana*, 2009 AIR SCW 1934.
329. Section 28 of the Indian Contract Act.
330. Under s. 23 of the Indian Contract Act.

case where a tenant agrees to waive the protection given under rent control legislation concerning amount of rent or eviction from the premises.[331]

A statute may restrict the power of a party to exclude or limit liability in particular classes of contracts. A carrier is liable for loss or damage arising from any criminal act of himself, his agents, or his servants.[332]

B. Consumer Protection Law

322. In case of contracts for providing goods or services to consumers to which the Consumer Protection Act 1986 is applicable, remedies of replacement, return of price, or compensation would be granted irrespective of any clause excluding liability. It appears, however, that a clause limiting liability will bind the consumer.[333]

V. Penalty Clauses

A. Penalty

323. A penalty has been described to imply a contract, subsidiary to the main contract, providing for some more drastic consequences (e.g., to pay something more than the debtor would be liable to pay under the primary contract) in event of the breach of the original and main contract.[334] A term would be a penalty where the real purpose is that by reason of its burdensome or oppressive character it may operate *in terrorem* over the promisor so as to drive him to fulfil the contract. A stipulation entitling a party to forfeit an amount lying in its hands, whether as earnest money or security deposit, may amount to a penalty.

B. Penalty and Liquidated Damages

324. Penalty differs from liquidated damages; the latter represent a genuine pre-estimate made by the parties at the time of making the contract of damages that may ensue in the event of breach.[335] Whether a stipulated sum is penalty or liquidated damages is a question of construction to be decided on the terms and the circumstances as they existed at the time of the contract and not at the time of its breach.

Under English law, a plaintiff may sue to enforce the clause enabling payment of an amount in case of breach or may disregard the clause and sue for unliquidated damages. If he chooses the first course of action, the amount will be recoverable

---

331. *Murlidhar Agarwal v. State of Uttar Pradesh* AIR 1974 SC 1924.

332. Section 12 of the Carriage by Road Act 2007; Clause 5 of Art. IV of the Schedule giving Rules relating to Bills of Lading under the Indian Carriage of Goods by Sea Act, 1925; ss 22–23 of the Carriage by Air Act 1972.

333. *Bharati Knitting Co v. DHL Worldwide Express Courier Division of Airfreight Ltd* AIR 1996 SC 2508.

334. *Sukkulal Sowcar v. A V Tirumala Row Sahib* AIR 1919 Mad 200.

335. For discussion on liquidated damages see paras 568–572 *infra*.

only if the court classifies it as a stipulation for liquidated damages, rather than as penalty, in which case it is irrecoverable.

Unlike in English law, section 74 of the Indian Contract Act, however, applies one uniform principle to both penalty and liquidated damages. In every case (except bail bonds or where the bond is given for the performance of any public duty) in which a sum is named as payable in case of breach of contract, the court can award only 'reasonable compensation' not exceeding the amount so named. All stipulations in a contract, whether in the nature of liquidated damages or penalty, are treated in the same manner. Where parties stipulate in express terms that the sum named as payable in case of breach is a genuine pre-estimate of damages, the burden of proving that it is not so would fall on the party so alleging.[336]

C. Penalty and Stipulations for Payment of Interest

325. Stipulations for payment of increased interest from date of default may be in the nature of penalty. Payment of higher rate of interest from the date of default is reasonable, but may be a penalty if applicable from the date of the loan. Stipulation of payment of interest on interest (compound interest) is not necessarily in the nature of penalty.

The following stipulations are not penalty – where a debtor is liable to pay an amount due in instalments and in default of any instalment, the whole amount shall become due; stipulation for payment of lower rate of interest if the debt is repaid in time; and a provision for capitalization of overdue interest and payment of interest on the whole amount.

D. Penalty and Specific Performance

326. A provision in a contract to pay an amount in case of breach does not bar specific performance. Even if the party in breach is willing to pay such amount, the court may order specific performance if the court finds that the sum was named only for the purpose of securing performance of the contract and not for the purpose of giving to the party in default an option of paying money in lieu of specific performance.[337] But the promisee cannot demand both specific performance and payment of such amount.

VI. Arbitration Clauses

A. Arbitration Agreement

327. A contract to refer existing disputes or future disputes to arbitration is valid. It is called an 'arbitration agreement'; so is a contract or stipulation that any dispute

336. *Oil and Natural Gas Corporation Ltd v. SAW Pipes Ltd* AIR 2003 SC 2629.
337. Section 23 of the Specific Relief Act 1963.

that may arise between the parties shall be referred to arbitration and that only the amount awarded in such arbitration shall be recoverable in respect of the dispute so referred.

Arbitration and its proceedings will be governed by the Arbitration and Conciliation Act 1996, based on the Model Law on International Commercial Arbitration adopted in 1985 by the United Nations Commission on International Trade Law (UNCITRAL).

An arbitration agreement is defined as an agreement by the parties to submit to arbitration all or certain disputes that have arisen or that may arise between them in respect of a defined legal relationship, whether contractual or not.[338] An arbitration proceeding can involve parties who have not been parties to the arbitration agreement.[339]

B. Form of Arbitration Agreement

328. It may be in the form of an arbitration clause in a contract or in the form of a separate agreement. It must be in writing, in the form of a document signed by the parties, or may be contained in exchange of letters or faxes. Parties have such an agreement even where the existence of the agreement is alleged by one party and not denied by the other in an exchange of statements of claim and defence. It is governed by the law of contract as regards formation, interpretation, and validity.

C. Freedom of Parties

329. Even under this Act, parties are free to determine the number of arbitrators, in odd numbers. They may choose an arbitrator of any nationality, may determine the procedure for appointing arbitrators or for challenging the arbitrator or the procedure to be followed by the arbitral tribunal in conducting its proceedings, including nature of hearing the tribunal shall conduct, or that the arbitral award need not state reasons. Parties can agree on the place of arbitration and the language to be used in the proceedings.

D. Powers of the Arbitral Tribunal

330. The arbitral tribunal may rule on its own jurisdiction and also on any objections about the existence or validity of the arbitration agreement. For this purpose, an arbitration clause forming part of a contract is treated as independent of terms of that contract, and the decision that the contract is void will not affect the validity of the arbitration clause.

338. Section 7 of the Arbitration and Conciliation Act 1996.

339. *Chloro Controls India (P) Ltd v. Severn Trent Water Purification Inc* AIR 2012 SC (Supp) 1017.

The arbitral tribunal has the power to take interim measure for protection of subject matter of the dispute and to require any party to provide appropriate security for the purpose. The Act of 1996 also gives powers to the court even while the arbitration proceedings are pending, to make orders as interim measures for protection, interim custody or sale of goods, for securing amount in dispute, or for detaining or preservation or inspection of any property or thing that is the subject matter of dispute. It may also issue orders of interim injunction or appointment of receiver.

E. Suits in Matters Governed by Arbitration

331. Where parties have an arbitration agreement, the further conduct of arbitration is governed by the provisions of the Act of 1996, and no court can intervene except in the manner provided under the Act. Any court before which a dispute is brought that is already a subject of an arbitration agreement, is bound to refer the parties to arbitration if any party applies to have it so sent.

F. Effect of Award and Its Enforcement

332. An arbitral award is final and binding on the parties and persons claiming under them. Under the Act of 1996, the award can be enforced directly as if it were the decree of the court.

§2. Interpretation

333. Although the parties to a contract may have expressly agreed to the terms, they may differ in their views about the meaning of these and their effect on their rights and obligations. It then falls to the court to settle these differences by the process of construction.

The purpose of construction is to discover the mutual intention of parties. It involves two things – ascertaining the meaning of the words used, and the legal effect to be given to them. The court is aided by rules of construction. These are guidelines meant to ascertain the presumed intention of the parties.

I. Intention of Parties

334. The intention of parties is determined objectively, by determining the intention of reasonable people placed in the same situation as the parties.

It is gathered from the language they have used, considered in the light of surrounding circumstances and the object of the contract, insofar as that has been agreed or proved. The surrounding circumstances will include, for example, circumstances in which it was written, drafting abilities of the parties, the intention that the writing was to convey and how the parties acted under it. If the language used is ambiguous, the court may also consider evidence of prior negotiations[340] or the conduct of parties subsequent[341] to making of the contract. Contents of other documents may be seen if the document supplements the other document.

II. Literal Interpretation

335. The court ascertains the intention primarily from the language employed. One must, therefore, look at the words used in the contract itself. In construing written documents, the grammatical and ordinary sense of the words will be applied. If the language used is on the face of the document ambiguous and defective, evidence cannot be given to show its meaning or supply defects.[342]

The document must be construed as a whole to ascertain the meaning of its several clauses. Where different parts of an instrument are inconsistent, effect must be given to that part which is calculated to carry into effect the real intention of parties as gathered from the instrument as a whole.

The form of the document or the name given by parties to their contract is not conclusive to determine its real legal nature and effect.

III. Use of Extrinsic Evidence

336. Sections 91 and 92 of the Indian Evidence Act provide for the circumstances in which documents are exclusive evidence of transactions they contain. Sections 9–398 provide allowing extrinsic evidence for interpretation of documents.

When the *terms* of a contract grant, or of any other disposition of property, have been reduced to the form of a document, and in all cases in which any *matter* is required by law to be reduced to the form of a document, no evidence shall be given in proof of the terms of such contract, grant, or disposition, or of such matter, except the document itself.[343] When such terms of a contract, and so on, are proved by producing the document, evidence of agreement, or statement cannot be admitted as between the parties to any such document for the purpose of contradicting, varying, adding to, or subtracting from its terms.[344] But any oral agreement or statement can be admitted to prove any fact that would invalidate the document; a separate oral agreement as to any matter on which the document is silent and that is not inconsistent with its terms; a separate oral agreement constituting a condition precedent to the attaching of any obligation under the document; a subsequent oral

340. *Joseph Darmanin v. Carmel Micallef* AIR 1946 PC 50.
341. *Godhra Electricity Co Ltd v. State of Gujarat* AIR 1975 SC 32.
342. Section 93 of the Indian Evidence Act 1872.
343. Section 91 of the Indian Evidence Act 1872.
344. Section 92 of the Indian Evidence Act 1872.

agreement to rescind or modify any such contract, any usage or custom not inconsistent with its express terms.

IV. Rules of Construction

337. Sections 93–98 of the Indian Evidence Act 1972 give rules for construction of documents.

When the language used in a document is, on its face, ambiguous or defective, evidence may not be given of facts that would show its meaning or supply its defects.

When language used in a document is plain in itself and when it applies accurately to existing facts, evidence may not be given to show that it was not meant to apply to such facts.

When language used in a document is plain in itself, but is unmeaning in reference to existing facts, evidence may be given to show that it was used in a peculiar sense.

When the facts are such that the language used might have been meant to apply to any one, and could not have been meant to apply to more than one, of several persons or things, evidence may be given of facts that show which of those persons or things it was intended to apply.

When the language used applies partly to one set of existing facts and partly to another set of existing facts, but the whole of it does not apply correctly to either, evidence may be given to show to which of the two it was meant to apply.

Evidence may be given to show the meaning of illegible or not commonly intelligible characters, of foreign, obsolete, technical, local, and provincial expressions; of abbreviations; and of words used in a peculiar sense.

§3. Conditional Contracts

I. Terms and Conditions

338. Unlike in English law, the Contract Act uses the term 'promise', but neither the word 'term' nor 'condition'. However, these words are often employed in contract language. A condition is a stipulation in the contract that imposes liability or obligation dependent on a future uncertain event.

When liability arises on the happening of an event or performance of a condition, it is a condition precedent. It is a suspensive condition preventing the existence of any obligation until the condition is satisfied. If liability ceases on the happening of an event or performance of a condition, it is a condition subsequent. It is a resolutive condition that terminates a pre-existing obligation. It provides that a previously binding contract determines on the occurrence of the event.

II. Types of Conditions

339. A condition may prevent the very formation of a contract when it is a condition precedent to the formation of contract, for example, where an agreement is made 'subject to contract' or 'subject to confirmation or approval'.[345] The contract is not made and does not bind until this contingency occurs.

A party may assume an immediate unilateral obligation subject to a condition, such as a sale on 'sale or return' basis, or an option to return the goods enjoyed by a purchaser under hire-purchase. This gives an option to the purchaser, and the seller cannot withdraw from the contract except under the terms of the transaction offered. Here the contract takes place immediately, but one party assumes an immediate obligation subject to a condition.

In a third category parties make a contract immediately binding, but (i) its performance may depend on the happening of a specified event, for example, where agricultural land is sold 'subject to permission of competent officer'; or (ii) the liability under the contract is to arise after occurrence of the specified event, such as the liability of an insurance company to pay the policy amount.

III. Types of Contractual Promises

340. Contractual promises may be absolute or conditional. An absolute promise may be unilateral, that is, outstanding on the part of one party only, or it may be a reciprocal promise, that is, outstanding in regard to both parties. Conditional promises under the Act would either be contingent contracts or reciprocal promises.

Where the performance of a promise depends on the performance by the other party of his promise, these are reciprocal promises, subject to provisions given in sections 51–58 of the Act. Where the operation of the contract or performance of a promise depends on the happening or non-happening of an event, collateral to the contract, the contract is a contingent contract. It is subject to special rules given in sections 31–36 of the Indian Contract Act.

IV. Reciprocal Promises

341. Promises that form the consideration or part of consideration for each other are reciprocal promises.[346] The Act provides for the obligation to perform them, the order in which they must be performed, and the consequences of non-performance.

A. Independent Reciprocal Promises

342. When promises are independent of each other, that is, where the performance of one promise does not depend on the performance of any promise by the

345. See paras 101, 119, 125 *supra*.
346. Section 2(f) of the Indian Contract Act.

other, both parties are under an absolute obligation to perform according to the agreed schedule.

B. Conditional Reciprocal Promises

343. Conditional reciprocal promises may be:

(i) *concurrent* promises to be simultaneously performed, in which case a promisor need not perform his promise unless the promisee is ready and willing to perform his reciprocal promise. Thus, where A and B contract that A shall deliver goods to B to be paid for by B on delivery, A need not deliver unless B is ready and willing to pay for the goods on delivery, and B need not pay unless A is ready and willing to deliver them on payment.
(ii) *dependent* promises, where one promise is dependent on and to be performed after the other is performed. The order in which these promises are to be performed may be expressly fixed by contract, in which case they must be performed in that order. Whether one promise is dependent on the other depends on the true construction of the contract.

C. Order of Performance

344. If the order is not fixed, they must be performed in that order in which the nature of the transaction requires. It is implied that any work must be completed before claiming payment. Thus, where A and B contract that A shall deliver goods to B at a stated price, and B promises to give security for the payment of money, A's promise need not be performed until the security is given. The nature of the transaction requires that A should have security before he delivers the goods.

D. Failure to Perform and Preventing from Performance

345. If the promisor who has to perform his promise before the performance of the other's promise, *fails* to perform it, he cannot claim performance of the other's promise and is also liable for compensation for his non-performance. Such failure will not give a right to terminate, unless the contract so provides or unless this failure amounts to a refusal to perform the whole of the contract.

However, if one party *prevents* the other from performing his promise, the contract becomes *voidable* at the option of the party so prevented, and he is entitled to compensation from the other party for any loss arising from non-performance. Prevention, thus, gives a right of termination.

V. Contingent Contracts

A. Promises Conditional on an Event

346. Contingent contracts are conditional promises to do or not to do something, if some event, collateral to such contract, does or does not happen.[347] Such an event is neither the performance directly promised, nor the consideration for the promise. A contract to pay for work done after it is completed is not a contingent contract because the completion of work being the very thing contracted for is not collateral to the contract. The performance of the work is a condition precedent to the payment of the wages. Further, the event must not only be contingent, that is, one that may or may not happen, but also one occurring in the future, and beyond the control of the parties.[348] A contract of insurance is an example of a contingent contract, so is a contract of indemnity. Although death is a certain event, a contract of life insurance is a contingent contract because it is uncertain whether death will occur within the specified time. The provisions about enforcement of contingent contracts is found in sections 31–36 of the Indian Contract Act.

B. Contract Dependent on Act of Third Party

347. The contract may be contingent because the performance of the promise also depends on any act or abstinence of any third party or even of any party to the contract. Thus, it has been suggested that a contract between a tenderer and his sub-contractor executed in anticipation of acceptance of tender is contingent on the tender being accepted.[349]

348. The liability under the contract may depend on the act of a third party. But if such third party does anything that renders it impossible that he may act so within a definite time, the event shall be considered impossible, and, therefore, the contract will be discharged.[350] But in cases in which the right to recover payment is made conditional on certification of the work by an architect or engineer, and the architect or engineer fails or refuses to do so, the court or arbitrator can determine the amount and order its payment.[351]

However, a contract in which one party has complete discretion whether he will perform or not is no contract. This can be justified on the basis of lack of consideration or the intention to create legal relations. This differs from the exercise of an option given under a contract,[352] which is enforceable.

---

347. Section 31 of the Indian Contract Act.
348. *Balwant Singh v. Rajaram* AIR 1975 Raj 73.
349. *UP Rajkiya Nirman Nigam Ltd v. Indure Pvt Ltd* AIR 1996 SC 1373.
350. Section 34 of the Indian Contract Act.
351. *South India Railway Co Ltd v. S M Bhashyam Naidu* AIR 1935 Mad 356; *Heavy Electricals (India) Ltd v. Pannalal Devchand Malviya* AIR 1973 MP 7.
352. See para. 28 *supra*.

Where a promise is dependent on the satisfaction of a party about the subject matter or about the quality of performance, the approval may not be withheld unreasonably.[353]

C. Contingent Condition and Promissory Condition

349. A contingent condition must be distinguished from a promissory condition, which the promisor promises to make good. Thus, a term in a contract for sale of goods stating 'the goods have been purchased by us from X and will be shipped to you as soon as delivered to us' creates an absolute and not a conditional obligation. The words indicate mode or manner of performance.[354]

D. Contract Stipulating Time for Performance

350. A contingent contract must also be distinguished from a contract stipulating the time for performance. Thus, where a seller agreed to sell his half share in a property, the sale to be completed one month after the property was partitioned and his share separated, the liability was not contingent but absolute, and the execution of the sale deed was merely postponed to a future date.

Where the operation of the contract or the liability under it is subject to such a condition: (i) neither party is under any obligation to perform before the event occurs; (ii) neither party undertakes that the condition or event will occur; (iii) the contract forms immediately, and neither party can withdraw unilaterally from the contract before the event occurs.

E. Duty to Take Effort for Fulfilling Condition

351. Although the obligations may not arise until the event occurs, a term may be implied that one or both parties will use all reasonable efforts to secure the fulfilment of the condition or bringing about the event.[355]

Thus, where a sale of land is made subject to a sanction under an applicable law, and the seller has applied for the sanction that has been refused, a distinction is made between the first obligation to seek sanction, and second, if the sanction is obtained, to complete the sale. The seller having sought sanction, has committed no breach if the sanction is refused; and the contract is discharged by the refusal. In any case such an agreement to transfer the property is subject to an implied condition that the transferor will obtain the sanction of the concerned authority.[356]

---

353. *Secretary of State for India in Council v. Augustus John Arathoon* (1882) ILR 5 Mad 173.
354. *Ganga Saran v. Firm Ram Charan Ram Gopal* AIR 1952 SC 9; *Harnandrai Fulchand v. Pragdas Budhsen* AIR 1923 PC 54.
355. See *Motilal v. Nanhelal* AIR 1930 PC 287.
356. *Nathulal v. Phoolchand* AIR 1970 SC 546.

VI. Rules Regarding Contingent Contracts

A. Enforcement of Contingent Contracts

352. Contingent agreement to do or not to do anything, if an impossible event occurs, are void, whether the impossibility of the event is known or not to the parties to the agreement at the time it is made.[357]

Contract contingent on the happening of an event can be enforced after that event occurs.[358]

The parties are under no obligation till such event occurs, except when a term is implied, as stated earlier, requiring one party to make reasonable efforts to bring about the event. It must be established for enforcement that the event occurred in the manner contemplated by the contract.[359] If the event becomes impossible, the contract 'becomes void' and enforceable from that time.[360] All parties are discharged from liability or from payment of damages. Later conditions or events will not affect it any more.

Contingent contracts to do or not to do anything if a specified uncertain event happens within a fixed time become void if, at the expiration of the time fixed, such event has not happened, or if, before the time fixed, such event becomes impossible.[361]

B. Contingent Contract and Impossibility

353. Discharge of a contingent contract differs from discharge by the doctrine of impossibility, though both belong to the doctrine of frustration under English law. Where the contract itself, as a matter of construction, contains impliedly or expressly a term according to which it would stand discharged on the happening of certain circumstances, the question of dissolution of the contract according to its terms falls to be determined under section 32 and not under the doctrine of impossibility of performance.[362]

357. Section 36 of the Indian Contract Act.
358. Section 32 of the Indian Contract Act.
359. *Toolsidas Tejpal v. M P Venkatachalapathy Aiyar* AIR 1921 PC 46.
360. See para. 453 *infra.*
361. Section 35 of the Indian Contract Act.
362. *Satyabrata Ghose v. Mugneeram Bangur & Co* AIR 1954 SC 44; *Naihati Jute Mills Ltd v. Khyaliram Jagannath* AIR 1968 SC 522.

Chapter 4. Privity of Contract

§1. The Rule of Privity of Contract

354. A contract cannot confer rights or impose obligations arising under it on any person except the parties to it.

The Indian Contract Act 1872 does not state this rule. But this English doctrine is very much part of Indian law relating to enforcement of contract,[363] and courts have held it to be so by interpreting definitions in the Act.[364]

I. Consideration and the Rule of Privity

355. It is usual to find a discussion of the rule of privity alongside consideration. But the two are essentially different. The rule of privity speaks of who can enforce a contract or against whom. The doctrine of consideration deals with kinds of promises or agreements which will be enforced.

A. Strangers to Consideration and to Contract

356. The rule of English common law that a party wishing to enforce a contract must furnish or have furnished consideration must be distinguished from the doctrine of privity.

As already discussed elsewhere, a promise can be enforced in Indian law even if the consideration has moved from a person other than a promisor.[365] The distinction between the two doctrines can be explained with these examples. A, B, and C together agree that A shall provide service to B and that B shall make payment to C. In the second case X and Y agree that X shall provide a service to Y and Y shall pay to Z the service charges. Under English common law, as it stood before the enactment of the Contracts (Rights of Third Parties) Act 1999, even as a party to the contract C cannot enforce the contract, being a stranger to consideration. Party C can sue under the Indian law because consideration for the promise can move from another person, A in this case. Party Z cannot enforce the payment under English or Indian law by operation of the rule of privity.

B. Need for Change

357. The rule of privity is likely to work injustice on parties, especially on third parties who rely on the terms. Like under English law, courts in India have also

363. *M C Chacko v. State Bank of Travancore* AIR 1970 SC 504.
364. *Krishna Lal Sadhu v. Promila Bala Dasi* AIR 1928 Cal 518.
365. See para. 134.

developed exceptions to the rule of privity, which are discussed later.[366] There are also statutes enabling third parties to sue on contracts to which they are not party.[367]

The Law Commission of India proposed in 1958 to amend this rule. It recommended that a contract be enforceable by the third party in his own name, if the contract expressly conferred a benefit on him, but subject to any defences available to contracting parties. It also proposed that parties to a contract should not be able to vary, rescind, or alter it, once the third party had adopted the contract. Recommendations in this report did not become law.

II. Third Parties and the Contract

A. *The Two Aspects of Privity*

358. The doctrine of privity has two aspects. First, none but the parties to it are entitled under it. Therefore, a stranger cannot sue on a contract to which he is not a party, nor can he take a defence based on that contract. This also means, for example, that an exclusion clause in a contract will not bind a stranger.

The second aspect is that parties to a contract cannot impose liabilities on a third party; that a person cannot be made liable on a contract to which he is not a party.

B. *Parties to the Contract*

359. It is essential to determine who are parties to the contract, and who are bound to perform under it. Parties are the persons who have made the agreement in any form or have reached agreement through an agent.

A contract binds the parties to it, and they must either perform or offer to perform their respective promises.

C. *Death of a Party*

360. If a promisor dies before performance, his representatives are bound by contract, unless the contract so provides, or a contrary intention appears from the contract.[368] The representatives may either actually perform as promised or be liable in damages for breach. The liability of representatives is restricted to the estate of the deceased promisor in their hands.

Representatives will not be liable in two cases: (i) where the contract expressly so provides and (ii) where the contract indicates an intention that the representatives will not be liable. Therefore, contracts involving personal confidence or

366. See paras 368 onwards.
367. See paras 376–380.
368. Section 37 of the Indian Contract Act.

exercise of personal skill by the promisor, for example, a contract to paint a portrait, cannot be enforced against representatives of the painter after his death.

361. The Indian Contract Act is silent about devolution of rights after death of the promisee. The representatives of a deceased promisee may enforce for the benefit of his estate contracts subsisting during his lifetime, unless parties intend or the nature of the contract is such that death of the promisee ends the obligation.

D. Remedy in Tort

362. A third party may seek remedy under the law of torts. He may sue a contracting party for failure of his obligation to use care. A professional, such as a solicitor or surveyor owing duty of care toward his client, may be held liable for misrepresentation to third parties relying on his representations.

E. Stranger Can Challenge the Contract

1. Rescission

363. A third party can have a right to avoid or challenge the transaction. He can rescind the contract simply by giving notice to the contracting parties or by taking this defence in a suit filed by any party to the contract. In addition he can have the contract rescinded through court by the remedy of rescission.[369] The manager (called the *karta*) of a Hindu Undivided Family has the power to alienate property belonging to all the members of a family, which power he can exercise only for necessity of the family or for benefit of estate. A member of such family is entitled to challenge the alienation as being beyond the powers. His remedy is of rescission. This is a discretionary remedy and may, for example, be refused where the contract has been ratified or third parties have acquired rights in good faith without notice and for value.

2. Cancellation of Instrument

364. Cancellation of instrument is another remedy available to a third party. Where any person apprehends that a written instrument, which is void or voidable, will cause him serious injury if left outstanding, he can sue to have it delivered up and cancelled. Fraudulent compromise decrees can be cancelled in this manner. Thus, where A, representing that the tenants on his land were all at will, sells the land to B and soon thereafter fraudulently grants to C a lease of part of lands of an earlier date and procures the lease to be registered under the Indian Registration Act,

369. A discretionary remedy under s. 27 of the Specific Relief Act 1963.

B may obtain the cancellation of this lease. A creditor may sue on behalf of himself and all other creditors to set aside a deed executed by his debtor by which the creditors are defrauded, defeated, or delayed.[370]

Any such instrument does not bind a third party at all, nor does it affect his rights, and he need not seek cancellation. But the remedy enables him to avoid the serious injury likely to be caused to him if the instrument is left outstanding.

III. Contract for the Benefit of a Third Party

365. A promisee in a contract is entitled to direct the manner in which the promise may be performed by the promisor. If indicated in the contract, the promisor will be bound to perform in that manner. In any case, if the promisor performs in the manner later directed by the promisee, he has discharged his obligation. Therefore, a debtor who pays into the creditor's bank instead of direct payment, or a seller who delivers goods directly to a third person according to the orders of the purchaser, are merely performing the promise under the contract. Such cases do not involve the rule of privity. Whether the parties perform the contract to benefit a third party, and whether that third party can sue for enforcing such term, are different issues.

366. Unlike the law in Germany, Austria, and Switzerland, and English law after the new legislation, a third party cannot enforce a contract under the Indian law merely because the parties to the contract have conferred benefit on him. Case law suggests that such enforcement is possible, some indicating that such third party may have a right to enforce in equity and others that the third party may sue on the ground of justice. But the view that person not a party to the contract cannot sue on the contract unless the case comes within one of the recognized exceptions is supported by the Supreme Court of India.[371] Thus, if A mortgages his property to B, and part of the consideration for the mortgage is B's promise to A to pay C the amount that A owed to C, C, not being a party to the contract, cannot sue B for the payment, unless the document has created a trust in favour of C. Nor can a purchaser's contract to pay off a mortgage be enforced by the mortgagee who was not party to the contract.

367. Warranty of goods as to fitness or quality can be enforced only by the buyer against the seller from whom the goods have been purchased and not against the seller's suppliers or the manufacturer.

IV. Exceptions to the Rule of Privity

368. Exceptions to the rule of privity are recognized. These are mainly those recognized under English common law. Strangers to contract also have rights by virtue of certain statutes. These are discussed in the following section.

370. See s. 53 of the Transfer of Property Act.
371. *M C Chacko v. State Bank of Travancore* AIR 1970 SC 504.

A. Trust

369. Trust is the main exception to the rule of privity. Where A makes a promise to B for the benefit of C, the promise can be enforced by C against A if B has constituted himself trustee of A's promise for C. This exception is applied to promises to pay money or to transfer property. It is necessary to establish an intention of the promisee to enter into the contract as a trustee. Use of the words 'trust' or 'trustee' may indicate such intention. A trust does not arise simply because a party to a contract undertakes to confer a benefit on a stranger.

In a case that went up to the Privy Council,[372] the father of a bridegroom contracted with the father of the bride to make the daughter an allowance if she married the son. She claimed the allowance after her marriage. The facts resembled the landmark English case[373] applying the rule of privity. But the Privy Council considered the common practice of such arrangements in Indian communities and held that she was entitled to proceed in equity to enforce her claim. In another case, certain persons collected dues for charitable purposes of an organization. That organization could recover the amount from them as they had constituted themselves as trustees for the organization.[374]

B. Marriage Settlements and Family Arrangements

370. A stranger can enforce a benefit due under a marriage settlement, partition, or other family settlement.[375] Thus, where two members of a family divided their properties and agreed at the partition that they would provide maintenance of their mother, she could enforce the promise. A contract is a settlement on marriage, and family arrangements can be specifically enforced at a suit of any person beneficially entitled thereunder.[376]

C. Charge over Property

371. A stranger to a contract can sue for the money made payable to him by it where the money is charged on immovable properties[377] or where specific money is allocated by the promisor in favour of such third party.[378]

D. Covenants Running with Land

372. A right to restrain enjoyment in a particular manner of property imposed for the more beneficial enjoyment of the transferor's property, and benefit of an

372. *Khwaja Muhammad Khan v. Hussaini Begam* (1910) 37 IA 152.
373. *Tweddle v. Atkinson* (1861) 1 B & S 393.
374. *Ram Dhan v. L Chauthmal* AIR 1935 Oudh 496.
375. *Dan Kuer v. Sarla Devi* AIR 1947 PC 8.
376. See s. 15(c) of the Specific Relief Act *infra*.
377. *Subbu Chetti v. Arunachalam* AIR 1930 Mad 382, FB.
378. *Iswaran Pillai v. Sonnivevaru* (1913) ILR 38 Mad 753.

obligation arising out of contract and annexed to the ownership of property, can be enforced against a transferee with notice or a gratuitous transferee, but not against transferee for consideration and without notice of the right or obligation.[379]

E. Estoppel

373. If the promisor agrees with the third party to pay or to perform directly, it may create privity by acknowledgment. Otherwise the promisor may become an agent of the third party. Such promise may also render the promisor liable in circumstances of estoppel.[380]

F. Other Devices

374. Certain other techniques are devised in decisions of cases to enable enforcement by persons who are not parties to a contract. One such device is to read the contract as one of agency. Thus, in a suit by a purchaser against the seller for damages for shortage of supply of goods by shipper, the shipper, as agent, was also entitled take benefit of the arbitration clause in the contract between the purchaser and the seller and to apply for stay of suit.[381]

375. A collateral contract between one of the parties to the main contract and associated with the main contract may enable a third party to enforce the main contract. Thus, a buyer of goods can enforce a manufacturer's guarantee, which is collateral to the contract of purchase of goods. This is enforceable because the third party is a party to the collateral contract.

375.1. An arbitration proceeding can involve parties who are not parties to the arbitration agreement.[382]

G. Statutory Exceptions

376. Certain statutes expressly give to a third party the right to enforce a contract between two other persons.

1. Specific Relief Act

377. The Specific Relief Act 1963, which states the circumstances in which specific performance of a contract (and consequently injunction in respect of contracts)

379. Section 40 of the Transfer of Property Act 1882.
380. *Subbu Chetti v. Arunachalam* AIR 1930 Mad 382, FB.
381. *Societe Commercial De Corealas & Financiers v. State Trading Corporation of India* AIR 1998 Guj 94.
382. *Chloro Controls India (P) Ltd v. Severn Trent Water Purification Inc* AIR 2012 SC (Supp) 1017.

can be granted, enables strangers to sue on a contract.[383] Thus, a person beneficially entitled under a marriage settlement and family arrangement can sue for such entitlement, so can a new company arising out of amalgamation of a contracting party (company) with another company sue and be liable for contracts made with that company. A new company can sue or be liable in respect to contracts entered into before its incorporation.

2. Consumer Protection Law

378. Under consumer protection law,[384] a user of goods using or taking benefit with the consent of the purchaser can file a complaint and obtain relief for defect in goods. In a similar situation, a beneficiary of services taking benefit of services with the consent of the person who has hired the services can obtain relief for any deficiency in services.

3. Insurance

379. Special provisions in statutes protect beneficiaries of insurance. A policy of insurance effected by any married man on his own life and stated to be for the benefit of his wife or children, is deemed to be made in trust for the benefit of his wife or such children.[385] A victim of an accident, who is the third party, can enforce the third-party liability against an insurer who has insured the motor vehicle involved in the accident. Such insurer is liable to satisfy any judgment or decree passed in favour of such third party.[386] A mortgagee, consignee, or other person having an interest in the subject matter insured may insure on behalf of and for the benefit of other persons insured as well as for his own benefit.[387]

4. Labour Statutes

380. A principal employer employing a contractor for execution of any work involved in his business or trade is liable to pay compensation under the Employees' Compensation Act arising out of accidents to the workmen employed by the contractor in doing such work and is entitled to indemnity for such amount from the contractor.[388] The same principle applies to payments made by the principal employer toward contribution of provident funds and of employees' insurance schemes in respect of employees of the contractor.

383. Section 15 of the Specific Relief Act 1963.
384. Section 2(d)(1) and (11) of the Consumer Protection Act 1986.
385. Section 6 of the Married Women's Property Act 1874.
386. Section 149 of the Motor Vehicles Act 1988.
387. Section 17 of the Marine Insurance Act 1963.
388. Section 12 of the Workmens' Compensation Act 1923.

§2. Transfer of Contractual Rights

381. The Indian Contract Act has no provision dealing with assignment of contractual rights and liabilities. An assignment of a contract might result by transfer either of the rights or of the obligations thereunder. An assignment may also occur by way of gift, or exchange, or by way of security for repayment of debt or performance of promise.

382. A right or benefit under the contract can be transferred by assignment only before any breach has occurred. If the contract is broken, the obligations under the contract are replaced by the rights and obligations to claim and pay damages. A claim for damages for breach of contract is not an actionable claim. It is a mere right to sue and cannot be transferred.[389] The right to sue arising out of or incidental to the right to property can be assigned with the property transferred. An assignment of right of action may also be valid where the assignee has a genuine commercial interest in taking the assignment. Hence, the transfer of the right of action of the insured to an insurer who has indemnified him under the policy of insurance is valid because the insurer has a genuine interest in recovering the loss sustained by the payment on the policy.[390]

I. Assignment of Rights and Liabilities

A. Assignment by Parties

383. Obligations under a contract cannot be assigned except with the consent of the promisee. This amounts to novation, resulting in substitution of liabilities. This principle is based on the premise that a person cannot be obliged to accept liability from a person other than one with whom the contract is made. Thus, services of employees cannot be transferred to another employer without employees' consent.[391]

On the contrary, rights under a contract are assignable unless the contract prohibits assignment or the rights are incapable of assignment, for example, as in the case of goods covered by personal licenses. In the case of goods covered by import licenses the buyer cannot assign his right to a non-holder of a license because the import licenses are personal.[392] A contract also is not assignable where considerations connected with the person of a contracting party are important. An arbitration clause is not a personal covenant and can be assigned.

389. Section 6(e) of the Transfer of Property Act 1882.

390. *Hindustan Corporation (Hyd) Pvt Ltd v. United India Fire and General Insurance Ltd* AIR 1997 AP 347; *United India Fire and General Insurance Co Ltd v. Pelaniappa Transport Corporation* AIR 1986 AP 32.

391. *BCPP Mazdoor Sangh v. NTPC* AIR 2008 SC 336.

392. *Khardah & Company Ltd v. Raymon & Co (India) Private Ltd* AIR 1962 SC 1810.

Where mutual obligations under a contract still remain to be enforced, the contract cannot be assigned as to discharge any original promisor and this can be done only with the consent of all the parties to the contract. Even where such assignment is effected, the assignor continues to be liable for his outstanding promises under the contract.

B. Assignment by Operation of Statute

384. Rights and obligations of a party might stand assigned by operation of statute, for example, by virtue of a law made for acquiring an undertaking or taking over management of a business organization. Such transfer of rights and obligations will be subject to the provisions of the statute. Employees are transferred from one undertaking to the new establishment. Such statutes might also give to the government or the transferee undertaking the power to cancel or vary any agreement.

C. Actionable Claims

385. Some contractual claims are actionable claims. An actionable claim is a claim of any debt (except secured debts), or to any beneficial interest in movable property not in the possession, either actual or constructive, of the claimant, whether such debt or beneficial interest be existent, accruing, conditional, or contingent.[393] These can be transferred in the manner specified in the Transfer of Property Act 1882. Thus, a contract for future delivery of goods can be assigned as an actionable claim.

Assignment of some claims in contract are prohibited by statute, such as claim to a provident fund, right to pension, and claims under the employees' state insurance scheme.

An actionable claim can be transferred by an instrument in writing, after which the rights and remedies of the assignor vest in the assignee, who can then sue the promisor of the original contract without joining the assignor as party to the suit. The right of a seller to call for payment of the price of goods on delivery is also an actionable claim.

D. Prohibition of Assignment

386. Parties may expressly prohibit assignment, in which event the rights or benefits under the contract cannot be assigned except with the consent of the promisee. Any assignment in the face of express prohibition is invalid as between the contracting parties. Thus, an assignee of a plot could not question the order of

393. Section 3 of the Transfer of Property Act 1882.

resumption of the plot by the Industrial Development Corporation where the assignment was made without the consent of the Corporation in breach of the terms of allotment by the assignor.[394]

Parties may prohibit assignment altogether or may prohibit assignment of some only of the rights, such as the right to claim future performance, right to claim amounts due, and so on.

As between the assignor and assignee, there is a valid contract that can entitle a claim in damages.

E. Formalities for Assignment

387. Unless the claim amounts to an actionable claim, or any other statute specifically provides for the manner or form in which assignment might be effected,[395] an assignment need not be in writing, nor need it be absolute. Therefore, an assignment may be made as security for payment of money.

Notice to the debtor or promisor is necessary only for binding the debtor. There is no prescribed mode of giving notice. It may be given directly by the assignor to the promisor or debtor. Giving notice is desirable for claiming priority. Further, if notice is not given, the debtor may give the payment to the promisee under the contract (the assignor) and get a valid discharge. If the debtor makes the payment or gives performance to the promisee under the contract even after receiving notice, the debtor is not discharged and must pay to the promisee again.

F. Assignment of Rights under Statutes

388. Some assignments are governed by statute, for example, actionable claims, bills of lading, negotiable instruments, policies of insurance, and rights and liabilities under a railway receipt. Thus, a holder of a promissory note, bill of exchange, or cheque is entitled to recover the amount due thereon.[396] Every consignee of goods under a bill of lading and every endorsee of a bill of lading has the right of suit and is subject to the same liabilities as if he were a party to the bill of lading.[397] A consignee of goods covered by railway receipt or the endorsee shall have all rights and liabilities of the consignor on delivery of railway receipt to him.[398]

389. One would have to look at the applicable statute to know the formalities for completing the assignment, requirement of registration, consequences of non-registration, extent to which rights can be assigned, whether notice need to

394. *Indu Kakkar v. Haryana State Industrial Development Corporation* (1999) 2 SCC 37.
395. See para. 389 *infra*.
396. Section 8 of the Negotiable Instruments Act 1881.
397. Section 1 of the Indian Bills of Lading Act 1856.
398. Section 74 of the Railways Act 1989.

given to the promisor, and the respective rights and liabilities of the assignor, assignee, and promisor.

An assignment failing to comply with the statutory requirements may still be valid.[399]

G. Effect of Assignment

390. An assignment will be effective from the date intended by the parties, else from the date of assignment. The debtor's creditor may have the amount attached in the hands of the assignee thereafter in execution. Failure to give notice to the debtor does not affect the validity of an assignment.

An assignee takes the assignment subject to equities. Hence, the debtor is permitted to take against the assignee all defences available to him against the original promisee-assignor, including the right to set-off.

An assignee cannot sue in his own name and without joining the assignor as a party,[400] unless he has the right under the statute providing for the assignment. An assignee can claim specific performance.[401]

An assignment transfers to the assignee all the interest of the assignor under the contract. Thus, where X assigned a mortgage to Y, agreeing to indemnify him against any loss on the mortgage, and Y assigned his rights to Z, Z was entitled to sue on the contract of indemnity.[402]

A transfer of a debt includes transfer of the securities for the debt, unless those securities secure other debts or claims not transferred to the transferee.[403]

II. Negotiation

391. Although an assignee acquires all right, title, and interest of the assignor only subject to equities between the assignor and the promisor, the transferee of a negotiable instrument (bill of exchange, promissory note, or cheque) obtains the rights of a holder in due course and can get a better title than the transferor, free from defects in title of prior parties. The Negotiable Instruments Act provides for transfer of negotiable instruments by negotiation. Negotiation of a negotiable instrument is effected by delivery in case of a bearer instrument, and by endorsement and delivery in case of an instrument payable to order. The endorsement must be made on the instrument itself.

399. *P R Viswanatha Iyer v. A Muthukumaraswami Pillai* AIR 1948 Mad 139; *Jethalal Nagji Shah v. Municipal Corporation, Greater Bombay* AIR 1954 Bom 167.
400. *P R Viswanatha Iyer v. A Muthukumaraswami Pillai* AIR 1948 Mad 139.
401. Section 15 of the Specific Relief Act 1963.
402. *Dharshi Monji v. Chandulal Girdharilal* AIR 1950 Kutch 84.
403. Section 8 of the Transfer of Property Act 1882.

§3. SUBCONTRACTING

392. The promisor under a contract may perform the promise himself or may employ competent persons to do it. For such employment he will have another contract – called the subcontract. Subcontracting differs from assignment of contract.

I. Personal Contracts

393. The Indian Contract Act provides:[404] if it appears from the nature of the case that it was the intention of the parties to any contract that any promise contained in it should be performed by the promisor himself, such promise must be performed by the promisor.

Such intention may be gathered from the express terms of the contract or may be inferred from the terms of the contract, its subject matter, and surrounding circumstances. In other cases the promisor or his representatives may employ a competent person to perform it. One useful question to ask would be whether the promisor promised personal performance or merely promised a result.

The Act in principle, therefore, entitles a promisor to employ a subcontractor or any competent person to perform the promise. This right may be restricted by express provision in the contract. A promise to paint a portrait must be performed by the promisor himself. A promise to pay a sum of money or supply goods might be performed by any other competent person. In cases in which the promisor can employ another person to perform the promise and the promisor dies before performance, his representatives are also entitled to employ another person to complete the promise.

394. The promisor must himself perform the contract that involves exercise of his individual skill, depends on the competency or personal qualification of the promisor, or is based on personal confidence between the parties. In such cases the death of the promisor or his disablement discharges the contract and frees the other party from liability.

II. Subcontractors and Doctrine of Privity

395. The doctrine of privity prevents any contractual relationship between the promisee of the original contract (the employer) and the subcontractor. The employer cannot sue the subcontractor for defective performance, but can only hold the promisor-contractor liable. The promisor-contractor continues to be liable on the contract, even for non-performance or defective performance of the main contract by the subcontractor in the execution of the work involved in the promise. The subcontractor cannot sue the employer for payment, enforcement of other terms, or breach.

404. Section 40 of the Indian Contract Act.

396. A principal employer is liable under statutes[405] for claims of employees engaged through a labour contractor for carrying out works at his place of business. Thus, a principal employer might be liable to pay in respect of workmen engaged by the labour contractor, their contributions to a provident fund, contributions to employees' insurance schemes, and compensation for injuries caused by accidents occurring at work place. Because these payments are the primary liability of the contractor for the employees he has employed, he is liable to indemnify the principal employer for such payments. These laws entitle the principal employer to recover the amounts from contractors.

§4. *ACTIO PAULIANA*

397. Indian law has no provision similar to the oblique action or the *Paulian* action in Belgian law, which enables creditors direct action in respect of their debtors contracts. A creditor cannot exercise any right or action of the debtor to bring an action in the name of the debtor.

398. If a contract is broken, the promisee has the following remedies: (i) self-help remedies – that is, remedies available under the contract, such as forfeiture, withholding performance, and so on; (ii) enforcement of securities offered for performance of that promise, such as guarantees, mortgage, pledge, lien, and so on; (iii) commence legal proceedings in the courts or in arbitration and enforce the judgment, award, or decree got in his favour. He may also take interim steps in the legal proceedings to prevent the promisor from dealing with his properties in a manner as may affect the ultimate enforcement of the award or decree; but this relief of seeking interim/interlocutory injunction or attachment before judgment is available only if he can show that the promisor is likely to dispose of his assets with the intention of defeating the judgment or decree as may be passed against him. In the course of enforcement of the decree in his favour, the promisee, now the judgment creditor, may enforce the payments or contracts of the promisor (judgment debtor).

399. He may have a right against the property of the debtor; the specific property is pledged or otherwise taken as security for the debt or performance of the promise.

405. See s. 8A of the Employees' Provident Funds Act 1952, s. 41 of the Employees' State Insurance Act 1948 and s. 12(2) of the Employees' Compensation Act 1923.

Chapter 5. The Discharge of the Contract

400. The term discharge is used in this chapter in both senses – discharge of any particular obligation under a contract affecting part only of a contract and discharge of an entire contract.

401. Parties to a contract are free to decide the circumstances in which their contract or any obligation under it would be discharged, and its consequences.

402. Obligations under a contract will be discharged in different ways:

(i) by performance or making an offer of performance;
(ii) by rescission on breach in certain cases;
(iii) by termination in exercise of powers under the contract;
(iv) by performance of contract becoming impossible or unlawful by some reason beyond the control of the promisor;
(v) by agreement – that is, by novation, rescission, or alteration of terms;
(vi) rescission of contract voidable for lack of free consent;
(vii) remission by act of promisee – by remission or dispensing with performance;
(viii) by operation of law;
(ix) discharge under the provisions of the contract; and
(x) by unauthorized material alteration of instrument.

403. The expression 'termination of contract' is used to indicate termination of a contract by any party in the exercise of a right of termination available to him under it. Such party may terminate the contract, that is, bring contractual relationship to an end, by giving notice to the other party.

§1. Performance and Breach

404. The normal method of discharge of contractual obligations is by performance or by offering performance.

The Indian Contract Act uses both terms – breach and non-performance. Any kind of non-performance, whether amounting to failure, refusal, or by reason of the promisor disabling himself in performing, amounts to breach unless excused. But the consequences differ.

Every breach enables a promisee to claim damages for loss incurred by reason of the breach, but does not lead to discharge of obligations.

405. The consequences for non-performance differ. If non-performance is excused on the grounds of subsequent impossibility, the obligation of restitution arises.[406] If the non-performance is not excused, it would excuse the other party from performing his part of the contract and also give rise to a claim for damages.

406. Section 65 of the Indian Contract Act, see paras 305, 454.

In certain cases only will the party have a right to terminate the contract upon non-performance by the other party.

I. Performance

406. The Indian Contract Act obliges parties to perform their respective obligations, which may consist of payment of money, providing service, supply of goods, or in the nature of any other act or forbearance. The term 'payment' refers to payment of money.

A. *Obligation to Perform*

407. Parties to a contract must either perform or offer to perform, their respective promises, unless such performance is dispensed with or excused under the provisions of the Indian Contract Act or any other law.[407] The promisee may dispense with performance. The Act excuses performance in some situations.[408]

Performance will be excused under other statutes, for example, under the laws relating to insolvency,[409] rent control legislation, or laws granting debt-relief to debtors, or under the rule of *damdupat*.[410] Performance may also be suspended under express provisions of statute.

B. *Offer of Performance*

408. The promisor is not responsible for non-performance if his offer of performance is not accepted by the promisee. Such offer of performance, or tender as it is called under English law, must be unconditional and made at the proper time and place, and the promisor must be able and willing to fulfil that obligation fully. A promisor offering to deliver goods must give an opportunity to the promisee to see whether the thing offered is that which was promised.[411] If the promise is owed to multiple persons, it is sufficient to offer performance to any one of them.

---

407. Section 37 of the Indian Contract Act.
408. (i) the event on which the performance of contract is contingent has not occurred (ss 32–36); (ii) where one party has refused to perform his promise, or has disabled himself from performing it (s. 39); (iii) if the promisor defaults in performance of a reciprocal promise (s. 54); (iv) when parties make a new contract, or rescind or alter the terms of the contract (s. 62); (v) when the promisee dispenses with or remits performance (s. 63); (vi) when a party rescinds the contract where such right is available under the Act (ss 39, 54 and 55), or under contract; (vi) when the promise becomes impossible for performance for reasons beyond the control of the promisor (s. 56); (vii) when the promisor fails to afford facilities to the promisor for performance (s. 67).
409. Sections 38–45 of the Presidency-Towns Insolvency Act 1909, and ss 41–44 of the Provincial Insolvency Act 1920.
410. This rule of Hindu law provides that the amount of principal and interest recoverable at one time in a lump sum cannot be more than double the money lent.
411. Section 38 of the Indian Contract Act.

Thus, if a debtor sends the amount of debt to his creditor at the proper time and place, but the creditor does not accept it, the debtor will not be liable for interest on the amount or to send that amount again. This does not discharge the obligation to pay.

409. The promisor must fulfil the entire obligation according to its terms. He cannot insist that the promisee accept performance in part. But if partial performance is offered, the promisee has an option to accept it. Even while the promisee does so, the promisee may reserve his right to seek damages for breach. In regard to payment of money on a contract of loan, the court may, under the law affecting usury, applicable to very few loans, reduce the rate of interest or vary terms of the loan.

C. Who Must Perform

1. Employ Another to Perform

410. Whether a promisor must perform himself or can employ another to complete the engagement depends on the nature of his obligation. In any case, the promisor continues to be liable for failure or faulty performance. Performance by another does not amount to assignment of contract.

2. Contracts of Personal Nature

411. A promisor must personally execute the engagement if it is the intention of parties that the promise must be performed by the promisor himself.

Such intention may be expressly stated. It may be gathered from the terms of the contract, its subject matter, and the surrounding circumstances. Such would be the intention if the performance requires skill or taste depends on the competency or personal qualification of the promisor, or is based on special personal confidence between the parties. Contracts of employment; services of an architect, lawyer, or another professional person; engagement of an author by a publisher; require such employee, professional, or author to perform personally. Such obligation also ends with the death of the promisor, and his representatives are not liable.

412. When there is no such intention of personal performance, a promise may be performed by the promisor and by his representative, and the representative may also employ a competent person to perform it.

3. Offer Performance to Whom

413. Performance may be offered to the promisee himself, to his agent having authority, or to such person as may be prescribed in the contract. A promisee may ratify payment made to a person not having authority.

D. *Acceptance of Performance from Third Party*

414. However, when a promisee accepts performance of a promise from a third person, he cannot afterward enforce it against the promisor.[412] This is so even if the promisor has not authorized or ratified the performance. Such a provision enables a promisee to release a debt at the instance of a third party. It also enables that promisor to take advantage of such a release. This release is effective only if the promise has been fully performed. The rights of subrogation of an insurer making payment or any other person are not lost.

E. *Contents of Performance*

1. Nature of Obligation

415. The content of performance depends on the nature of obligation incurred. It may be strict, for example, a promise to supply goods of the specified quality. It may be an obligation to take best or utmost efforts, for example, a promise to take best efforts to obtain government permission required for a contract. The promisor may have undertaken to exercise only reasonable care or due diligence, such as in a contract for services. Whether the performance rendered is sufficient according to contract is a question in each case of construction of the terms of that contract.

2. Strict Obligation

416. In any case, the promisor must perform strictly what he has promised to do. Otherwise he will be liable for breach and the promisee may not be liable for his reciprocal promise.

The promisee may, however, waive this requirement and accept any other performance. In such a case he cannot claim the original promise. Such substituted performance accepted by the promisee will discharge the obligation.[413] Such acceptance is the unilateral act of the promisee, and differs from novation, in which both parties agree to substitute a new contract for the old one.[414] Such remission or waiver does not require consideration under the Indian law. However, novation must be supported by consideration.

The promisee cannot be forced to accept performance other than agreed. This is not a valid offer of performance as stated earlier and hence does not discharge the obligation.

---

412. Section 41 of the Indian Contract Act; *Citibank NA v. Standard Chartered Bank* (2004) 6 SCC 1.
413. Section 63 of the Indian Contract Act.
414. Section 62 of the Indian Contract Act.

F. Payment of Money

1. Mode of Payment

417. Payment of money must be offered in the manner expressly or impliedly provided in the contract. No formality is required. The debtor would naturally choose a mode that would enable evidence of the offer of payment. He might, therefore, send the payment by postal money order, or by an instrument sent by registered post with acknowledgment from the creditor. Payment by cheque, credit card, or charge card may be accepted by the creditor. A creditor is not bound to accept a cheque, but once accepted cannot object to it. It is usual practice to make large payments by cheque or demand draft.

2. Income-Tax Law

418. The law relating to income-tax imposes a disability if certain types of payments are not made by crossed cheque or demand draft.[415] It provides that if any payment of amount of more than INR 20,000 is made toward any expenditure otherwise than by an account payee cheque or bank draft, such amount cannot be deducted as expenditure while computing income from business. Certain expenditures are also excepted by rules. Similarly, repayment of deposits may be made only by account payee cheque or bank draft drawn in the name of the person who has made the deposit, where the deposit or interest is held by such person.

3. Negotiable Instrument Is Conditional Payment

419. If a creditor accepts payment by cheque or other negotiable instrument, it is presumed that he has received it as conditional or qualified payment and not in absolute satisfaction of debt. This means that if the cheque is dishonoured, the obligation is not discharged but entails consequences of breach.

G. Currency

420. Where the promisor is bound to pay money, he must pay in the manner, at the time, and at the place provided in the contract. Where there is no such express provision, he is bound to tender the current legal tender – in rupees.

1. Principle of Nominalism

421. Where the obligation is to pay an amount in a particular currency, the principle of nominalism applies. This principle is that if a debt is payable in the

415. See ss 40A(3), and 269T of the Income-tax Act 1961.

future, it involves an obligation to pay the nominal amount of debt at the time of payment in whatever is the legal tender for that currency at that date, irrespective of the fluctuations in the currency between the date of the contract and the date of payment. The date on which payment *becomes due* is the crucial date.

Parties may contract out of this principle and protect themselves from depreciation in the value of currency by adopting gold clauses or clauses linking payment with cost-of-living index or other index.

2. Rate of Exchange

422. The parties can agree on the exchange rate. Otherwise, currency will be converted with reference to the exchange rate on the date of payment.[416] In case of amount payable on a note or negotiable instrument, the exchange rate of the date of maturity will apply.[417] Whether increase in exchange rate can be claimed from the other party is a matter of construction of the term.[418]

3. Rate Fixed by Court or Arbitrator

423. A court in India as well as an arbitrator have jurisdiction to pass a decree for a sum expressed in foreign currency by making the payment of foreign currency subject to permission of the foreign exchange authorities if necessary.[419] There will be an alternative for payment of a sum of money in Indian rupees.

In regard to the date for converting foreign currency into Indian rupees, the court must select a date that puts the plaintiff in the same position in which he would have been had the defendant discharged his obligation when he ought to have done, keeping in mind that the rate of exchange is not a constant factor but fluctuates from time to time. The Supreme Court has held that the date of passing of decree (final judgment) as the date for conversion was fairest to both parties. In this judgment the Supreme Court also laid down the practice to be followed in suits in which a sum of money expressed in foreign currency is claimed by the plaintiff and decreed by the court; but specified that execution can issue only in the rupee equivalent specified in the decree.

An arbitrator can make an award in foreign currency convertible at a rate of exchange on the date of award or a very close date.

424. A promisor may have agreed to perform his promise in two ways:

(i) requiring that the promisee demand performance, called application for performance; or
(ii) directly without requiring such application.

---

416. *Renusagar Power Co Ltd v. General Electric Co* AIR 1994 SC 860.
417. As stated in *Syndic in Bankruptcy of Khoury v. Khayat* [1943] AC 507, [1943] 2 All ER 406.
418. *Pure Helium India Pvt Ltd v. Oil and Natural Gas Commission* AIR 2003 SC 4519.
419. *Forasol v. Oil and Natural Gas Commission* AIR 1984 SC 241.

If the promisor is to perform without application by promisee, and no time is fixed, he must perform within reasonable time, which is a question of fact dependent on particular circumstances of that case. If it is to be so performed on a certain day, it must be performed within business hours, and at such place where it ought to be performed.

425. If the place of performance is fixed by contract, he must perform it or offer its performance at that place. If the promisor is to perform the promise without application by the promisee, but no place is fixed for performance in the contract, the promisor must apply to the promisee to fix the place and then perform at that place. The place fixed by the promisee must be reasonable.

If the parties have fixed the day, but the promisee is to apply for performance, the promisee must indicate the proper place.

In regard to payment of money, if no place is named expressly or impliedly, 'the debtor is to find the creditor'. The debtor cannot insist that the creditor come to him for taking the money.

426. The promisee may prescribe or sanction the manner or time for performance by the promisor, and the promisor may perform in that manner and at that time.

H. Time for Performance Is Specified

427. If the promisor fails to perform his promise at the time *specified* for that purpose in the contract, the solution or remedy depends on whether the parties intended that *time shall be of the essence* of the contract.[420]

If it is of the intention of the promisee at the time of making the contract that time specified shall be of essence, and the promisor fails to perform within the time specified, the promisee has the option to avoid the contract. If he does not exercise this option, and accepts performance at the time due, he cannot claim compensation for the delay unless he asserts such claim while accepting.

If it is not the intention of the parties that time should be of the essence in the contract, the contract does not become voidable by such failure, but the promisee is entitled to damages for loss caused to him by such failure. Even in such contracts, the promisee may make time of essence by giving notice to the promisor, giving him reasonable time and requiring performance.

Unlike in English law, time is not of essence merely because of an express stipulation in the contract that time shall be of its essence; it is but one of the factors to be considered in deciding the intention of the parties. The intention of the parties can be ascertained from (i) the express words used in the contract stating time is important, (ii) the nature of the property that forms the subject matter of the

420. Section 55 of the Indian Contract Act.

contract, (iii) the nature of the contract itself, and (iv) the surrounding circumstances. Later conduct of the parties might indicate such intention.[421]

Except in commercial contracts, the ordinary presumption is that time is not of the essence of the contract, especially in contracts relating to immovable property or building construction contracts. This presumption can be rebutted by giving evidence of a contrary intention.

428. This provision of law is not a popular one. Although parties may believe that performance at the specified time is very important, what the court decides in the case might belie their expectations. The promisee who has expressly provided that time shall be of essence and has terminated the contract in terms of the contract for non-performance within that time may not find support in court. The court is quite likely to come to a conclusion that the intention of the parties was not that time was of the essence. Exercising the right of termination for failure to perform within time, therefore, must be exercised very cautiously.

I. Appropriation of Payments

429. The Act makes provisions for appropriation of payments. Where a debtor owes several distinct debts to another and makes a payment, a question arises as to which debt must such payment be applied.

The appropriation would be made according to the provisions, if any, for the same in the contract.

If there is no provision in the contract:

(i) The debtor has the right to indicate the debt toward which the payment shall be applied. If the creditor accepts the payment, which he need not, the payment must be applied toward that debt.[422]
(ii) If the debtor has not indicated any choice, the creditor may apply the amount toward any lawful debt, even if barred by the law of limitation.[423]
(iii) If it appears that neither the debtor nor the creditor have made such choice, the payments will be applied toward the debts, whether time-barred or not, in the order of time.[424]

430. Payment made toward a single debt (including a debt payable under a decree[425]) is first applied toward the interest and costs and then toward the principal, unless the contract provides otherwise. This is an old rule of common law.[426]

421. *Amteshwar Anand v. Virender Mohan Singh* AIR 2006 SC 151.
422. Section 59 of the Indian Contract Act.
423. Section 60 of the Indian Contract Act.
424. Section 61 of the Indian Contract Act.
425. Subject to any express provisions made by the court in the decree.
426. *Industrial Credit and Development Syndicate v. Smithaben H Patel* AIR 1999 SC 1036.

The rules relating to several distinct debts, given earlier, does not apply in such a case and the debtor has no right to demand application towards the principal.

J. Subrogation

431. The expression 'subrogation' refers to a transfer of rights from one person to another, without assignment or assent of the person from whom the rights are transferred. It occurs by operation of law. The transfer will comprise all rights, actions, securities, of such person and be subject to all claims or exceptions against such person.

1. Insurer

432. The right of subrogation is available to an insurer[427] when the insurance is a contract of indemnity, for example, insurance against loss of property. It is the right of the insurer who has paid a loss to be put in the place of the insured so that he can take advantage of any means available to the insured to extinguish or diminish the loss for which the insurer has indemnified the insured. It is not available in cases of life or accident insurance.

The right arises only after the insurer has paid in full the claim of an insured, though it is possible to provide by condition in the contract that the insurer shall have the right of subrogation even before he has indemnified the insured.

The insurer is entitled to the benefit of all remedies of insured against third parties responsible for the loss, whether in contract or in tort. The insurer is also entitled to receive all benefits received by the insured from third parties in compensation for the loss for which the insurer has given indemnity. Thus, an insurer will be entitled to claim from the insured the amount received by the insured toward his loss from the third party that has caused the loss.[428] The insurer is entitled to sue in the name of the insured or to compel the insured to take proceedings against third parties for the benefit of the insurer. The insurer cannot sue in his own name unless there is a specific contract of assignment of rights.

If the insurer recovers more than the amount paid to the insured, this excess must be paid to the insured; this excess need not be paid to the insured where the insurer has a legal assignment of the insured's right of action and, therefore, sues the third party in his own name.

2. Surety

433. A surety in the contract of guarantee also enjoys a statutory right of subrogation. Where a guaranteed debt has become due, or default of the principal

427. Summary of law in *Economic Transport Organization v. Charan Spinning Mills (P) Ltd* (2010) 4 SCC 114.

428. *Union of India v. Sri Sarada Mills* AIR 1973 SC 281.

debtor to perform a guaranteed duty has taken place, the surety, on payment or performance of all that is liable for, is invested with all the rights that the creditor had against the principal debtor.[429] This gives the surety the right to sue the principal debtor for the amount, to all securities, the creditor had from the debtor (whether known to him or not at the time he became surety),[430] including the right of lien, the right to claim in the administration of the debtor's estate, the right to the same priority as the creditor in any winding-up or insolvency proceedings relating to the principal debtor. If he is a surety for payment of price, he can also exercise the seller's right to stop the goods in transit and the seller's right of lien and of resale.

This right of the surety is automatic and does not require any further action by the creditor or the surety. Neither an assignment nor any document of transfer is necessary.[431]

434. The mere fact that one person has advanced money to another to enable him to pay specific debts or buy some property does not give such lender any rights of the other, unless there is a specific contract giving such rights to the lender. This would be properly classified as a contractual claim and would be subject to the agreed terms.

II. Rescission for Breach

435. A party is said to have broken a contract either when he has (i) renounced his liabilities under it by refusing to perform it; (ii) disabled himself from performing it; and (iii) failed to perform his part of the promise. In these three cases there is repudiation of contractual obligations. In the first two cases, breach may occur either before or at the time for performance. In the last case, breach occurs at the time of or during performance of the contract.

436. Although every breach gives rise to a claim for damages,[432] not every breach gives the right to the promisee to rescind the contract. The promisee may rescind the contract for breach only in the following cases:

(i) where the promisor has refused to perform or disabled himself from performing his promise in its entirety;[433]
(ii) where parties have specified a time for performance of a promise and the promisor fails to perform at the specified time, time being intended to be of the essence of the contract;[434]

429. Section 140 of the Indian Contract Act.
430. Section 141 of the Indian Contract Act.
431. *Amrit Lal Goverdhan Lalan v. State Bank of Travancore* AIR 1968 SC 1432.
432. Under s. 73 of the Indian Contract Act.
433. Section 39 of the Indian Contract Act.
434. Section 55 of the Indian Contract Act.

(iii) where one party prevents the other from performing the promise of the other;[435]
(iv) where the contract gives him the power to terminate the contract for such breach. In such a case, the promisee can exercise the right strictly in the manner and subject to the terms and conditions of the contract.

§2. Impossibility, Frustration, and Hardship: 'The Unforeseen'

I. Initial Impossibility

437. An agreement to do an act impossible in itself is void.[436] Thus, where A agrees with B to discover treasure by magic, the agreement is void.

Where performance of the contract is impossible at the time of making of contract because the subject matter does not exist, the parties are labouring under a mutual mistake, and the agreement is void because their consent is caused by mistake,[437] the impossibility exists, the parties may discover it later, and hence such a case appears at first sight to be a question of the doctrine of impossibility.

II. Subsequent Impossibility

A. *The Doctrine of Subsequent Impossibility*

438. Section 56 (paragraph 2) of the Indian Contract Act states the effect of subsequent supervening impossibility on a contract. It provides:

> A contract to do an act which, after the contract is made becomes impossible, or, by reason of some event which the promisor could not prevent, unlawful, becomes void when the act becomes impossible or unlawful.

1. Application

439. Subsequent impossibility ends a valid contract from the moment it becomes incapable of performance. Further performance is excused. It includes not only physical or literal impossibility, but also to events that render performance impracticable and useless from the point of view of the object and purpose the parties had in view or where the event or change of circumstances frustrates the whole purpose or basis of the contract.[438]

---

435. Section 53 of the Indian Contract Act.
436. Section 56, para. 1 of the Indian Contract Act.
437. Section 20 of the Indian Contract Act; see paras 237 onwards.
438. *Naihati Jute Mills Ltd v. Khyaliram Jagannath* AIR 1968 SC 522; *Satyabrata Ghose v. Mugneeram Bangur & Co* AIR 1954 SC 44.

2. Doctrine of Narrow Limits

440. The doctrine is applied within very narrow limits and will not be lightly invoked.[439] The doctrine cannot be permitted to become a device for destroying the sanctity of contract. The court will also not apply the doctrine of impossibility to assist a party that does not want to fulfil its obligations under the contract.

3. Conditions for Applicability

441. The following conditions are essential before section 56 becomes applicable: (a) a valid and subsisting contract between the parties, (b) some part of the contract yet to be performed, and (c) the contract becoming impossible of performance after it is made.

4. Not Available to Party at Fault

442. There is no discharge where the event is caused by the fault of either party. This fault may occur because of deliberate choice not to perform or by putting the performance out of one's power. Also, impossibility is not a defence for the party that has failed to perform its obligations. It has been stated: 'it is not accurate to say that impossibility excuses breach, without further qualification. It would be more correct to say that precisely opposite is the rule'.[440]

5. Not Applicable to Transfers of Property

443. The doctrine, unlike in English law, affects contracts for sale of land in India, but not completed sales. It does not apply to transfers of property or interest in land, such as leases.[441] If a leased land is wholly destroyed or rendered substantially and permanently unfit for the purpose for which it was let by reason of fire, tempest, flood, and so on, the lessee has an option to determine the lease.[442]

B. Frustration and Impossibility

444. Frustration occurs when circumstances arise after the formation of the contract that occur by the fault of neither party and that render performance of the contract by one or both parties impossible. The court regards these sets of circumstances as releasing the parties from any further obligations.

---

439. *Twentsche Overseas Trading Co Ltd v. Uganda Sugar Factory Ltd* AIR 1945 PC 144.
440. *Grant Smith and Company and McDonell Limited v. Settle Construction and Dry Dock Company* AIR 1919 PC 85.
441. *Raja Dhruv Dev Chand v. Raja Harmohinder Singh* AIR 1968 SC 1024.
442. Section 108(e) of the Transfer of Property Act 1882.

445. Where the contract itself, as a matter of construction, contains impliedly or expressly a term according to which it would stand discharged on the happening of certain circumstances, the question of dissolution of the contract according to its terms falls to be determined under another provision of the Indian Contract Act – section 32, although under English law such cases will be treated as cases of frustration.

Section 32 provides:

> Contingent contracts[443] to do or not to do anything if an uncertain future event happens cannot be enforced by law unless and until that event has happened. If the event becomes impossible such contracts become void.

Thus, contracts requiring permissions or consents for performance of contract may become void if the performance is made conditional on such permission or consent; the refusal of permission rendering the contract void. This is because the parties have stated this condition and not because of the doctrine of impossibility.

C. Only One Doctrine of Impossibility in Indian Law

446. The statutory provision about impossibility gives a positive rule of law and excludes consideration of principles and theories of frustration discussed often as part of English law. The provision is exhaustive. In a leading case on the subject[444] the Supreme Court has observed: 'In deciding the cases in India, the only doctrine we have to go by is that of supervening impossibility or illegality as laid down in section 56 of the Indian Contract Act, taking the word "impossible" in its practical and not literal sense'.

D. Instances of Impossibility

447. Performance may become impossible because of the following:

(i) The specific thing essential to the performance has been destroyed. In case of sale of specific goods, where after the agreement to sell and before sale, and before the risk passes to the buyer, the goods perish or become so damaged as no longer to answer to their description without any fault of the seller or buyer, the agreement is avoided.[445]

(ii) The state of things on which the performance depended and that formed the basis of the contract do not exist.

443. Section 31 of the Indian Contract Act defines: 'A "contingent contract" is a contract to do or not to do something, if some event, collateral to such contract, does or does not happen'; see para. 346 onwards.

444. *Satyabrata Ghose v. Mugneeram Bangur & Co* AIR 1954 SC 44.

445. Section 8 of the Sale of Goods Act 1930.

(iii) In a contract requiring an act involving personal skill or qualifications of the promisor, the death or insanity of the promisor before performance.
(iv) Changes in law after the making of the contract prohibiting the act, or restricting its performance; these would include not only statutory changes but also restrictions placed by executive orders of government.
(v) Conditions of war.

This list is not exhaustive.

E. No Discharge Despite Performance Being Impossible

448. The contract will not be discharged even if performance is rendered impossible if:[446]

(i) the obligation undertaken is absolute;
(ii) the contract makes full and complete provision for a given contingency; for example, where they make provision for the supervening event foreseen by them, where they expressly provide that the risk for specified events shall be borne by one or other of them, or they apportion the risk, provide for remedies, or provide for total discharge in various ways;
(iii) the event is such that it can be supposed to have been contemplated by the parties when they made the contract or would have foreseen with reasonable diligence. The fact that the parties have foreseen the event but have not provided for it, indicates that either of them has assumed the risk for the event.

F. Hardship and Difficulty in Performance

449. A contract is not frustrated because its performance has become more onerous or burdensome or there is any extreme or unforeseen cost or difficulty of performance.[447] Thus, the following events are ordinary risks of business and do not excuse performance: abnormal rise or fall in prices, abnormal increase in expenses, scarcity of labour, scarcity of raw materials, depreciation of currency, insolvency or inability to obtain finance for completing performance, and strikes and lockouts or other industrial disturbances. Nor do disappointed expectations even of both parties discharge obligations. Parties may however, provide in the contract, that the contract shall be discharged on happening of such contingencies.[448]

---

446. See *Satyabrata Ghose v. Mugneeram Bangur & Co* AIR 1954 SC 44; *Afshar M M Tacki v. Dharamsey Tricamdas* AIR 1947 Bom 98; *Alopi Parshad & Sons Ltd v. Union of India* AIR 1960 SC 588; *Ramayya v. Firm of Gulfarosh Mohdeen Saib Shaik Saib* AIR 1958 AP 576.
447. *Alopi Parshad & Sons Ltd v. Union of India* AIR 1960 SC 588; *Naihati Jute Mills Ltd v. Khyaliram Jagannath* AIR 1968 SC 522; *Keshavlal Brothers & Co v. Diwan Chand & Co* AIR 1923 PC 105.2. Force majeure clauses, see para. 451 *infra*.
448. Force majeure clauses, see para. 451 *infra*.

G. No Right to Demand Revision of Contractual Relationship

450. When an unforeseen event occurs rendering performance impossible, the contract is discharged. No party has a right to demand renegotiation to adapt the original terms of the contract to changed circumstances. Nor does the court have such power to revise the contract. Parties are free to together renegotiate the terms in the changed circumstances, which will then be a new contract.

H. Allocation of Risks by Contract: Force Majeure Clauses

451. A provision relating to force majeure indicates an intention of saving the performing party from the consequences of anything over which he has no control. Such a provision is enforceable. It also indicates that parties take the risks of the events covered by such provision, in the manner indicated.

Parties can provide:[449]

(i) provisions for supervening events foreseen by the parties, including those events that might not otherwise have given an excuse for performance;
(ii) for discharge of contract on occurrence of any specified supervening event;
(iii) for the procedure or course of action to be followed by one or either party on occurrence of such event;
(iv) that risk for any such event shall be borne by one or either of them;
(v) remedies available if such specified events occur.

I. Subsequent Illegality

452. A contract may become incapable of performance if it becomes unlawful by some event that the promisor could not prevent. An order of the government prohibiting import or restricting transactions in specified goods can render void performance of transactions in such goods.

J. Consequences of Supervening Impossibility or Illegality

453. When an act becomes impossible of performance or unlawful because of supervening events, the contract 'becomes void'; that is, it ceases to be enforceable. It discharges both parties from further performance at the time the event happens.

Discharge of the contract is automatic on the happening of such event and does not require any act or election by any party, nor does it require any repudiation by any party. It is not necessary that the parties be aware of the effect of the event.

449. *Afshar M M Tacki v. Dharamsey Tricamdas* AIR 1947 Bom 98.

The aggrieved party cannot keep it alive, nor can discharge be waived. The issue has to be decided by the court ex post facto on the actual circumstances of the case.

Yet the contract will exist for resolving disputes, including whether the contract has been discharged on these grounds. Therefore, an arbitration clause is not discharged by supervening events.[450]

K. Remedies

454. When a contract 'becomes void', the obligation in the nature of restitution lies. The party who has received any advantage under it is bound to restore it or make compensation for it to the other party.[451] Performance rendered must be paid under the contract.

Where one person has promised to do something that he knew or with reasonable diligence might have known, and that the promisee did not know to be impossible or unlawful, such promisor must make compensation to such promisee for any loss that such promisee sustains through the non-performance of the promise.[452] This is an exception to the doctrine of frustration, in which instead of declaring the contract discharged, the promisor is saddled with the liability to pay compensation to the promisee for the non-performance of the promise.[453]

§3. Discharge by Agreement

455. If the parties to a contract agree to substitute a new contract for it, or to rescind or alter it, the original contract need not be performed.[454] Thus, the parties to a contract are free to substitute the entire contract, or to rescind it entirely, or to modify, alter, vary, or rescind some of its terms.

Such mutual novation, cancellation or rescission must be clearly expressed. It can also be inferred from the conduct of parties.

Such novation, modification, or rescission cannot be effected unilaterally by one party or forced by one party on the other. It requires consent of all parties.[455] It may take place in the same manner as a contract. Thus, if a party proposes a substitution or change in terms and the other party accepts this proposal, the earlier contract (to the extent of change in terms) is discharged and a new contract on fresh terms takes place.

---

450. *Union of India v. Kishori Lal Gupta & Bros* AIR 1959 SC 1362; *Khardah & Company Ltd v. Raymon & Co (India) Private Ltd* AIR 1962 SC 1810.
451. Under s. 65 of the Indian Contract Act.
452. Paragraph 3 of s. 56 of the Indian Contract Act.
453. *Satyabrata Ghose v. Mugneeram Bangur & Co* AIR 1954 SC 44.
454. Section 62 of the Indian Contract Act.
455. *Y A J Noorbhai v. S P L K R Karuppan Chetty* AIR 1925 PC 232.

Despite rule of parol evidence,[456] oral evidence can be given to prove a subsequent variation, modification, or novation, unless such change is required by law to be in writing.[457]

I. Novation

456. Novation occurs when the parties substitute a new contract for the existing one. This may be done in two ways: (i) between the same parties or (ii) between different parties, on same or different terms.

Novation has two elements: (i) discharge of the existing contract or a promisor and (ii) substitution of a new contract or a promisor. Its essence is substitution. Consideration for the new contract is the mutual discharge of the old one.

A. *Intention of Parties*

457. Whether the transaction amounts to a novation or is supplementary to the old agreement would depend on the intention of the parties, as seen from the substance of the agreement and not merely the form or its name. This depends on the facts and circumstances of each case. The test of novation is: are the two contracts so inconsistent that they cannot stand together or are the terms of the new contract such that it is impossible to perform the terms of the old contract. There is no novation if the nature of rights and liabilities parties has not changed.[458]

But where a negotiable instrument, such as a bill of exchange or promissory note, is given in discharge of a debt, it is presumed to operate as a conditional payment. If the instrument is dishonoured, the creditor can claim his original debt.

B. *Form*

458. The new contract may be oral, in writing, or may be implied. Even where the old contract is in writing, section 92 of the Indian Evidence Act allows oral evidence to prove the existence of any distinct subsequent oral agreement to rescind or modify such contract, unless such new contract is required by law to be in writing or registered.

C. *Effect of Novation*

459. Upon novation, the new contract will govern the relationship between the parties. The old contract is discharged, and the promisor is relieved of his

---

456. Section 92 of the Indian Evidence Act 1872, see para. 186 onwards.
457. Proviso 4 to s. 92 of the Indian Evidence Act 1872.
458. *Chatterjee Petrochem Co v. Haldia Petrochemicals Ltd* AIR 2014 SC (Supp) 699, 2014 AIR SCW 237.

obligations under it. The new contract gives a new cause of action, and the period of limitation for filing the suit will be determined with reference to the new contract. The old contract is not revived by non-performance or breach of the new contract.

With the replacement of the old contract, any arbitration clause in it also ceases, and hence cannot be invoked even to decide whether that contract subsists or has been discharged.[459]

D. *Novation by Substitution of Debtor*

460. To supersede one contract by another, all the parties to the first contract must be parties to the second contract. A novation cannot be forced on a person intended to be the substituted party without his agreement. This is because in a novation the promisee might be prejudiced, whereas it is immaterial to a promisor to whom he renders performance, so long as he gets a good discharge for it. It is necessary to find not only whether the new promisor has consented to assume liability, but also whether the promisee has agreed to accept his liability in substitution to that of the original promisor.

In a partnership, a new partner does not become liable for any act of the firm done before he became a partner, unless he has so agreed. To determine whether an incoming partner becomes liable to an existing creditor of the firm, it must be seen first whether the new firm has assumed the liability to pay the debt and second whether the creditor has agreed to accept the new firm as his debtor and to discharge the old partnership from its liability.

E. *Assignment and Novation*

461. An assignment of rights under a contract can be effected without the consent of the promisor, unless it is prohibited by the contract. A novation will require the consent of the promisor. An assignment of liabilities cannot be done without the consent of the promisee and hence when effected, will necessarily involve novation.

F. *No Novation after Breach*

462. A new contract can be substituted only where the original contract subsists, and not after the original one has been broken. It has been suggested that a new contract be enforceable whether made before or after the breach, especially when it

459. *Union of India v. Kishori Lal Gupta & Bros* AIR 1959 SC 1362; *Damodar Valley Corporation v. K K Kar* AIR 1974 SC 158.

is a common practice among parties to compromise through mediation after the breach.[460]

II. Cancellation

463. The parties together can cancel the entire contract or some only of the terms. Such rescission may be express or implied. There is an implied rescission of the contract when new and independent terms inconsistent with the first contract are agreed regarding the same subject matter between the parties.

Such rescission is effective only if made by all parties to the contract. A contract cannot be cancelled or terminated unilaterally, unless such power is given under the contract itself.

The consideration for such rescission is the release by one party of the other from its obligations or the mutual abandonment of obligations.

464. A contract can be mutually rescinded even after its breach. It is a question of construction whether or not it rescinds the original contract totally, in which case the arbitration clause also stands rescinded.

465. Any contract between the creditor and the principal debtor that has the effect of releasing the principal debtor, or any act of the creditor that has the effect of discharging the principal debtor, discharges the surety, unless the surety has consented in the guarantee to such power to the creditor.[461] Thus, acceptance of a new debtor instead of the old one puts an end to the liability of a surety for old debt.

III. Variation

466. Parties to an agreement may vary some of its terms by a subsequent agreement in such manner that the modified terms are read into and become part of the original contract. The original terms are binding except to the extent they are inconsistent with the modifications. In the absence of power to that effect under the contract, a contract may not be varied except with the consent of all the parties.

A. Unilateral Variation

467. A contract may give to one of the parties the power to vary unilaterally specified terms in the contract, such as the price, the extent of works, and so on. Such a provision is valid. The extent and the mode of exercising such power depend on the provisions of the contract. Any variation beyond such provisions would

460. The Law Commission of India 13th Report, 1958, para. 77.
461. Section 134 of the Indian Contract Act.

amount to breach. The extent of the power of variation is a matter of contruction of such provision in the contract.

B. Effect on Surety

468. If the creditor and principal debtor vary their contract without the consent of the surety, the surety is discharged in respect of transactions made after the variation,[462] even if the surety is not injured by the variation. Liability already incurred is not affected.

§4. Rescission of Contract Voidable for Lack of Free Consent

469. A contract is voidable at the option of that party whose consent is not free by reasons of coercion, undue influence, misrepresentation or fraud. The party rescinding the voidable contract, as well as the other party, are relieved from further performance.[463]

§5. Remission by Promisee

470. The promisee, being the party having the right to demand performance may:[464]

(i) dispense with or remit the performance, in which case the promisor is discharged to the extent of the remission. Thus, where A promises to paint a picture for B, and B afterward forbids him to do so, A is no longer bound to perform the promise. Where X owes Y INR 5,000, Z pays to Y INR 1,000 and Y accepts it in satisfaction of his claim on X, the payment of INR 1,000 is a discharge of the whole claim;
(ii) accept any other satisfaction instead of performance, which will discharge the promisor.

Neither consideration nor an agreement is necessary for enabling a promisee to dispense with or remit the performance of a promise or accept any satisfaction instead of the promise.[465] This is an obvious departure from English law. The obligation will be discharged where there is an actual remission or dispensation or acceptance of satisfaction. A promise to do so will require consideration.

462. Section 133 of the Indian Contract Act.
463. Section 64 of the Indian Contract Act.
464. Section 63 of the Indian Contract Act.
465. *Firm Chhunna Mal Ram Nath v. Firm Mool Chand-Ram Bhagat* AIR 1928 PC 99.

§6. Discharge under Operation of Law

471. The promisor under a contract is discharged on the being declared insolvent by a competent court.[466] A promisor will also be discharged where a law excuses performance by promisor fully or partially.[467]

§7. Discharge under Provisions of the Contract

472. A contract may itself contain a provision for its own discharge. A contract for a fixed period will end when the period expires. The parties may agree that the contract will end on the happening or non-happening of an event, or that in such cases, any one or either of the parties shall have an option to terminate the contract.

I. Termination by Parties

473. Parties can stipulate expressly or impliedly that one or other or both parties may terminate the contract in certain circumstances, such as:

(i) notice at the option of any one or of either party without assigning any reason; or
(ii) on happening of a event; or
(iii) non-performance or breach of a term of the contract.

II. Procedure of Termination

474. Any such termination must be communicated. Such notice must be given in the manner and according to the terms provided in the contract. If the contract requires notice of a specified length of time, notice of that length of time must be given. If the contract does not prescribe any period, the notice must be reasonable. There is no obligation that a party must act reasonably when deciding to exercise a contractual power to terminate. But such a stipulation is to be construed according to its natural meaning subject to the principle that a party shall not take advantage of his own wrong.[468]

§8. Unauthorized Material Alteration

475. Any material alteration in an instrument made by a party, or by anyone while it is in the party's custody or in that of his agent, without the consent of the

466. Under the provisions of the Presidency-Towns Insolvency Act 1900 or the Provincial Insolvency Act 1920.
467. For example by operation of laws giving relief to debtors.
468. *Chotelal Lallubhai v. Champsey Umersey & Sons* AIR 1923 Bom 75.

party or parties liable thereunder, disables him from relying on it either as plaintiff or as defendant.[469] Indian decisions have accepted this principle of English common law.

An alteration is material if it varies the rights, liabilities of the parties, or their position or affects the substance of a contract expressed in the document, alters the legal effect of the document.

An alteration will not affect the rights if it merely expresses what was already implied in the document or corrects clerical errors. The Negotiable Instruments Act 1881 expressly allows filling up blanks in instruments, converting endorsement in blank to endorsement in full and crossing of uncrossed cheques.[470]

The party responsible for the alteration cannot maintain an action on it and cannot claim any relief. However, if the alteration is made in a document effecting a transfer of interest in immovable property including mortgages, the document is not rendered void for all purposes, but only as affected by the alteration.

469. *M S Anirudhan v. Thomco's Bank Ltd* AIR 1963 SC 746.
470. Sections 20, 49 and 125 of the Negotiable Instruments Act 1881.

Chapter 6. Remedies

§1. General Provisions

I. Consequences of Breach

476. The Indian Contract Act speaks of consequence of breach, rather than remedies for breach. However, it is usual to find reference to remedies in respect of contractual obligations in books on contract law.

Section 37 of the Indian Contract Act provides: 'the parties to a contract must either perform, or offer to perform, their respective promises, unless such performance is dispensed with or excused under the provisions of this Act, or of any other law'. Parties are thus obliged to perform their promises, unless the performance is dispensed with or excused. The Act itself provides for circumstances when performance of a promise is dispensed with or excused. These are discussed elsewhere as circumstances discharging the contract.[471]

The Indian law uses both terms – 'breach' and 'non-performance', but neither have been defined.

II. Breach

477. When any party refuses or fails to perform the obligation under his promise, he has committed breach. The Act defines obligations of parties as stated above and states the consequences of breach in Chapter VI.

A promise creates an obligation that must be performed, unless dispensed with or excused, else the party who suffers by such breach is entitled to receive from the party who has broken the contract compensation for any loss or damage caused to him thereby.[472] Thus, where one party breaks an obligation, a new obligation arises, that of compensating the aggrieved party for loss caused to him because of breach.

The Act does not make any distinction between promises, that is, in the nature of obligation of result or of best efforts. Failure to perform any promise will be breach.

The promisor is liable for breach, even where the breach is caused by the conduct of his delegate or by any other person performing on behalf of the promisor or any subcontractor.

III. Requirement of Fault

478. Unlike the civil law systems, Indian law does not require the promisee to prove any 'fault' of the promisor to be able to claim relief.

---

471. See para. 402 *supra*.
472. Section 73 of the Indian Contract Act.

IV. Remedies

479. A party aggrieved by breach of contract or non-performance may have four remedies, as follows:

(i) compensation or damages;
(ii) specific performance;
(iii) rescission and termination;
(iv) discharge from own performance.

V. Difference between Continental and Common Law Systems

480. The primary remedy under Indian law is compensation, that is, damages.[473] Specific performance that compels the other party to perform the promise is an exceptional remedy and rests with the discretion of the courts.[474]

An action for damages is always available as of right when a contract has been broken, as against the relief of specific performance, which lies in the discretion of the court. Sections 73–75 of the Contract Act deal with the remedy of damages, and sections 9–24 of the Specific Relief Act deal with specific performance.

A promisor can be restrained from committing breach, especially in cases of negative covenants, by an order of injunction, also governed by sections 36–42 of the Specific Relief Act.

VI. Types of Breach

481. A breach may occur in any of the following ways:

(i) repudiation of liability;
(ii) disabling oneself from performing;
(iii) failure to perform, including breach of warranty;
(iv) defective performance;
(v) delay in performance;
(vi) preventing the other party from performing his promise.

482. Every breach does not discharge the innocent party from performance. In fact, breach does not discharge a contract at all. Where one party repudiates all liability under the contract, or disables himself from performing his part under the contract in its entirety, the other party has *an option* to treat the contract as

473. Sections 73–75 of the Indian Contract Act.
474. Sections 9–24 of the Specific Relief Act 1963.

discharged.[475] This is the right of rescission. If the innocent party does not avoid, and the contract continues, he would still be entitled to damages for the defective performance.

In all other circumstances of breach, the aggrieved/innocent party has to rest content with damages, except cases in which he can seek specific performance.

§2. Faulty Behaviour of Promisor

483. A party is liable for default of himself and of his agents or employee or of the person appointed by him for completing the performance.

484. A party aggrieved by breach need not prove faulty behaviour of the other party to recover damages. Non-performance is dispensed with or excused in circumstances given under the Indian Contract Act or under the provisions of their contract. In the absence of such circumstances, non-performance amounts to breach and renders the defaulting party to damages.

Even in cases in which breach entitles the promisee to a discharge, the discharge follows breach and rescission, without requirement of any fault of the promisor.

485. Where the promisor has agreed, expressly or impliedly, to use care, the promisee seeking remedies will have to prove that he failed to use care.

A consumer seeking relief under the Consumer Protection Act for defect in goods or deficiency in services provided by the supplier can seek replacement or repair of goods or refund of price. If he seeks compensation, he must show that he has suffered loss or injury as a result of negligence of the supplier.[476]

§3. Specific Performance and Injunctions

486. Indian law follows the common law tradition. Specific performance of a contract or injunction in relation to a contract are exceptional remedies, available only when compensation for its breach is either unascertainable or inadequate. Unlike civil law systems, damages are the normal and presumptive remedy.

A contract may be specifically enforced in three ways:

(i) A promise to do an act is enforced by a decree of specific performance.
(ii) A promise not to do an act is enforced by a decree of injunction.
(iii) A promise to pay an ascertained sum of money, such as a contract to repay a loan or pay the price of goods purchased, is enforced by a judgment and decree for the amount. It is a claim for money.

475. See paras 521–523 *infra*; s. 39 of the Indian Contract Act.
476. Section 14(d) of the Consumer Protection Act 1988.

I. Specific Performance

A. *Specific Performance in Two Cases*

487. Specific performance of a contract can be claimed in two cases – first when there is no standard to ascertain the actual damage caused by non-performance of an act and second if compensation will not afford adequate relief for its non-performance.[477] The plaintiff is required to prove these circumstances.

B. *Presumptions*

488. There is a presumption that in cases of contracts to transfer immovable property, compensation will not be adequate. Hence, a contract for transfer or any dealing of immovable property will generally be specifically enforced. This is a rebuttable presumption, and the defendant may show that the object of purchase was not for use, but by way of investment.

On the contrary, in cases of contract to transfer movable property there is a presumption that compensation is an adequate remedy for its breach, unless the property is not an ordinary article of commerce, or is of special value or interest to the plaintiff, or is not easily available in the market; or is held by the defendant as an agent or trustee of the plaintiff.

There are no presumptions for other types of contracts. The plaintiff, having no benefit of presumption, will have to show that compensation for non-performance is unascertainable or inadequate.

C. *No Specific Performance in Certain Contracts*

489. Specific performance cannot be granted of certain contracts, because of difficulties of supervision or enforcement. These are as follows:

(i) a contract, the non-performance of which is adequately relieved by money, however, an agreement to execute a mortgage deed can be enforced;
(ii) a contract that runs into details or involving performance of a continuous duty that the court cannot supervise, for example, a contract to construct a building, except where the building is described with precision, the plaintiff has substantial interest in its performance, and the defendant has obtained possession of the land;
(iii) a contract dependent on personal qualifications or volition of the other party. Thus, an artist cannot be compelled to paint, and an author cannot be compelled to write. Contracts of employment cannot be enforced by the employer or the employee, unless the employee's services are protected by statutes;

477. Section 10 of the Specific Relief Act 1963.

(iv) a contract that is determinable, that is, a contract that can be terminated by a party at any time.

D. Who Can Claim and against Whom

490. Specific performance can be claimed by any party to a contract, his legal representative, persons beneficially entitled under settlement on marriage, or family arrangements.

Specific performance can be enforced against not only the parties to the contract, but also a subsequent transferee, unless he has paid value in good faith and does not have notice of plaintiff's contract.

A company can claim specific performance of a contract made by its promoters before its incorporation, and a contract made by its promoters can be enforced against the company, if the contract is warranted by the terms of incorporation and the company has accepted the contract and communicated the acceptance to the other party.

E. Discretionary Remedy

491. Even in the limited cases in which specific performance is available, it is not a remedy available as of right. Its grant is discretionary. Conduct of the plaintiff, therefore, affects the grant. A plaintiff who has become incapable of performing the contract, acts in fraud of the contract, or wilfully acts in variance of the relationship between the parties cannot enforce the contract.

The plaintiff must plead and prove that he was and has always been ready and willing to perform the terms of contract that remain to be performed by him. This is a strict requirement. Thus, a purchaser enforcing an agreement to purchase immovable property will have to show his ability to pay the price of the land and his willingness to do so.

492. The remedy, as already stated, is discretionary. Section 20 of the Specific Relief Act 1963 states:

> The jurisdiction to decree specific performance is discretionary, and the court is not bound to grant such relief merely because it is lawful to do so; but the discretion of the court is not arbitrary but sound and reasonable, guided by judicial principles, and capable of correction by a court of appeal.

F. Exercise of Discretion

493. A plaintiff will have the benefit of discretion in his favour if he has done substantial acts or suffered losses under the contract. A court may not decree specific performance in certain cases. The main concern of a court is whether it is inequitable to make such a decree considering the circumstances of the case, the conduct of the parties and their respective interests under the contract.[478]

Specific performance may be refused where a contract, though not voidable for lack of free consent, gives the plaintiff an unfair advantage over the defendant, if granting the remedy would impose great hardship on either of the parties, or because it would be inequitable to enforce specific performance. Although unfairness or unconscionability do not vitiate the contract, these are factors affecting discretion of the court in granting specific performance. Relief cannot be refused merely on the grounds that the price of suit property has risen pending proceedings.[479] The Supreme Court has ordered specific performance on terms that the plaintiff shall pay an enhanced amount to compensate for the rise in prices pending proceedings;[480] but it has also observed later that such direction need not be given in all cases.[481]

Unexplained delay in approaching the court for remedy is often a defence to such a suit. Delay can defeat such a decree, even if otherwise the suit is within limitation if granting the relief will prejudice the rights of the defendant or where he has altered his position.

II. Specific Delivery of a Thing

494. The remedy of recovery of specific movable property differs from the remedy of specific performance of a contract to transfer movable property. The latter is a remedy in contract, the former a remedy for delivery of property and based on the right to possess. It is the remedy of *detinue* under English law.

The claim for delivery of specific movable property can be made not only by the owner, but also by any other person entitled to an immediate right to possession, such as a bailee, finder of goods, or holder of a right of lien.[482] The plaintiff seeking delivery of the article can seek its delivery or its value. In such a suit the court can order delivery, also stating the amount of money to be paid in the alternative if delivery cannot be had.[483] The court can also only decree payment of its value.

An order for specific delivery of movable property can be ordered against a defendant, not being the owner of that property, only in the following four cases:[484]

(i) where the defendant holds it as the trustee or agent of the plaintiff;
(ii) when its possession has been wrongfully transferred from the plaintiff;
(iii) if compensation for its loss will not be an adequate relief;
(iv) if the actual damage caused by its loss is extremely difficult to ascertain.

---

478. *Mademsetty Satyanarayana v. G Yellogi Rao* AIR 1965 SC 1405.
479. *S V R Mudaliar v. Rajabu F Buhari* AIR 1995 SC 1607.
480. *Nirmala Anand v. Advent Corporation (P) Ltd* AIR 2002 SC 3396.
481. *P D'Souza v. Shondrilo Naidu* AIR 2004 SC 4472.
482. Section 7 of the Specific Relief Act 1963.
483. See O XX, R 10 of the Code of Civil Procedure.
484. See s. 7 of the Specific Relief Act 1963.

In the first case, the plaintiff has to prove the relationship, and in the second case the wrongful transfer. In the last two cases, the burden of proof lies on the defendant that compensation in money is ascertainable or is adequate.

III. Injunction

495. A plaintiff can seek injunction to enforce a negative covenant, that is, a promise not to do something, and also to restrain the defendant from interfering with the plaintiff's exercise of rights under the contract.

An injunction will not be issued to enforce any promise under a contract for which specific performance will not be granted,[485] except to enforce a negative covenant when it accompanies an affirmative covenant.[486]

A civil court can grant temporary injunction to aid the final order of specific performance that may be passed in the suit after trial. The defendant can thus be restrained from transferring or disposing of the property involved. Such an order can be by a civil court in any proceeding for preserving the *status quo* pending litigation.[487]

IV. Execution of Decrees of Specific Performance and Injunction

496. The procedure for execution of decrees of specific performance or injunction are given in the Code of Civil Procedure.[488] Where the act ordered in a decree of specific performance can be done by employing any another person, the court may appoint a person to do it. Thus, an order of executing a sale deed can be enforced by requiring the judgment debtor in the first instance to execute it or by appointing a person to execute it on behalf of the judgment debtor. If the decree is for executing a document, detail rules provide for preparing the draft and its execution.

A party who wilfully fails to obey a decree of specific performance is liable to be detained in civil prison. His property may also be attached. If the decree is not obeyed, the attached property can be sold, and compensation awarded to the person in whose favour the decree of specific performance has been passed.

V. Compensation in a Suit for Specific Performance or Injunction

497. A plaintiff is not entitled to specific performance as of right even if he satisfies the threshold requirement of inadequacy of damages. He should not be forced

485. Sections 38 and 40 of the Specific Relief Act 1963.
486. Section 42 of the Specific Relief Act 1963; *Niranjan Shankar Golikari v. Century Spinning and Manufacturing Co Ltd* AIR 1967 SC 1098.
487. Section 94 and Order 31 rules 1, 2 and 2A of the Code of Civil Procedure.
488. Order 21, rules 32 and 34.

to another suit for compensation after the suit for specific performance or injunction was dismissed. A plaintiff can combine the two otherwise independent remedies and can ask in the same suit for compensation in addition or in the alternative to the claim for specific performance[489] or injunction.[490] He cannot file another suit for claiming compensation.

§4. Non-performance as Bar to Enforcement

498. The defence of non-performance as described in Belgian law is a defence that the promisee of the relevant promise shall not be able to enforce it. This defence is available to a promisor under the Indian law in certain circumstances enumerated in the Indian Contract Act.

I. Reciprocal Promises

499. This defence is peculiar to contracts involving reciprocal promises,[491] that is, synallagmatic contracts. Reciprocal promises may be independent, dependent, or concurrent.

A. Independent Reciprocal Promises

500. If the reciprocal promises are independent and one party fails to perform a promise, the other party is bound to perform his promise and can merely claim damages for non-performance. Neither party is excused from performance, unless the non-performance amounts to a refusal entitling the other party to rescind the contract.

B. Concurrent Reciprocal Promises

501. If the promises are concurrent, that is, to be simultaneously performed, one party need not perform unless the other party is ready and willing to perform and one party can demand performance only if he is ready and willing to perform his own.[492] In a contract for sale of goods, delivery of goods and payment of price are concurrent conditions unless otherwise agreed.[493]

489. Section 21 of the Specific Relief Act 1963.
490. Section 40 of the Specific Relief Act 1963.
491. See para. 341 onwards.
492. See s. 51 of the Indian Contract Act.
493. Section 32 of the Sale of Goods Act 1930.

C. Dependent Reciprocal Promises

502. Sometimes promises are to be performed in a sequence, because it is the order of performance fixed by parties, it is the natural order in which promises must be performed, or because the performance of one is a condition for claiming the performance of the other.

If the first promise is not performed, such non-performing party cannot claim performance from the other party and is also liable for paying compensation sustained by such non-performance. Once parties have prescribed the order of performance, the defence of non-performance is available, however minor is that promise to be performed first. The other party cannot rescind the contract merely for the reason that the first promise is not performed, unless circumstances bring his case within the provisions entitling him to rescind the contract.[494] The other party is bound to accept performance if offered later.

II. Non-acceptance of Tender of Performance

503. In another case one party offers to perform his promise but the other does not accept performance. The party offering is not responsible for non-performance, nor does he lose rights under the contract, that is, sue for damages or rescind as the case may be.

In a contract for sale of goods, if the buyer refuses to take delivery when the seller has offered it, he is liable to the seller for any loss occasioned by his neglect or refusal to take delivery and also for a reasonable charge for the care and custody of the goods. If the refusal to take delivery amounts to repudiation of the contract, the seller has a right to avoid under the general principles of contract law.[495]

III. Effect of Non-performance

504. Non-performance by one party can thus have one of the following effects:

(i) the other party will be entitled to rescind the contract only in certain circumstances and on rescission will be discharged from liability;[496]

(ii) in all cases he cannot claim performance from the other party. The other party need not perform his part of the promise and will not be liable for non-performance of his own promise. The non-performing party can offer performance later, which the other party will be liable to accept. Thus, the liability of the other party is not discharged totally.

Unlike Belgian law, there is no suspension of obligations.

494. See para. 345 *supra*.
495. Section 44 of the Sale of Goods Act 1930.
496. See para. 530 *infra*.

§5. SELF-HELP REMEDIES

I. Lien

505. The right of lien is the right of a person to retain possession of another's property until the present and accrued claims of the former are satisfied. The right cannot be exercised if there are no goods in possession of the person having a claim. The person holding a lien on property is a 'secured creditor' and has a priority in insolvency proceedings. Moreover, his rights as a lien-holder are not lost by commencement of insolvency proceedings against the party against whom he claims the lien.

The right of lien is expressly conferred under statutes in certain types of contractual relationships. Apart from these provisions, parties can enable the right of lien in any contract, including the right of sale or disposal of property held under lien.

A. Unpaid Seller's Lien

506. An unpaid seller having the goods sold in his possession can exercise the right of lien until payment or tender of price. He does not have this right to withhold goods sold if he has given credit to the debtor, unless the credit has expired. Nor does he have this right if he has agreed to deliver the goods independent of payment of price. A seller can also resell the goods if price is not received.[497]

B. Bailee's Particular Lien

507. A bailee who has rendered a service involving labour and skill on the goods bailed, has a right to retain the goods until he receives due remuneration for services. This is subject to any contrary contract.[498] This is a particular lien, available only over the goods in respect of which he has rendered services.

C. Bailees' General Lien

508. Bankers, factors, wharfingers, and attorneys of High Court and policy brokers have a general lien over goods bailed to them. They can retain the goods as security for a general balance of account. Any other person can have such right of retaining goods for a general account and can do so by making express contract to that effect.[499]

497. Sections 47 and 54 of the Sale of Goods Act 1930.
498. Section 170 of the Indian Contract Act.
499. Section 171 of the Indian Contract Act.

D. Agent's Lien

509. An agent can retain his principal's goods, papers, and other property, movable or immovable, which he has received, until he has received the amounts due for his commission, disbursements, and services.[500]

E. Contractual Lien

510. The right of selling or disposing of the goods under lien, except in the case of the right of an unpaid seller, can be acquired only by express provision in the contract.

511. Provisions in contract can also entitle a party to retain any money or goods of the other party for dues or as security of performance in respect of other contracts between them.

It is often a term in government contracts that any amount kept by the contractor with the government as security deposit, or any amount due by the government to the contractor under any contract, can be retained by the government toward any dues or claims from that contractor under *any other* contract with the government. The government might also have a right under the contract to adjust the amount toward such claims under another contract. Such right of adjustment must be expressly provided in the contract.[501]

It is also usual for bankers to provide that any amount of its debtor lying with the bank can be retained by the bank until any dues or claims under any other transaction are paid, and that the bank can set-off such amounts against the dues and claims.

II. Retention of Deposit

512. Retaining deposit for due performance of the contract, returnable if the contract is performed to the satisfaction of the party retaining the deposit, is also one method of enforcing performance. Such security deposit can be forfeited for breach under provisions of the contract and adjusted toward compensation for breach. Any such forfeiture is subject to the provisions applicable to liquidated damages.

III. Enforcement of Bank Guarantees

513. It is common to require a party to give a guarantee issued by a bank for his due performance of the contract. Such a guarantee is a separate contract, independent of the primary contract it guarantees, and is governed by its own terms. When the bank undertakes to pay 'on demand without demur', its beneficiary can invoke the guarantee at will.

---

500. Section 221 of the Indian Contract Act.

501. *H M Kamaluddin Ansari & Co v. Union of India* AIR 1984 SC 29.

Bankers as a matter of policy do not refuse to honour such guarantees. Courts also refrain from stopping payment under such guarantees, and will not issue injunctions for such purpose.[502]

Hence, this is a popular method of enforcing the performance, else receiving payment, which might cover compensation. If the payment recovered under the guarantee exceeds the true amount of compensation, or if the party who has given the guarantee has not committed breach, he is forced to move the court for recovering back the amount.

IV. Enforcing Property Secured

514. If property is pledged (pawned) as security for performance of a promise, the pledgee has the right to sell under law. If goods are hypothecated, and possession is with the hypothecator, the hypothecatee can seize and sell the goods, in the manner provided in the hypothecation contract. The power of a mortgagee of goods to sell the goods depends on the terms of the mortgage.

§6. Rescission and Termination

515. Under Indian law, rescission[503] is the right of a contracting party and can be exercised in the circumstances discussed later. It results from his communicating rescission to the other party and does not need any judgment of court. It is, of course, his option whether to rescind the contract or not. If he does not rescind, the contract continues and must be performed according to its terms by both parties. The exercise of the right of rescission does not prejudice other rights of that party, for example, defence of non-performance or compensation.

I. Rescission

516. A party to a contract can rescind it in the following three circumstances:

(i) where the contract is voidable because his consent to it is not free,[504] being caused by undue influence,[505] fraud, misrepresentation, or coercion;[506]

---

502. *Mahatma Gandhi Sahakara Sakkare Karkhane v. National Heavy Engg Coop Ltd* AIR 2007 SC 2716; *U P Co-operative Federation Ltd v. Singh Consultants and Engineers (P) Ltd* (1988) 1 SCC 174; *Tarapore and Co v. V/O Tractoroexport Moscow* AIR 1970 SC 891.

503. The term 'rescission' is used for the right of one party to end a contract voidable at his option. This includes avoidance because his consent is not free, as also putting an end to a contract where the other party has refused to perform his part of the contract. The term 'termination' is used where a party seeks to terminate in exercise of his power under the terms of his contract.

504. For rescission of voidable contracts, see para. 236 onwards.

505. See s. 19A of the Indian Contract Act.

506. See s. 19 of the Indian Contract Act.

(ii) where it is voidable by reason of a major breach[507] of other wrong conduct of the defendant in the course of performance of the contract;[508] and
(iii) where it is terminable because he has reserved the right to terminate the contract under its terms.

The exercise of the right of rescission or termination is also described as a self-help remedy, its exercise does not require assistance of courts, though its use can be challenged in courts by the other party.[509]

II. Rescission for Breach

A. Power to Rescind under Law

517. Every breach does not entitle a party to rescind. A contract is voidable for certain breaches or conduct of a party. Such circumstances are given in the Indian Contract Act as follows:

(i) A party has refused to perform or disables himself from performing his promise in its entirety, that is, where a party has repudiated his obligations under the contract, by renouncing his obligations, by his own act making its performance impossible, or failure of performance. Failure to perform the promise will entitle to rescind only if the conduct of failure is such as amounts to refusal to perform, or an abandonment of the contract. This depends upon whether the failure shows that the party does not wish to go on with the contract, or whether the failure would lead a reasonable person to conclude that he did not intend to fulfil his part of the contract.
(ii) If one party prevents the other from performing his part of the promise in a contract consisting of reciprocal promises, the contract can be rescinded. The party preventing performance is also liable to compensate the other party.
(iii) Where a contract specifies a time for performance of a promise and the promise is not performed at that time, the contract can be rescinded if it is the intention of the parties that the time shall be of essence of the contract. If time is not of the essence, the party in default is liable to pay compensation for delay.

A contract cannot be avoided for breach except in the above cases.

B. Contractual Power to Rescind

518. Parties, however, can provide for a power to terminate the contract for minor breaches, or specified breaches, or without giving any reason.

---

507. See ss 39 and 55 of the Indian Contract Act.
508. See s. 54 of the Indian Contract Act.
509. P.S. Atiyah, *An Introduction to the Law of Contract* 419–444 (5th edn, 1995).

C. Rescission Subject to Scrutiny by Court

519. If the circumstances exist entitling rescission, the contract can be rescinded. Courts will often be required to decide whether the circumstances exist entitling a party to rescind and whether the procedure of its exercise is correct. There is no requirement of reasonableness in the exercise of the power to rescind. If a buyer has avoided a contract because the seller has failed to deliver at the specified time and the buyer files a suit for damages, the court will decide whether time was intended to be of essence. If yes, the rescission is valid and the suit will succeed. If time is not held to be essence, the rescission is invalid, the buyer is now guilty of breach, and the buyer's suit will be dismissed. A seller's counter-claim for damages, if made, will succeed.

III. Mode of Rescission

520. Rescission must be communicated in the same manner as a proposal. It becomes effective only when it is received by the other party.

A party can rescind or terminate the contract simply by communicating his rescission.[510] He need not file any suit for the purpose. He can also exercise his option to rescind as a defence in a suit for enforcing rights under the contract.

IV. Option to Rescind

521. Rescission is the option of the person at whose option the contract is voidable or terminable. He can, instead of avoiding the contract, elect to continue with it, without losing his right to claim damages if any breach has occurred.

One exception to this rule is not rescinding for failure to perform at specified time in contracts where time for performance is of the essence. In such a case, if the promisee accepts performance later, he cannot claim loss caused by non-performance unless he has given notice of such intention at the time of accepting performance.[511]

In these situations, the promisee is automatically discharged after he has rightfully rescinded. His discharge is not provisional, but absolute and permanent. The promisee need not do any further act to claim relief of non-performance. He need not approach the court to seek a discharge; but whether the circumstances entitle the promisor to take the defence of non-performance is always subject to scrutiny. He can, if he wishes, seek a decree of rescission from the court.

522. A promisee can put an end to a contract repudiated by the promisor, unless he has signified his acquiescence in its performance.[512] The right to rescind is, therefore, lost by acquiescence. In any case the promisee has an option to end the

510. Section 66 of the Indian Contract Act.
511. Section 55, para. 3 of the Indian Contract Act.
512. Section 39 of the Indian Contract Act.

contract and may decide to continue with the contract. In such a case the contract remains in force for the benefit of both parties. The promisee can perform his part and insist on performance from the other party according to the terms agreed. He does not lose his rights to claim damages for breach.

523. This gives rise to a peculiar position in which both parties have been guilty of breaches of a type entitling the other to rescind. Thus, if X commits repudiatory breach, and later Y also commits a repudiatory breach, X's breach gives to Y the right to terminate. If Y terminates, his own breach is not a breach. But if Y does not rescind, the contract continues, and Y's breach gives to X the option to terminate. This means that Y cannot allege X's repudiatory breach in defence of X's claim for damages on Y's breach.

V. Rescission in Addition to Non-performance, and Compensation

524. Even where a party has a right to avoid a contract for failure or breach by the other party, but does not rescind, he does not lose his other rights, such as of claiming the defence of non-performance or of compensation for breach.

VI. Suit for Rescission

525. A suit for rescission can be filed by any person interested where the contract is voidable or terminable at his option when he has reserved under its terms a right to rescind. This remedy is not confined to parties to a contract. Any person, though not a party, may sue for rescission if his interests are affected by it.

A suit for rescission is really one for declaration that the rescission already exercised by one party is valid. The court merely declares the validity of a rescission already exercised.[513]

The court refuses to rescind in certain circumstances if the plaintiff has expressly or impliedly ratified the contract. Relief in a suit for rescission is discretionary. The court will not rescind where the parties cannot be restored to the position in which they stood at the time of making the contract or where third parties have, during the subsistence of the contract, acquired rights in good faith without notice and for value. Delay in filing suit indicates that the plaintiff has waived his right or abandoned it or has acquiesced in the continuance of the contract. In such circumstances it will defeat the right even if suit is otherwise within limitation.

On adjudging the rescission of a contract, the court may require the party to whom such relief is granted to restore, so far as may be, any benefit that he may have received from the other party and to make any compensation to him that justice may require.[514] This is based on the principle that he who seeks equity must do equity. Both parties must be restored to the *status quo ante*. A court can order the plaintiff to make compensation to the defendant as justice may require.

513. *Hungerford Investment Trust Ltd v. Haridas Mundhra* AIR 1972 SC 1826.
514. Section 30 of the Specific Relief Act 1963.

VII. Termination

526. The expression ‘termination’ is used to indicate termination of contract in the exercise of right of termination available to him under the contract.

Parties can agree that the contract can be terminated by any one or all of them. Such a term is valid,[515] but might be restricted or denied by law.

Thus, the government or statutory corporation cannot terminate the services of its employees except according to service rules, which usually will confer this power only if the employee has committed grave misconduct. Tenancies protected under rent control legislation applicable to urban areas cannot be terminated; the landlords can seek possession only on establishing certain grounds of eviction in the courts.

A. *Power of Termination*

527. A contract may provide that any or all parties[516] to it can terminate it, on occurrence of any event, or on any or specified breach by the other party. A clause empowering any party to terminate without assigning any reason is also valid.[517] Parties can also agree that the contract shall stand terminated on the happening of an event, even on specified breach by one of the parties.

The government also enjoys the freedom to terminate in such cases, and the courts will not normally interfere to cancel the termination if it has been done according to the terms of the contract.[518]

B. *Mode of Termination*

528. Such a contract is terminated by giving notice to the other party. The notice must be clear and unambiguous. Such notice must comply strictly with the procedure and term given in the contract.[519] Any such requirement might be waived. A party guilty of breach cannot terminate the contract.[520]

C. *Effect of Termination*

529. Such termination will not affect any liability already incurred under the contract.[521] Any clause giving power to cancel the contract at any time without

---

515. *Food Corporation of India v. Jagannath Dutta* AIR 1993 SC 1494.
516. *Central Bank of India Ltd v. Hartford Fire Insurance Co Ltd* AIR 1965 SC 1288.
517. *Hajee S V M Mohamed Jamaludeen Bros & Co v. Govt of Tamil Nadu* AIR 1997 SC 1368; *Food Corporation of India v. Jagannath Dutta* AIR 1993 SC 1494.
518. *Radhakrishna Agarwal v. State of Bihar* AIR 1977 SC 1496.
519. *Ramachandra Narayan Nayak v. Karnataka Neeravari Nigam Ltd* 2013 AIR SCW 5913.
520. *Chotelal Lallubhai v. Champsey Umersey & Sons* AIR 1923 Bom 75.
521. *Central Bank of India Ltd v. Hartford Fire Insurance Co Ltd* AIR 1965 SC 1288.

assigning any reason is void and cannot be enforced to the extent any liability has been incurred.[522]

In all cases, the party whose contract has been terminated can challenge the termination as plaintiff or defendant, and it would fall on the court to decide whether termination was valid, that is, whether the circumstances for its exercise arose and whether it has been exercised in the manner provided in the contract.

Parties can also provide in their contract for consequences of termination, for example, liability to compensate, restitution, or that there will be no liability on the party terminating to compensate the other party.

VIII. Effect of Rescission: Restitution, Discharge, Compensation

530. Section 64 of the Indian Contract Act gives the double effect of rescission of a voidable contract, release from obligation and obligation of restoration. The person rescinding the contract is released from his obligation to perform. The guilty party also need not perform any outstanding obligations.[523] The party guilty of breach is liable for damages for the breach committed.

Rescission for major breach is effective from the date it is communicated to the other party. If validly done, it discharges the contract from such time. Parties are, however, liable for all acts performed or things done until rescission.

IX. Some Clauses Survive

531. Where a contract is rescinded, certain clauses in it survive such rescission, for example, clauses governing choice of law, choice of jurisdiction, arbitration, and so on. The extent of the right of rescission and its correct exercise will be determined by the law applicable, by the courts chosen, or will fall on an arbitrator for decision.

X. Right of Rescission under Other Laws

532. If a buyer of goods does not take delivery of goods offered by the seller, such failure might amount to repudiation. In such a case, the seller has the option to rescind the contract under the provisions of general law of contract. However, if the failure is not repudiatory, the buyer is liable to the seller for loss caused by such neglect or refusal and for charges for care and custody of goods.[524]

---

522. *Maddala Thathiah v. Union of India* AIR 1957 Mad 82.
523. Section 64 of the Indian Contract Act.
524. See s. 44 of the Sale of Goods Act 1930.

§7. Restitution

533. Section 64 of the Indian Contract Act requires that the party rescinding the contract is liable to restore the benefit to the person from whom it was received. This obligation arises on the principle that the parties are to be placed, as far as possible, in a situation in which they would have stood, if there had never been any transaction between them.

The obligation is to restore the benefit received *under* the contract, and only to the extent it is possible. The principles are also found in section 30 of the Specific Relief Act, which requires that in a suit for rescission, a court granting rescission may order restoration of benefit. There must be restoration of benefit as a condition of rescission of the contract. In a suit for rescission, therefore, the defendant's claim for restoration is a defence, and not a claim for set-off.[525]

This principle is available for all contracts voidable, be they for lack of free consent or rescission for default by one party. Earlier, courts held that the principle applied only to first category. But later, the Privy Council applied the principle also to a contract voidable under section 39 of the Indian Contract Act for repudiation of obligations by one party.[526] It decided that where a person has elected to put an end to the contract under section 39, he is bound to return any benefit that he has received under the contract, but he is entitled to set-off the damages for the defaulting party's breach.

534. Parties can contract that there shall be no restoration in the event of breach. Hence, where an insurance policy is avoided by an insurer for non-disclosure or breach of any other condition by the insured, the forfeiture clause in the insurance policy entitles the insurer to retain the premium paid for insurance, rather than return the amount to the insured.[527]

§8. Damages

I. Compensation

535. 'Compensation' refers to the pecuniary recompense a person is entitled to receive for damage or loss suffered other than arising out of an actionable wrong. The latter are 'damages', awarded by the court for loss suffered as a result of an actionable wrong. The Indian Contract Act prefers the term 'compensation' to damages. Compensation for loss arising out of breach is really 'damages' in that sense. The familiar term 'damages' is used in this chapter.

---

525. *Pramada Prasad Mukherji v. Sagarmal Agarwalla* AIR 1954 Pat 439.
526. *Muralidhar Chatterjee v. International Film Co Ltd* AIR 1943 PC 34.
527. *Mithoolal Nayak v. Life Insurance Corporation of India* AIR 1962 SC 814.

II. Section 73 of the Indian Contract Act

536. Section 73 of the Indian Contract Act gives the law relating to damages.[528] It declares the common law relating to damages, and its language is closely based on the decision of the English case *Hadley v. Baxendale*.[529] In its four paragraphs it provides the following:

(i) that compensation can be recovered for loss or damage that arose in the usual course of things from such breach or that the parties knew at the time they made the contract as likely to result from such breach;
(ii) that no compensation is payable for any remote or indirect loss or damage;
(iii) that the same principles apply if any obligation resembling contracts[530] is broken;
(iv) that the plaintiff has a duty to mitigate, which will affect assessment of compensation.

The principles of section 73 apply in case of all types of contracts, even those covered by special laws, unless that law gives a special provision affecting damages.

III. Damages and Claim for Agreed Sum

537. A claim for damages differs from a claim for debt or money promised under a contract, for example, claim for repayment of debt, price of goods, wages of an employee, arrears of instalments in a hire-purchase, or under a guarantee or a policy of insurance. Enforcement of claim for such a debt resembles specific performance and is available as of right. The promisee can claim the debt only if he has performed his part under the contract. If he has been prevented from performing, his remedy is in damages and not for the amount agreed. There is no obligation of mitigation or remoteness.

There is one very vital advantage if such a contract is in writing. Such amounts can be recovered in summary proceedings.[531] The defendant needs permission to

528. Section 73 provides: *Compensation for loss or damage caused by breach of contract.* When a contract has been broken, the party who suffers by such breach is entitled to receive, from the party who has broken the contract, compensation for any loss or damage caused to him thereby, which naturally arose in the usual course of things from such breach, or which the parties knew, when they made the contract, to be likely to result from the breach of it. Such compensation is not to be given for any remote and indirect loss or damage sustained by reason of the breach. *Compensation for failure to discharge obligation resembling those created by contract.* When an obligation resembling those created by contract has been incurred and has not been discharged, any person injured by the failure to discharge is entitled to receive the same compensation from the party in default as if such person had contracted to discharge it and had broken his contract. *Explanation.* In estimating the loss or damage arising from a breach of contract, the means which existed of remedying the inconvenience caused by the non-performance of the contract must be taken into account.

529. (1854) 9 Exch 341, [1843-60] All ER Rep 461.

530. See para. 791 onwards.

531. Under Order XXXVII of the Code of Civil Procedure.

defend such proceeding, which he can have only if he shows a substantial defence leading to a triable issue. Often the court will require him to give security so that the decree will be satisfied.

In a suit for such a claim, damages might also be awarded for loss caused to the promisee because the amount was not paid in time.

IV. Primary Remedy

538. Award of damages is the primary and presumptive remedy for non-performance of a contract under Indian law. The claim for damages is a matter of right of the promisee who has suffered by the promisor's breach.

V. Nature of Remedy: Compensatory

A. Expectation Interest

539. Damages for breach of contract are awarded to place the injured party in the same position as far as money can do it, as if the contract was performed. In terms of Fuller and Perdue,[532] this is the 'expectation interest' of the promisee that the remedy of damages seeks to satisfy. This is a positive interest.

The aim of the remedy is to redress the innocent party's defeated financial expectation and to compensate him for his loss of bargain. Such expectation is broadly of two types.[533] First, the innocent party wishes to receive the performance. Therefore, he wants delivery of goods or performance of services promised under the contract. Second, he has an expectation to be able to put such a thing to intended use. Therefore, he wishes to use the goods for manufacture or resale or the services for the purposes of his trade and to earn a profit. Damages must protect both these interests.

B. Reliance Interest

540. The 'reliance interest' that the remedy can serve aims at putting the innocent party in as good a position as he was in before the contract was made. The innocent party can claim pre-contract expenditure, expenses incurred for his performance, and expenses incurred after breach.

Reliance losses are easier to prove than expectation losses and will be chosen where the innocent party will not be able to prove the likely benefits if the contract were performed. Expectation losses are prospective and look forward to a position that the promisee would have occupied if the promise were performed. Reliance

532. Lon *Fuller* & William Perdue, *The Reliance Interest in Contract Damages*, (1936–1937) 46 Yale LJ 52.

533. See Treitel, *The Law of Contract* 875 (10th edn).

losses are retrospective and look backward to look at what position he would have been in if the promise was not made.

C. Choice between the Two

541. The plaintiff has to choose between the two types of losses. He can choose to claim the expenses or losses he suffered in reliance in making and performing the contract or the profits lost in expectation that the contract will be performed. It is rare, but possible, that the court will award loss on account of both.

D. Claim for Defendant's Profits

542. The basis is the loss of the plaintiff and not gain to the defendant. It is to be seen whether the Indian courts recognize a remedy for account of profits for breach of contract in the manner recognized by the House of Lords in the United Kingdom.[534]

VI. Punitive Damages

543. The amount of damages cannot exceed the loss actually suffered by the plaintiff. Damages must compensate, not punish. This is the general principle of civil jurisprudence.

The Consumer Protection Act 1986 was amended in 2002 enabling the adjudicating authorities under it to grant punitive damages in appropriate cases of consumer disputes.

VII. Valid Contract and Its Breach

544. The party complaining of breach and seeking damages has to prove that a valid contract existed between the parties. There is no question of paying damages if the court finds that the parties do not have a contract according to the rules of its formation or that the agreement is void.

Whether there is breach cannot be decided by a party; it must be adjudicated and proved.[535] A court deciding breach and damages must then necessarily ascertain its exact terms, so that it can decide whether breach has occurred. It must then find that a contract has been broken. A plaintiff cannot succeed in damages simply by showing that the defendant has obtained profit from non-performance.

Breach includes failure to perform altogether, fully, at the right time, right place, or where performance falls short in some way than what was promised under the

534. In *Attorney General v. Blake* [2000] 4 All ER 385, HL.

535. *J G Engineers Pvt Ltd v. Union of India* AIR 2011 SC 2477; *P Radhakrishna Murthy v. NBCC Ltd* (2013) 3 SCC 747.

contract. It may consist of delay in performance, breach of warranty, partial performance, faulty performance, and so on.

The promisee is not required to give notice to the promisor or any protest, whether any time is fixed for performance or not. The claim for compensation does not depend on such demand.

VIII. Actual and Anticipatory Breach

545. A breach may occur at the time of performance, which is actual breach. It may occur before the time fixed for performance, for example, where there has been a refusal or a party has disabled himself from performing. It is common to term this 'anticipatory breach'. If the promisee chooses not to rescind the contract on breach, the contract continues until the date due for performance. If the promisor fails to perform then, the promisee can proceed to claim compensation. If the promisee has chosen to rescind the contract earlier, loss is assessed with reference to the date of refusal. If the promisee has chosen to wait, loss is assessed on the date of actual breach, whether promisee's loss is increased or decreased in the meantime.

IX. Freedom of Parties

546. Parties have the freedom to provide for ending their contract. They may also give the power to one or both parties to terminate the contract, on any or specified breaches or without reasons, and its consequences.[536] Likewise, they can also control the consequences or aftermath of breach. They can provide that in the event of breach, no relief can be claimed unless notice of specified period or in a specified manner is given. They can also provide that in the event of breach only amount paid shall be refunded, with no further liability. They can exclude or limit liability for breach or provide for measure of damages.

X. Contract and Tort

547. The law of damages in tort differs in certain aspects from the law of compensation in contract. In the case of both, the burden of proving all conditions of liability rest on the plaintiff. The requirement of causation and that loss not be remote are also common. Both seek to compensate with reference to the date of breach of contract or the date of commission of tort.

Damages in tort protect the reliance interest and put the plaintiff in a position as if the tort had not occurred. The plaintiff's contributory negligence affects liability in tort. The conduct of the plaintiff or his role if any in the breach of contract does not reduce his compensation.

536. See paras 473–474, 526–529.

The plaintiff claiming from breach of contract must show that the loss flowed naturally and in the usual course of things from the breach or was within the reasonable contemplation of the parties at the time of making of the contract; whereas the plaintiff in tort must show only that the loss was reasonably foreseeable by the party in breach.

XI. Who Is Liable to Compensate and to Whom

548. A defendant will be liable for damages only if he is a party to the contract and is guilty of breach. Therefore, if he has agreed to do something requiring government permission, and the government permission is obtained but later cancelled, he will not be liable for breach, unless his obtaining the license is a direct promise under the contract. A person not party to a contract cannot be liable under it, even if he has made an independent promise to be liable.[537]

549. The plaintiff claiming damages must have suffered by the breach. He should have performed or was ready to perform his part of the obligations arising under the contract.[538] Thus, where a party failed to provide facilities for loading, he could not claim demurrage.[539] In a contract of sale of land, the purchaser who cannot pay the balance purchase price cannot recover damages from the vendor who has refused to sell.[540]

XII. Cause of Non-performance Irrelevant

550. A party who has given a promise is absolutely bound to perform, unless he is excused by any provision of law, the breach is waived by the promisee, or the promisee has accepted some other satisfaction for the promise. He must compensate, irrespective of the reason for his breach. Neither the conduct nor intention of the innocent party, nor the conduct of the guilty party, can affect the assessment of damages. Motive or intention of the parties in committing breach is not relevant.[541]

551. A consumer seeking redressal under the Consumer Protection Act can claim compensation for loss under that Act only if he can show that he has suffered a loss arising of the negligence of the trader or service provider.[542]

In such cases, consumer disputes redressal agencies also have power to grant punitive damages in appropriate cases. It is possible that conduct of the guilty party and his motive or intention in breaking the contract will be relevant to decide whether the case deserves granting punitive damages.

537. See paras 354 onwards.
538. *Tan Ah Boon v. State of Johore* AIR 1936 PC 236.
539. *Timblo Irmaos Ltd v. Jorge Anibal Motos Sequeira* AIR 1977 SC 734.
540. *Abdullah Bey Chedid v. Tenenbaum* AIR 1934 PC 91.
541. *Yarlagadda China Rattayya v. Donepudi Venkataramayya* AIR 1959 AP 551.
542. Section 14(d) of the Consumer Protection Act.

XIII. Awarded on Adjudication

552. Damages are said to be liquidated when they have been agreed and fixed by the parties. In all other cases damages are unliquidated and the court assesses and quantifies the damages.

553. A claim for damages is a claim for an unliquidated amount and is not instantly due and payable. It cannot, therefore, be assigned.[543]

It becomes a debt only after the amount has been ascertained by a judgment of a court. The defendant is not liable to pay any amount until the court has determined it. It is clear that there is no liability. A breach merely gives to the promisee a right to sue. Therefore, when the court determines the amount of damages, it is not determining a pre-existing liability.[544]

For example, a contractor having a contract with the government has agreed that the government can retain and adjust the security deposit or any pending bills, toward any claim under any other contract. The government has a claim for damages against him for his breach under another contract. The government cannot retain any money or adjust it against such claim, unless such a claim is adjudicated on by a court or by any authority, that is, by an independent person or body who is not party to the contract.[545]

XIV. Kinds of Damages

A. General and Special Damages

554. The law in section 73 follows English law in recognizing general and special damages. The innocent party is entitled to receive those damages that arise naturally in the normal course of events. He can also claim special damages, that is, which do not so naturally arise, if these were in contemplation of parties at the time they made the contract. Special damages must be pleaded and proved.

B. Nominal Damages

555. Even where the plaintiff fails to prove any actual damage, he will receive nominal damages. Such grant is for recognizing the plaintiff's right and breach by the defendant. These might be granted where the plaintiff has not suffered any loss, or is unable to prove the loss.

---

543. Section 6 of the Transfer of Property Act specifically provides that a mere right to sue cannot be transferred.
544. *Union of India v. Raman Iron Foundry* AIR 1974 SC 1265.
545. *State of Karnataka v. Shree Rameshwara Rice Mills* AIR 1987 SC 1359.

C. Aggravated Damages

556. A court might grant aggravated damages, which are an amount more than normal damages. It is appropriate to grant them where the loss of the plaintiff has increased by the manner in which the defendant has committed the wrong and thereby caused mental distress. Where the banker has dishonoured the cheque of its customer, the customer will be entitled to aggravated damages, in converse proportion of the value of the cheque.

XV. Losses

557. The loss or damage to the plaintiff may be harm to his person (injury, disability, inconvenience, mental stress, injured feelings, loss of reputation), harm to his property (damage or loss to property), or injury to his economic position (loss of profits, expenditure incurred, compensation paid to third parties, and so on.).

The plaintiff can also claim losses arising after breach, such as cost of engaging another person to complete the contract work, liability of the plaintiff under his contract with third party, or expenses of procuring substitute goods.

Damages for loss of enjoyment, loss of amenity, inconvenience, vexation, or mental distress are not generally awarded in ordinary commercial contracts.[546] Such losses will normally be awarded where the purpose of the contract is to provide enjoyment, pleasure, comfort, and peace of mind.

XVI. Remoteness

A. Test of Foreseeability

558. The principle of remoteness concerns which losses the plaintiff can recover and the tests to ascertain these losses. The plaintiff can recover compensation for only those losses that were reasonably foreseeable at the time of making the contract as liable to result from breach. Whether loss is foreseeable depends on the knowledge of the parties at the time of making the contract. The defendant will be liable only if loss is reasonably foreseeable by a normally prudent person standing in his place and possessing the information he has.

B. Natural Loss

559. Certain types of losses naturally arise from the breach, and this is assumed as known to any reasonable person. Thus, when goods are not delivered, the natural loss is the difference between the contract price and market price as on the date of breach.

---

546. *Ghaziabad Development Authority v. Union of India* AIR 2000 SC 2003.

C. Special Loss

560. The other type of knowledge is of special circumstances, after knowing which the parties can foresee additional loss arising out of such circumstances. When goods are not delivered, and the purchaser cannot complete the further contract of sale of those goods, the profits lost on such further contract can be recovered only if the fact that the goods were purchased for further sale was known or within contemplation of the parties. As to what was within the contemplation of reasonable parties depends on the relevant degree of likelihood that particular kind of loss may occur. It is not necessary that the plaintiff had made the defendant aware of the special circumstances. It is sufficient if the defendant would have been aware of them as a reasonable prudent person. The knowledge is as on the date of making the contract.

The word contemplation is considered more accurate to describe the state of mind required for operation of the second branch of the rule than foresight or reasonable foresight. In regard to contemplation, the plaintiff need not show that the parties contemplated the breach or that the defendant actually considered the loss likely to result from it, but that a reasonable person in the position of the defendant would have concluded on consideration of the matter that the given type of loss was likely to result.[547]

D. Loss of Profits

561. Loss of profit does not arise in the usual course of things. But where a seller sells goods in large quantities to a purchaser in trading business and is aware of the business, loss of profits lies in contemplation of parties. This loss naturally arises out of usual course of things. The plaintiff can prove profits lost with reference to his other contracts, or other contracts in business, or the general profits earned by persons in that trade. In any case, even in absence of such evidence, the court can still grant a reasonable percentage on the contract price.[548]

E. Restricting Losses Recoverable

562. Parties can by contract restrict the types of losses recoverable. Statutes also may put a restriction on types of losses that can be recovered. A railway is not responsible for indirect or consequential damages or for loss of particular market arising out of loss, destruction, damage, deterioration, or non-delivery of any consignment.[549]

547. *The Heron II, Koufos v. C Czarnikow Ltd* [1969] 1 AC 350, [1967] 3 All ER 686, HL.

548. *Mohd Salamatullah v. Government of Andhra Pradesh* AIR 1977 SC 1481; *Dwarka Das v. State of Madhya Pradesh* AIR 1999 SC 1031.

549. See s. 102(d) of the Railways Act 1989.

XVII. Causation

563. The plaintiff can claim compensation for such loss as is caused by the breach, and not if the real or effective cause of the loss is some other event. It is essential to see the dominant cause; subsidiary and contributing causes might be ignored.

XVIII. Measure

564. Even where the plaintiff has proved his loss, an award of damages may not necessarily fully compensate him.

XIX. Assessment

565. Difficulty of assessing damages is no bar to granting them.[550] This is particularly true when the amount of loss depends on contingency or on the chance or other speculative factors. The court must calculate the loss on the basis of sufficient material and at times decide when there is no evidence of amount. At times the court might make a pure guess. An arbitrator can apply one formula where different formulae are available for calculating damages.[551]

XX. Assessed Once and for All

566. Damages resulting from any one breach must be assessed and recovered once and for all. The promisee is required to estimate all future losses arising out of the breach and claim them in one suit for all losses, past, present, and future. But separate suits can be filed for successive breaches, for example, in the case of instalment contract.

XXI. Mitigation

567. The principle of mitigation qualifies the principle that the innocent party must be placed in the position as if the contract has been performed. The innocent party is required to take all reasonable steps to mitigate the loss, and the opportunity for such mitigation will affect the assessment of damages. As stated in section 73, it is not a duty but a restriction on damages recoverable.[552] It does not entitle the faulty party to sue, but is a defence in the quantum of damages. The plaintiff is not expected to spend for mitigating his losses, but if he does spend, he can also

550. *K Narendra v. Riviera Apartments (P) Ltd* AIR 1999 SC 2309.
551. *Associate Builders v. Delhi Development Authority* AIR 2015 SC 620.
552. *M Lachia Setty and Sons Ltd v. Coffee Board Bangalore* AIR 1981 SC 162.

recover expenses incurred by him for taking reasonable steps for avoiding the loss. This liability can be excluded by express contract.

§9. LIQUIDATED DAMAGES

I. Liquidated Damages and Penalty

568. Contracting parties can agree while making the contract, that in event of a breach, the defaulting party will be a stated amount of money to the other. If such an amount represents a genuine pre-estimate of damages likely to result from breach, it is liquidated damages. If the purpose of stating such an amount is to secure performance of the contract, it may be a penalty. If the defaulting party has kept a deposit or amount with the innocent party under the contract, they can agree that such amount can be forfeited in case of breach.

Unlike under English law, under section 74 of the Indian Contract Act, liquidated damages and penalty are treated alike.

If damages have been liquidated for any particular breaches only, as regards other breaches, damages are unliquidated.

II. Reasonable Compensation

569. Section 74 provides that where parties have agreed to any such sum, the court will award to the innocent party only reasonable compensation not exceeding the amount named. Thus, the stated amount represents the limit of the amount of awardable damages.

III. Proof of Loss

570. The question whether the plaintiff seeking to recover liquidated damages must prove his loss recently came up for judgment before the Supreme Court.[553] It decided as follows:

(1) If the terms of the contract stipulating liquidated damages is clear and unambiguous, the party who has committed breach must pay compensation, unless it is found that such estimate of compensation is unreasonable or is by way of penalty.
(2) The person aggrieved by the breach is not required to prove actual loss or damage suffered by him before he can claim a decree. The court can award reasonable compensation.
(3) In some contracts, it would be impossible for the court to assess compensation arising from breach. If the stipulated amount is not penalty or unreasonable, the

553. *Oil and Natural Gas Corporation Ltd v. SAW Pipes Ltd* AIR 2003 SC 2629.

court can award if it is a genuine pre-estimate by the parties as the measure of reasonable compensation. The fact that loss is difficult to assess with precision strengthens the presumption that the sum agreed represents a genuine pre-estimate of compensation.[554]

(4) The party against whom the amount is claimed can show that the stipulated amount is unreasonable or in the nature of penalty.

IV. Stipulations about Payment of Interest

571. Much case law has been developed to decide whether stipulations for payment of interest are in the nature of penalty and, therefore, can be relieved by the courts. Thus, where simple interest is payable on the debt, but the contract provides for payment of compound interest in the event of default, but from the date of contract, such stipulation is in the nature of penalty, and the court can award lower interest. Terms requiring payment of a higher rate if the amount is not paid in time might amount to penalty.

V. Forfeiture of Deposit

572. Where a party has deposited an amount as security for performance, with power to the other party to forfeit it in case of breach, the forfeiture is subject to the provisions of section 74. But the forfeiture will not be interfered with, if reasonable in amount.[555]

§10. Exemption Clauses

573. These have been considered earlier in paragraphs 316–320.

§11. Limitation of Actions

574. The enforcement of claims must be subject to the limit of time. This ensures security of rights. Evidence supporting rights weakens as time passes – documents are destroyed, human memory dims. Setting a time limit for filing proceedings ensures that claims and demands are contested soon after the events, when it is easier to discover truth. The law of limitation provides for such time limits. It forces litigants to be diligent in seeking remedies.

---

554. *BSNL v. Reliance Communication Ltd* 2011 AIR SCW 525, (2011) 1 SCC 394.

555. *Fateh Chand v. Balkishan Das* AIR 1963 SC 1405; see also *Maula Bux v. Union of India* AIR 1970 SC 1955.

I. Laws Relating to Limitation

575. The law relating to limitation is given in the Limitation Act 1963, which is the general law of limitation applicable throughout India to any proceedings. It is very comprehensive, clear, and universally applicable. The Act deals with limitation for filing suits, appeals, revision applications (including some criminal proceedings), and other applications. It is also applicable to arbitration proceedings.[556] The period of limitation for filing criminal proceedings is provided in the Code of Criminal Procedure 1973.

However, special laws might make special provisions relating to limitation to commence action. These may vary or change the general rules by either shortening or extending the time provided in the general law. Even in such cases, the general provisions of the Limitation Act apply insofar as, and to the extent to which, they are not expressly excluded by such special or local law.

II. The Limitation Act 1963

576. The Limitation Act is divided in two parts. The first part contains in sections with provisions general principles applicable to all proceedings. These relate to computation of limitation period, the commencement of the period, and exclusion or suspension of the period. The limitation period for filing specific proceedings are listed in the Schedule. The proceedings are classified on the basis of subject matter. If any suit is not specified, residuary provisions enable the suit to be filed within three years from the time when the right to sue accrues. There is generally a uniform period of limitation for proceedings of the same nature. The periods prescribed range from thirty days for filing appeals to thirty years for suits by government or suits to redeem mortgages.

The period of limitation computed according to the Limitation Act is called the 'prescribed period'. It is the period specified for that category of suit in the Schedule, as may be extended or suspended by the provisions of that Act.

III. Limitation Bars the Remedy, and Not the Right

577. Limitation as a rule bars the remedy, but does not extinguish the right. A debt continues to be due even after the expiry of the period. A creditor of such a debt can realize or enforce his claim by any method except by suit. If the debtor pays the amount after the limitation period has expired, he cannot claim to recover it back on the ground that it was not money due or owing. A promise to pay a time-barred debt is one without consideration, but is nevertheless enforceable.[557]

578. The law also deals with two provisions of prescription. The two cases relate to certain easement rights and suits for possession.

---

556. Section 43(1) of the Arbitration and Conciliation Act, 1996.
557. Section 25 of the Indian Contract Act 1872.

Thus, when the period prescribed for filing a suit for possession of property, movable or immovable, expires, the right to property extinguishes.

This extinction of right directly confers the original holder's right to the opposing claimant, giving him a title against the whole world. Such extinctive prescriptions properly belong to law of property. Limitation as applied to contracts does not have an extinctive effect.

IV. The Bar of Limitation

579. The bar of limitation is contained in section 3 of the Limitation Act, which provides:

> Subject to the provisions contained in sections 4 to 24 (inclusive), every suit instituted, appeal preferred, and application made after the prescribed period shall be dismissed although limitation has not been set up as a defence.

580. The question of limitation can fall for determination in every case. It is the duty of the court not to proceed with the matter if it is made beyond the period of limitation, whether the plea of bar of limitation has been set up in defence or not.[558] The court has no choice in the matter.[559] Moreover, parties cannot extend or alter the period of limitation independently by consent, agreement, or waiver, except as provided in the Limitation Act or special statutes.

581. The bar of limitation is absolute. There is no relief to a plaintiff who comes even one day after the period of limitation has expired. The court cannot relieve a party from the bar of limitation on the grounds of hardship, mistake, or injustice. Therefore, a judge cannot on equitable grounds extend the time allowed by the law of limitation or postpone its operation. Other special laws, however, give courts discretion to allow a party having sufficient cause to file proceedings after the period of limitation has expired.

582. The Limitation Act does not differentiate between any other types of persons commencing proceedings, be they individuals or organizations, or between matters – commercial or non-commercial. The governments (Central and state) have a special limitation period of thirty years for all types of suits (and not appeals or applications). Except for this, the bar operates equally against an individual and the government.

V. No Bar of Limitation in Suits against Trustees

583. Under the Limitation Act, suits against trustees or their legal representatives or assignees for following in their hands trust property, or for account of

558. *Rama Shankar Singh v. Shyamlata Devi* AIR 1970 SC 716.
559. *Manindra Land and Building Corporation Ltd v. BhuNath Banerjee* AIR 1964 SC 1336.

property, are never barred by any time. Time never runs in favour of a trustee so as to enable him to claim the trust property himself. This provision applies to express and not implied trusts.

The provisions of the Limitation Act do not apply to any suit or other proceeding under any law relating to marriage and divorce, unless that special law makes it applicable. There is no period of limitation for certain applications filed in courts, for example, (i) application for succession certificate to collect debts due to the estate of a deceased person, or (ii) application for probate.

VI. Calculation of the Period of Limitation

584. The limitation period commences from the date enumerated in the Schedule for that respective proceeding. The last column in the Schedule gives the time when the right to sue arises. The Schedule specifies the point of time from which the period of limitation begins to run. Any suit for which no period of limitation is provided elsewhere in this Schedule must be filed within three years from the time the right to sue accrues.

Traditionally, different calendars are followed in India, for example, Samvat, Shaka, Malayali, Bengali, and so on. However, calculation of any period is done with reference to the Gregorian calendar. Thus, where parties refer to any traditional calendar in their contract, the first step is to arrive at the date on the basis of that calendar according to the Schedule and reckon the date according to the Gregorian calendar. Further calculation of limitation period, or exclusion and so on, is done with reference to the Gregorian calendar.

The date from which the period is to be counted is excluded, but the day on which the prescribed period ends is counted. If the last day of the prescribed period falls on a day when the court is closed, the proceeding can be filed on the day the court reopens.

Where in a suit a new plaintiff or defendant is added or substituted as a party, limitation is to be calculated with reference to the date he is added or substituted. But if he had been omitted because of a mistake made in good faith, the court might order that the addition or substitution is effective from an earlier date.

VII. Commencement Is Postponed

585. If the applicant is a minor or suffers from mental disability to file a suit at the time when the prescribed period *begins*, the starting point of prescribed period is postponed. The minor or such disabled person can file the suit within the same period after the disability ceases. But the period cannot be extended beyond three years from the cessation of disability or minority. This benefit applies where such minor or disabled person wishes to sue after disability has ceased.

Suits for benefit of such persons can be filed within the normal period of limitation by their guardians or 'next friends' representing them.

VIII. Continuous Running of Time

586. Once time has begun to run, no subsequent disability or inability to institute a suit or make an application stops it, even though subsequent events make it impossible for bringing proceedings.

IX. Exclusion from Calculation

587. Certain time may be excluded from calculating the prescribed period. In calculating period for filing appeals, the date of judgment and the time required for obtaining certified copies of the judgment and decree are excluded.

A plaintiff in civil proceedings who has filed it in a court having no jurisdiction and then files it in the proper court can seek to exclude from the period of limitation the period during which he bona fide prosecuted the proceedings in the court without jurisdiction.

A law may require that the plaintiff give notice of specified period or obtain sanction of an authority before filing a suit. For example, a notice of two months must be given to the government before filing a suit against it. This notice period or the time for obtaining sanction can be excluded.

For a plaintiff who is prevented from filing a suit because of an order of stay or injunction, the period during which the stay order or injunction continues is excluded.

In computing the period of limitation for any suit, the time during which the defendant was absent from India shall be excluded. This applies to a defendant who was present in India, but has been absent, whatever the cause and despite the defendant having in India an agent to receive notices. The Supreme Court has held that this provision also applies to a foreign companies having business presence in India, and if a foreign company carried on activities in India and had presence in India (an agent or office in India, or held meetings in India), it was not absent from India.[560]

X. Fraud and Mistake

588. The period of limitation does not begin to run in cases of fraud or mistake until the plaintiff knows of the fraud or becomes aware of his mistake. This applies where:

(i) the suit is based on the defendant's fraud;
(ii) the knowledge of the right or title on which the suit is founded is concealed by fraud of the defendant;
(iii) the suit is for relief based on mistake; or
(iv) a document necessary to establish the right has been fraudulently concealed from the plaintiff.

560. *Turner Morrison and Co Ltd v. Hungerford Investment Trust Ltd* AIR 1972 SC 1311.

In such cases, time does not begin to run until the plaintiff has discovered the fraud or with diligence could have discovered it. Bona fide transferees for value without knowledge of fraud or mistake are protected, and the described provision cannot be invoked in suits against them or to set aside their transactions.

XI. Fresh Period of Limitation

589. A fresh period of limitation is computed in two cases: when the debtor has acknowledged his debt in writing and when the debtor has made a payment toward the debt.

A. Acknowledgment in Writing

590. A person against whom any property or right is claimed can acknowledge his liability in respect of such property or right. If he has done this during the prescribed period in writing and has signed it, a fresh period of limitation is computed from the date of acknowledgment. Such acknowledgment need not specify the exact nature of right. It does not matter if the debtor has stated that the time for payment has not yet come or refuses to pay. Such an acknowledgment may be made to any person. Thus, an admission of liability in the balance sheet of the debtor submitted to income-tax authorities can extend the period of limitation under such provision.

591. An acknowledgment is of no effect if made after the prescribed period. However, a promise to pay a time-barred debt is an enforceable contract and gives a fresh right to sue; the creditor can file a suit based on such promise. A time-barred debt can, therefore, be revived, not by an acknowledgment, but by a promise.

B. Payment toward Debt

592. If a debtor makes a payment toward the debt before prescribed period has expired, a fresh period of limitation is computed from the date of payment.

593. The operation of these two provisions can be explained with a simple example. X has given a loan to Y repayable on 23 March 2007. X can file a suit for its recovery on or before 23 March 2010. Y sends a letter signed by him on 20 March 2010 that he is in difficulties and will need time to pay. A fresh period of limitation begins from 20 March 2010, and the suit can now be filed on or before 20 March 2013. Y gives a cheque for part of the amount on 10 February 2013, which is cashed by X on 20 February 2013. A fresh period of limitation has again begun, and the suit can now be filed on or before 20 February 2016.

C. *Joint Promisors*

594. In both the previously presented cases, acknowledgment or payment by one of joint promisors does not extend the limitation period against others, unless such promisor had authority, express or implied, to do so.

XII. Pleadings

A. *Reckoned with Reference to Plaint*

595. Very often, the issue of limitation arises from pleadings of parties. The person filing proceedings, that is, the plaintiff, must show on his own allegations that the claim is not barred by limitation. The period is calculated with reference to the allegations in the plaint and the reliefs claimed. The Civil Procedure Code requires that if the suit appears barred by limitation, the plaintiff must state the grounds on which he claims exemption from limitation.[561] He must plead and prove the facts that entitle him to excuses from limitation.

B. *Duty of Court to Decide*

596. Often the other party, that is, the defendant, would plead the bar of limitation. Even if he does not do so, it is the duty of the court to raise and decide the issue of limitation, irrespective of parties' pleadings. The Code of Civil Procedure also requires the court to reject a plaint if it is barred on the face of it.

C. *Does Not Apply to Defences*

597. The law of limitation applies to proceedings brought in a court by a party. It does not apply to a right set up by a defendant in defence. Therefore, a defendant can set up a plea that he could not enforce by way of suit, even if his claim is barred on the date on which it is taken. Thus, in a suit to enforce a contract, a defendant can plead that the instrument is voidable, even if his suit for challenging the transaction would have been time barred.[562] Further, a defendant can plead set-off (a defence answering the plaintiff's claim wholly or partially) even after his claim in defence cannot be raised by him by a separate suit being barred by limitation. However, a defendant's counter-claim, that is, his own claim against the plaintiff, must stand the test of limitation.

---

561. Order VII rule 6 of the Code of Civil Procedure 1908.
562. *Lakshmi Dass v. Rooplal* (1906) ILR 30 Mad 169.

D. Issue in Appeal

598. In the case of a pure question of law, the bar can be set up even in appeal.[563] But if limitation is based on questions of facts, the Appellate Court or Second Appellate Court can refuse to entertain the plea of bar of limitation if not taken in lower courts. But the plea can be considered if it arises from facts already before the court, is obvious from the record, or does not require any fresh evidence.[564]

XIII. Effect of Death

599. The cause of action for a person in whom the right to sue is vested devolves on the person on whom right devolves. The cause is the same.

XIV. Extension of Prescribed Period

600. If the applicant shows sufficient cause for not filing appeal or an application in time, the court may condone the delay and allow the appeal or application to be filed after the prescribed period. This provision does not apply to suits or applications for execution of decree. There is no extension in these two cases. It is usual to find such provisions of condoning of delay in many special statutes, even in respect of original proceedings. Where an applicant seeks such favour, he has to explain every day's delay.

XV. Continuing Breach of Contract

601. In case of continuing breach of contract, a fresh period of limitation begins to run at every moment of time during which the breach continues.

Examples of such breach are breach of covenant to repair or lessee using leased premises contrary to covenant. This is different from successive breaches. Non-payment of rent is not a continuing breach.

XVI. Conflict of Laws

602. In Indian law, the law of limitation belongs to the branch of procedural laws. It will apply to all proceedings before Indian courts and authorities, irrespective to the substantive law applicable in the particular case.

Section 11 of the Limitation Act expressly provides that suits instituted in India on contracts entered into in a foreign country shall be subject to the provisions of

563. *Town Municipal Council Athani v. Presiding Officer Labour Court* AIR 1969 SC 1335.
564. *Banarsi Das v. Kanshi Ram* AIR 1963 SC 1165.

the Limitation Act. A rule of limitation in laws of a foreign country can be set up as a defence only if (i) the rule has extinguished the contract and (ii) the parties were domiciled in the foreign country during the period prescribed by such rule.

XVII. Limitation and Laches

603. The doctrine of *laches* applies independent of the bar of limitation. Mere delay does not bar a person from filing a proceeding that is otherwise within limitation, unless the delay amounts to waiver or abandonment of rights. Delay does not matter so long as matters remain in status quo. Delay might also defeat grant of discretionary reliefs, such as specific performance, rescission or injunction. It is one factor that courts might consider in deciding not to exercise discretion in granting these reliefs.

XVIII. Period of Limitation for Suits Relating to Contracts

604. Part II of First Division of the Schedule to the Limitation Act provides for the period of limitation in suits relating to contracts. The same principles apply to express or implied contracts, as also to *quasi*-contracts. The period is generally three years from the date of obligation under the respective rules. This is of course a general statement. The Schedule states the type of suit, the period of limitation, and the time from which it is to be calculated.

A. *Illustrative List*

605. An illustrative list relating to commencement of periods of limitation for some suits on contracts is as follows:

(i) For wages in the case of any other person – When the wages accrue due.
(ii) Against a carrier for compensation for losing or injuring goods – When the loss or injury occurs.
(iii) For the balance of money advanced in payment of goods to be delivered – When the goods ought to be delivered.
(iv) For the price of goods sold and delivered where no fixed period of credit is agreed on – The date of the delivery of the goods.
(v) For the price of goods sold and delivered to be paid for after the expiry of a fixed period of credit – When the period of credit expires.
(vi) For money payable for money lent – When the loan is made.
(vii) Like suit when the lender has given a cheque for the money – When the cheque is paid.
(viii) For money lent under an agreement that it shall be payable on demand – When the loan is made.

(ix) For money deposited under an agreement that shall be payable on demand, including money in the hands of his banker so payable – When the demand is made.

(x) For specific performance of a contract – The date fixed for the performance, or, if no such date is fixed, when the plaintiff has notice that performance is refused.

(xi) For compensation for breach of a promise to do anything at a specified time or on the happening of a specified contingency – When the time specified arrives or the contingency happens.

(xii) For compensation for the breach of any contract, express or implied, not herein specially provided for – When the contract is broken or (where there are successive breaches) when the breach in respect of which the suit is instituted occurs or (where the breach is continuing) when it ceases.

The Schedule provides for other suits also relating to negotiable instruments, guarantees, and so on.

B. Limitation for Loans and Deposits

606. Article 21 provides for a suit for recovery of money lent under an agreement that it shall be payable on demand. Limitation is to be calculated from the date of the loan, and not the demand. On the contrary, if the amount is a deposit repayable on demand, limitation is to be calculated under Article 22 from the date the demand is made.

Considerable case law has developed around the question of whether a transaction is one of loan or of deposit. In the case of a loan, money passes from the payer to the payee at the instance of, and for the requirement or use of, the payee. In case of a deposit, the payee receives money at the instance of the payer and the requirement or use of the payee is not a relevant fact for consideration. The court will take into account the surrounding circumstances, relationship of parties, character of the transaction, and manner in which the parties treated the transaction, including the name used by parties for the transaction.[565]

C. Instalment Contracts

607. In case of amounts payable in instalments, rent, or other periodic payments, limitation period begins in respect of each instalment of payment when such instalment is due. Failure to pay one instalment does not entitle the creditor to claim the whole amount, unless the contract so provides, and in the latter case, period of limitation for recovery of the entire amount will commence from the date the whole amount becomes due under the contract. If the bond provides that in event of default

565. *Ram Janaki Devi v. Juggilal Kamlapat* AIR 1971 SC 2551.

made in payment of one or more instalments, the whole shall become due, the suit can and must be filed within three years from the date of default, unless the obligee waives benefit of the provision. The creditor cannot sue for instalment counting limitation from due date of each instalment.[566]

566. *Vishwanath v. Sadashiva* AIR 1932 Nag 1; *Jawahar Lal v. Mathura Prasad* AIR 1934 All 661.

Part II. Specific Contracts

Chapter 1. Agency

608. Chapter X of the Indian Contract Act 1872 states special provisions applicable to a contract of agency. It deals with appointing an agent; extent of his authority; termination of authority and its effect; delegation of powers; principal's rights, duties, and obligations and of the agent and his relations with third persons; and personal liability of an agent.

§1. Agency, Agent, and Principal

609. An 'agent' is a person employed to do any act for another or to represent another in dealings with third persons. The person for whom such act is done, or who is so represented, is called the 'principal'.[567] The essential feature of agency is that when an agent deals for his principal with a third person, he effects a contract between the principal and that third person. This makes the principal liable under that contract directly to the third person and entitles the principal to sue the third party.

The law of agency protects third persons dealing with an agent; they are protected as if they have dealt with the principal. A third person need not recognize the agent or may refuse to deal with an agent. But when a third person has recognized the agent's authority, he is estopped from questioning that authority in a suit on that contract.

I. Agent and Servant

610. An agent is bound to use his authority with all lawful instructions given to him, but is not subject to the direct control or supervision of the principal. He deals with third persons and creates contractual relations on behalf of his principal with them. Within the limits of his authority he can use his discretion and judgment.[568] He is neither a servant nor an independent contractor.

A servant acts under the direct control and supervision of his master, who directs how the work shall be done, and is bound to conform to all reasonable orders given

567. Section 182 of the Indian Contract Act.
568. *Lakshminarayan Ram Gopal and Sons Ltd v. Government of Hyderabad* AIR 1954 SC 364.

to him in the course of his work. An independent contractor is entirely independent of any control or interference and undertakes to produce a specified result employing his own means.

II. Agent and Independent Contractor

611. Persons doing business and calling themselves 'agents' need not necessarily be so; they may not be 'contracting' as agents. Insurance agents solicit business for insurers. Distributors and franchisees usually purchase for resale. Dealers of a particular product who call themselves agents would be dealing on their own account with each other. They act on their own behalf and take the business risk and liability for transactions they make.

The true nature of relationship of principal and agent is, therefore, determined with reference to all circumstances, dealings between parties, the functions and responsibilities of the alleged agent. The name used by the parties for the relationship does not matter. The real nature of relationship is important, because if it is of an agency; the agent gets indemnity for his acts from his principal and will not be held personally liable to the third person for acts done within his authority.

III. Classes of Agents

612. The Act does not make any distinction between different classes of agents. An agency need not always arise out of contractual relationship. It may arise out of necessity or by ratification.[569] Yet the distinction between general and special agents is important to decide the nature and extent of authority conferred on an agent. A general agent, such as a broker or a factor, has authority to act for his principal in all matters or in all matters concerning a particular trade or business. A special agent has authority only to do some particular act for some special occasion or purpose usually not within the ordinary course of his business or profession.

§2. Creation of Agency

I. Appointment of Agent

613. An agent may be appointed orally or in writing. Agency can be inferred from the circumstances and conduct of the parties or from correspondence. An implied agency arises from the act or position of parties or from necessity. Thus, where A receives goods purchased by B and deals with them, an agency can be inferred. It may also arise when the principal ratifies the unauthorized acts of the agent or by estoppel. Thus, if a principal allows a person to transact with third

569. See para. 634 *infra*.

parties on his behalf and induces them to believe that the person is transacting as agent, the principal will be bound by such transactions.

II. Formalities

614. The Indian Contract Act does not require any form for appointing an agent. Special statutes may prescribe formalities for appointing agents. An agent for executing and registering a document under the law of registration can be appointed by making a power-of-attorney executed and authenticated before officers under that law or other prescribed officers.[570] A proxy for attending meetings of a company must be appointed in writing and signed in the prescribed manner.[571] An advocate for appearance in court must be appointed by a document in writing, usually referred to as the *vakalatnama*.[572] A power-of-attorney given by a company to its director or to any other person must bear its common seal.[573]

III. Power of Attorney

615. When an agent needs to be appointed by a deed or the appointment needs to be formal for a transaction or for series of transactions, the principal may make an instrument called power-of-attorney.[574] This is an instrument empowering a specified person to act for and in the name of the person executing it.[575] The agent, called donee of the power or the attorney, gets a right to use the name of the principal. The law of agency applies to relations created by such power-of-attorney.

IV. Consideration

616. No consideration is necessary for creating an agency, that is, for appointing an agent. The agency may benefit the principal, or the agent, or both. It may provide for payment of remuneration to the agent for doing the business of the agency. An agent is not entitled to remuneration unless the agreement provides.

V. Competency

617. The principal must be capable of doing in law what he wants his agent to do. Therefore, a person can appoint an agent if he is major and of sound mind.[576] An agent of a minor or incompetent person is directly liable under the transaction

570. Sections 32 and 33 of the Registration Act 1908.
571. Section 105 of the Companies Act 2013.
572. Order 3 rule 4 of the Code of Civil Procedure 1908.
573. Section 22 of the Companies Act 2013.
574. The Powers-of-Attorney Act 1882.
575. Section 1A of the Powers-of-Attorney Act 1882.
576. Section 183 of the Indian Contract Act.

to the third person he deals with. A corporation or a company can also appoint an agent; its general competency will be determined by terms of its incorporation. Promoters are personally liable when they contract on behalf of companies not yet incorporated, because when a person is not in existence there cannot be any appointment. However, pre-incorporation contracts made by promoters warranted by terms of incorporation and accepted by the company after its incorporation, may be enforced by or against the company.[577]

A minor or incompetent person can be an agent and bring about a valid contract between the principal and the third party. But such an agent will not be responsible to his principal for breach of his obligations under the agency.

A principal may give authority to co-agents to act for him, who may be appointed to act jointly, separately, or in a certain number forming a quorum. Co-principals can jointly appoint an agent to act for them in their joint or separate business or affairs.

VI. Subject Matter of Agency

618. Generally a person may appoint an agent to do whatever he can do himself. Conversely, what a person cannot do himself, he cannot do by means of an agent.

An agent cannot be appointed in the following instances:

(i) The act to be performed is personal in character, such as swearing an affidavit.
(ii) A statute requires that the transaction shall be done or signed by the principal himself.
(iii) The competency to do the act arises by virtue of the holding of some public office.
(iv) Competency arises by virtue of some power, authority, or duty of a personal nature and requiring skill or discretion for its exercise.
(v) A statute imposes on a person a duty that he is not free to delegate, such as appearing on behalf of an accused in a criminal case.

The Indian Contract Act does not specify the acts for which an agent may be appointed.

§3. Authority of an Agent

619. The authority of an agent is his power to affect his principal's position by doing acts on his behalf. Authority of an agent may be express or implied.[578]

577. Section 15 of the Specific Relief Act 1963.
578. Section 186 of the Indian Contract Act.

I. Express and Implied Authority

620. It is express when it is given by words spoken or written. It is implied when it is inferred from conduct of the parties, nature of employment or other circumstances of the case, such as things spoken or written, the course of dealing between the parties.

Implied authority may be:

(i) incidental authority – to do things ordinarily or necessarily incidental to due performance of the express authority;
(ii) usual authority – to do that which other persons in the particular trade or business would ordinarily do;
(iii) customary authority – to do acts according to customs and usages of the place where the agent acts.

II. Authority to Do Necessary Acts

621. An agent with authority to do an act has authority to do every lawful thing that is necessary to do such act. The implied authority of an agent carrying on business extends to do every lawful thing necessary for the purpose of the business and to do all things that are usually done in the course of business.[579] An agent also has authority, in an emergency, to do all such acts for the purpose of protecting his principal from loss.[580]

III. Limitation on Authority

622. A principal may limit or restrict the authority of an agent, but such limitation would not bind the third person unless he knows of such limitation or restriction. The burden of proving such limitation or restriction lies on the principal.

IV. Apparent Authority

623. Apparent or ostensible authority is that authority of the agent that appears to others. The principal is bound to third parties for acts done by the agent falling within his apparent authority, which may be beyond the actual authority given to him, or any limitation or restrictions on his authority. The principal is liable for acts of the agent if he has by word or conduct induced a belief in the third party dealing with the agent, that the acts of the agent were within the scope of his authority.[581]

579. Section 188 of the Indian Contract Act.
580. Section 189 of the Indian Contract Act.
581. Section 237 of the Indian Contract Act.

§4. Personal Liability of Agent

624. An agent cannot personally enforce contracts made by him on behalf of his principal, nor is he personally liable on such contracts.[582] He may by contract agree to be personally liable.

An agent will be presumed to be personally liable:

(a) where the contract is made by an agent for sale or purchase of goods for a merchant resident abroad;
(b) where the agent does not disclose the name of his principal;
(c) where the principal, though disclosed, cannot be sued.

When an agent is personally liable, the person dealing which him may hold the principal or the agent or both of them liable.[583]

An agent has been held entitled to sue or will be liable if he has an interest in the contract made by him for his principal.[584]

§5. Relationship with Third Party

I. Effect of Acts of Agent

A. *Acts of Agent Bind the Principal*

625. Contracts made by an agent and obligations arising from acts done by an agent, may be enforced in the same manner and will have the same legal consequences as if the contracts had been entered into and the acts done by the principal in person,[585] even though the act does not turn out to the benefit of the principal.[586] The principal is bound by the acts of the agent falling within his apparent authority.[587] Any contract made by an agent with the authority of his principal may be enforced by or against the principal where his name or existence was disclosed (though not identified) to the other contracting party at the time when the contract was made.

B. *Undisclosed Principal*

626. Sometimes an agent might deal without disclosing the principal, and the third party does not suspect that he is only an agent. In such a case (i) the principal

582. Section 230 of the Indian Contract Act.
583. Section 233 of the Indian Contract Act.
584. *Subrahmania Pattar v. Narayanan Nayar* (1900) ILR 24 Mad 130; *Firm Hardayal Mal – Mohri Lal v. Firm Kishan Gopal Jhanji & Sons* AIR 1938 Lah 673.
585. Section 226 of the Indian Contract Act.
586. *Bank of Bengal v. Ramanathan Chetty* AIR 1915 PC 121.
587. See para. 623 *supra*.

can demand performance; and (ii) the third party can claim against the principal the same rights he had as against the agent as if he had been the principal. But if the principal reveals himself before the contract is completed, the third party can refuse to fulfil the contract if he can show that he would have refused to make the contract if he had known who is the principal or that the agent was not the principal.

C. Pretended Agent

627. Where the agent represents himself to a third party to be an agent of another without having authority, and that other does not ratify his acts, the purported agent must compensate the third party for any loss or damage incurred by so dealing.[588] Where an agent who has no principal, disclosed or undisclosed, but nevertheless poses as an agent, he cannot demand performance from the third party if he has been acting in reality on his own account and not as agent.

§6. Relationship between the Principal and Agent

628. An agent enjoys discretion in exercising the powers; he is not bound to exercise his authority. The contract of agency may impose on the agent the duty to exercise powers granted to him. The Act specifies certain rights, powers and duties of an agent.

I. Rights and Powers of an Agent

629. An agent is entitled to indemnity against the consequences of his lawful acts.[589] He may enforce indemnity not only by suit, but also by exercising the right of lien or set-off.

An agent is entitled to remuneration only if agreed. He can receive it according to the conditions in the contract and after he has carried out all that he agreed to do under the agency.

An agent is bound to pay to his principal all sums received on his account. He can retain and deduct out of any money received on account of the principal, the amount due to him for advances made, expenses incurred, and the agreed remuneration. He can also retain by way of a right of lien any of the principal's goods, papers, or any other movable or immovable property in his hands until the amounts due for his commission, disbursements and expenses, and services are paid to him.[590]

588. Section 235 of the Indian Contract Act.
589. See also paras 633, 641 *infra*.
590. Section 221 of the Indian Contract Act.

II. Duties of an Agent

630. He must conduct the business of agency according to directions of the principal; in the absence of any direction, he must act according to the custom that prevails in doing business of the same kind at the place where the agent conducts business. He will then be entitled to any agreed remuneration. If he fails to do so, he is liable to the principal for loss sustained and must account for profits, if any, to the principal.[591]

An agent must communicate with the principal in case of difficulty and obtain his instructions.[592]

An agent is bound to render proper accounts to his principal on demand[593] during and after termination of agency. Subject to deductions stated earlier, he is bound to pay to his principal all sums received on account of the principal.[594]

An agent should not deal on his own account in the business of agency, without consent of the principal.[595] An agent cannot, therefore, even after termination of the agency, use for making a profit for himself his position as agent, his principal's property, or confidential information arising from the agency. If the agent deals on his own account without knowledge of the principal, the principal is entitled to claim all benefits resulting from the transaction.

The fiduciary element in agency is the key to much of the law governing this relation, but it is not its essential element.[596]

III. Disabilities of an Agent

A. *No Delegation*

631. As a rule, an agent cannot delegate his authority. But he can appoint a sub-agent when the nature of agency permits it or demands it or the ordinary custom of trade in a particular business allows it.

If the sub-agent is thus properly appointed (i) the principal is liable to third parties for acts of the sub-agent; (ii) the agent is liable to the principal for acts of the sub-agent; and (iii) except in cases of fraud or wilful wrong, the sub-agent is not liable to the principal, but he is liable to the agent. The rule of privity prevents any obligations or rights between the principal and sub-agent.

Where the sub-agent is not properly appointed (i) the agent stands as a principal toward such a sub-agent; (ii) the agent is responsible to his principal and to the third parties for acts of the sub-agent; (iii) the sub-agent does not represent the principal; (iv) the principal is not liable to third parties for acts of the sub-agent; and (iv) the sub-agent is not responsible to the principal, but only to the agent.

591. Section 211 of the Indian Contract Act.
592. Section 214 of the Indian Contract Act.
593. Section 213 of the Indian Contract Act.
594. Section 218 of the Indian Contract Act.
595. Section 215 of the Indian Contract Act.
596. *Southern Roadways Ltd v. S M Krishnan* AIR 1990 SC 673.

IV. Rights and Powers of the Principal

632. Even after appointing an agent to do business or effect a transaction, a principal may conduct or complete the transaction himself.[597] He does not lose this power unless he has expressly agreed not to use it.

Where the agent has acted without authority or has exceeded his authority, the principal has an option to ratify[598] the transaction or disown it.

V. Duties of the Principal

633. It is the primary duty of the principal to indemnify his agent against consequences of his lawful acts.[599] The agent is, therefore, entitled to recover expenses incurred in doing the business of agency and any loss, liability, and so on incurred in exercising his authority. An agent is entitled to indemnity from the principal for acts done in good faith at the instance of the principal, though such acts cause injury to third persons.[600]

§7. RATIFICATION

634. The principal may elect to ratify or to disown any act of an agent done without or in excess of his authority. A person ratifying an unauthorized act ratifies the whole transaction of which it forms a part.[601] If the unauthorized act is ratified, that act will be deemed to have been done with the principal's authority and the agent is relieved from personal liability to the principal and to third party for acting in excess of authority. He can claim commission and expenses and is entitled to indemnity.

§8. TERMINATION OF AGENCY

635. Agency being a contract, it can be terminated in any manner in which any other contract is discharged, that is, by mutual agreement, by expiry of the term (period) of agency, by destruction of the subject matter of agency, or if the agency subsequently becomes unlawful. Where a partnership firm has appointed an agent, its dissolution will terminate the agency. An agency is also terminated in the ways discussed in the following sections.[602]

---

597. *Deb Ratan Biswas v. Anand Moyi Dev* AIR 2011 SC 1653.
598. See para. 634 onwards.
599. Section 222 of the Indian Contract Act.
600. Section 223 of Indian Contract Act.
601. Section 199 of the Indian Contract Act.
602. See ss 203–209 of the Indian Contract Act.

I. Revocation of Authority by the Principal

636. The principal can revoke the authority of the agent by giving notice to the agent.

A. Agency Always Revocable

637. The authority of an agent is revocable in all cases at any time but before the agent has exercised authority, even though the revocation may be wrongful as between the principal and agent. The only exception is where the agency is irrevocable in terms of section 202 of the Indian Contract Act.

Agency can be revoked even if it (i) is for a specified period, (ii) is stated as irrevocable; or (iii) has been given for a consideration. It can be revoked whether the agent is formally appointed by a power-of-attorney or informally. But if the principal revokes the agency before the agreed time, he must compensate the agent for earlier revocation, if the revocation is without sufficient cause. The notice of revocation must be reasonable.

The termination of authority is effective against the agent when it becomes known to him and as against third persons when it becomes known to them. The principal remains liable to the third party in respect of dealings already effected by the agent in the exercise of his *apparent* authority until the third party had notice of revocation. The principal is also liable to the agent in damages if the revocation is wrongful, for example, where an agency for a particular period is revoked before expiry of that period.

B. The Irrevocable Agency

638. Section 202 of the Indian Contract Act provides for the only case in which an agency is *irrevocable*. Where an agent has been appointed in respect of a subject matter and he has an interest in that subject matter, such an agency cannot be terminated in any manner so as to prejudice such an interest, unless there is an express contract to that effect. Such an agency can neither be revoked by the principal nor terminated by his death, unsoundness of mind, or insolvency. Thus, where X gives a power-of-attorney to his lender to sell or assign X's property given as security for that loan and to apply the proceeds toward the loan, such a power is irrevocable. Such an agency may be revoked only if the contract of agency contains an express provision to that effect, or the agent has committed misconduct in the business of agency.

II. Renunciation of Agency by Agent

639. An agent can also renounce his authority by giving a notice at any time before completion of the agency business. The notice must be reasonable. If he renounces without sufficient cause before the agreed period of agency, he is liable to the principal for damages caused by such renunciation.

III. Other Modes of Termination

640. An agency stands terminated when the business of agency is completed, on death of the principal or agent, when the principal or agent becomes of unsound mind, or if the principal is adjudicated as insolvent.

IV. Effect of Termination

641. The termination of an agency ends the relationship between the principal and agent and determines the authority of the agent. But the agent would still be entitled to indemnity for acts done and to receive remuneration earned for the period before termination.

Chapter 2. Bailment

§1. Contract of Bailment

642. A 'bailment' is the delivery of goods by one person to another for some purpose on a contract that they shall, when the purpose is accomplished, be returned or otherwise disposed of according to the directions of the person delivering them.[603] The essence of bailment lies in delivery of possession of goods and the duty on the bailee to return the goods according to bailor's directions. Issues in bailment arise in commercial transactions such as deposits of instruments or shares, goods delivered for carriage, hire-purchase transactions, hire for work and labour, pledges,[604] goods given as security, warehousing, and so on.

Very often, a question has arisen in the context of sales tax laws, whether transactions in question were bailment or sale, especially contracts providing for return of packing material of goods sold. The true test is that of the real intention of parties. The court ascertains the true nature of the transactions on the basis of all facts and circumstances of the case.[605]

A bailment may benefit the bailor or the bailee. The purpose of the bailment may be deposit or custody, hire, security, carriage, use, or loan, for work on the goods. A bailment may be gratuitous or for consideration.

§2. Bailment Otherwise Than on Contract

643. The Contract Act provides for bailment by contract. But a bailment may arise without a contract. It may arise, for example, if a person voluntarily takes custody or charge of goods of another, even without his consent.[606] It arises where a person lawfully comes into possession of goods belonging to another and holds them under circumstances whereby he ought, on principles of justice, to keep them safely and restore them or deliver them to the owner. A finder of goods has the same obligations as a bailee. A bailment can arise where a deposit is made under stress of circumstances. The government seizing goods under law, as in the case of violation of customs law, is liable like a bailee to return the goods or to pay its price if the goods cannot be returned.[607]

§3. Duty of Care

644. In all cases of bailment, whether gratuitous or for consideration, the bailee is bound to take as much care of the goods bailed to him as a man of ordinary

603. Section 148 of the Indian Contract Act; ss 148–171 of the Indian Contract Act deal with bailments.
604. See paras 744 onwards.
605. *Kalyani Breweries Ltd v. State of West Bengal* AIR 1998 SC 70; *United Breweries Ltd v. State of AP* AIR 1997 SC 1316.
606. *Trustees of the Port of Bombay v. Premier Automobiles Ltd* AIR 1981 SC 1982.
607. *State of Gujarat v. Memon Mahomed Haji Hasam* AIR 1967 SC 1885; *State of Tripura v. Bina Choudhary* AIR 2007 SC 2169.

prudence would, under similar circumstances, take of his own goods of the same bulk, quality, and value as the goods bailed.[608] All bailees, including pawnees, are subject to the same duty of care. The actual degree of care would depend on the facts of each case. A bailee is not an insurer of goods. Once he has taken such care, he is not liable to the bailor for loss or damage to goods while in his possession, unless he has agreed to undertake increased liability.

The bailee must use the goods according to the conditions of bailment. He cannot mix the goods with his own goods without the bailor's consent.

§4. Return of Goods

645. A bailee is liable to return to the bailor the same goods or to deal with them according to bailor's directions as soon as the time agreed has expired or the purpose of bailment is accomplished. The bailor need not demand their return. This duty is implied in every bailment, even if the contract is silent about return of goods. If the bailment is gratuitous, the bailor can ask for its return at any time, even before the time for which he has lent it. This duty also applies to any increase or profit accruing from the goods bailed. If the bailee fails to return or deliver the goods as discussed earlier, he is liable thereafter to the bailor for the loss or damage to goods from the date of default.

Unexplained failure to return the thing bailed is presumed to arise of the bailee's default, and the court would presume negligence.[609]

A bailee who in good faith returns the goods bailed to the bailor or his order is not liable to the true owner of goods. If a person other than the bailor claims the bailed goods, the bailee may apply to the court to stop delivery of the goods to the bailor and to decide the title to the goods.

§5. Expenses and Remuneration

646. The bailee is entitled to expenses and remuneration according to terms of bailment. A bailee who has rendered service involving labour and skill upon the goods is entitled to retain the goods by way of right of lien, until he receives his remuneration.[610] Where a bailee is to keep or carry goods or work on them and is not entitled to remuneration, he is nevertheless entitled to necessary expenses incurred by him for the purpose of bailment.

608. Section 151 of the Indian Contract Act.
609. *Kush Kanta Barkakati v. Chandra Kanta Kakati* AIR 1924 Cal 1056.
610. See paras 507–508 above.

Chapter 3. Gaming and Wagering

§1. Wagers

647. A wagering agreement is void and unenforceable. It is a promise to give money or money's worth on the determination or ascertainment of an uncertain event.[611] The following features make an agreement a wager:

(i) a promise to pay money or money's worth on happening of an event;
(ii) each of the two parties having a mutual chance of gain or loss, that is, one party to win and the other to lose on the determination of the event;
(iii) the event is uncertain;
(iv) the parties have no interest in the happening of the event other than the money they have promised.

648. The policy of the law is not to prevent or discourage betting. Wagering agreements are merely void and hence unenforceable.[612] A winner cannot sue to recover any amount won. Nor can a winner sue the stakeholder for any money entrusted to him to abide by the result of any game or event on which wager is made.[613] However, certain subscriptions or contributions in connection with horse races are saved.

Wagers are not unlawful or illegal except in a part of India,[614] what was once Bombay state.[615] In that area, wagering agreements are illegal. Therefore, collateral transactions, such as loans given for such purposes, are also illegal and unenforceable.

649. This provision does not apply to awards made to winners in horse racing or to games involving skill, training, attention, or experience.

Speculative contracts may not necessarily be wagers. An agreement to purchase or sell goods or shares on a future date, else to pay difference between the agreed or market price at that time, is a wager if the true intention of the parties is not to deliver goods, but merely to pay the difference.

Derivatives can be traded on a recognised stock exchange or settled on the clearing house of the recognized stock exchange, in accordance with the rules and byelaws of such stock exchange.[616] The Reserve Bank of India has issued circulars enabling and permitting transactions in derivatives and financial instruments for transferring or hedging risk.

611. A wager is not defined in the Indian Contract Act.
612. *Gherulal Parakh v. Mahadeodas Maiya* AIR 1959 SC 781.
613. Section 30 of the Indian Contract Act.
614. Now parts of the states of Maharashtra and Gujarat.
615. Act for Avoiding Wagers (Amendments) Act, 1865.
616. Section 18A of the Securities Contracts (Regulation) Act, 1956.

§2. Contracts of Insurance

650. A transaction of insurance resembles a wager. But it lacks one feature of a wager – the insured person as well as the insurer have an interest that the event constituting the risk shall not occur. It is essential that the insured have an insurable interest in the subject matter of insurance, that is, such an interest that the risk would cause damage to the assured, causing him to lose a benefit or incur a liability. In the absence of such interest, the insurance policy would amount to a wager and would be void. Thus, a life insurance on the life of a stranger will be void, but not, for example, insurance on the life of one's child.

Often certain contracts of life insurance lack the element of uncertainty because the specified amount becomes always payable by the insurer to the insured. Amount due under a policy of life insurance is considered property and is also assignable. A contract for payment of a specified amount an annuity of a specified amount assured on death is a contract of life insurance and governed by laws of insurance.[617]

617. The Insurance Act 1938 and principles laid down by higher courts in case law.

Chapter 4. Sale of Goods

651. The Sale of Goods Act 1930 applies to contracts of sale of goods. The general principles of contract in the Indian Contract Act 1872 also apply unless they are inconsistent with the express provisions of Sale of Goods Act 1930.[618] Provisions affecting sale of immovable property are found in the Transfer of Property Act 1882.

The Act applies to a sale of goods, that is, every kind of moveable property, including stock and shares, growing crops, grass, and things attached to or forming part of the land that are agreed to be severed before sale or under the contract of sale. It does not apply to actionable claims[619] and money.

§1. Contract of Sale of Goods

652. A contract of sale of goods is a contract by which the seller transfers or agrees to transfer the property in goods to the buyer for a price, that is, money consideration. This excludes application of this law to a barter or exchange of goods, which will be governed by the general provisions applicable to contracts. There may be a contract of sale between one part-owner and another. The contract may be absolute or conditional.

A contract of sale may be a sale or an agreement to sell. If the property in goods is transferred from the seller to the buyer at the time of contract, it is a sale. Where the property in the goods is to transfer at a future time or subject to some condition to be fulfilled, it is an agreement to sell. An agreement to sell becomes a sale when the time elapses or such conditions are fulfilled. This distinction affects the rights and liabilities of parties.

The seller may own and possess the goods at the time of contract. Otherwise he may contract for sale of goods that he has yet to acquire, or that have not yet been manufactured or produced, in which case the contract is an agreement of sale.

653. A contract of sale is made by an offer to buy or sell goods for a price and acceptance of such offer. The contract may provide for immediate delivery of goods or immediate payment of price of both, for the delivery or payment by instalments, or that the delivery or payment or both shall be postponed. Unless any other law provides, the contract may be oral or in writing or may be implied from conduct of parties.[620]

Compulsory sales to the government of goods on price fixed by it have been held to be contracts of sale. Such questions have often arisen in matters of assessment of sales tax.[621]

---

618. Section 3 of the Sale of Goods Act 1930.
619. See para. 385 *supra*.
620. Section 5 of the Sale of Goods Act 1930.
621. *Vishnu Agencies v. Commercial Tax Officer* AIR 1978 SC 449; *U P Co-op C U Federations v. West U P Sugar Mills Assocn* AIR 2004 SC 3697.

§2. Performance of Contract: Delivery and Payment of Price

654. The parties enjoy full freedom to decide the time and terms of delivery and payment of price. Unless otherwise agreed, delivery and payment of price are concurrent conditions.

I. Delivery

655. The parties can agree on the manner in which delivery will be made. It may be effected by any agreed act that has the effect of putting the goods in the possession of the buyer or of any person authorized by him.[622] Where the seller is required to send the goods to the buyer, delivery to any carrier is delivery to the buyer, unless the seller has reserved the right of disposal.

Delivery might be made in any of these ways: (i) actually handing over the goods or the warehouse keys where the goods are located; (ii) the seller acknowledging that he holds goods after sale on behalf of the buyer as the buyer's agent; (iii) an acknowledgment by a third person holding the goods that he agrees to hold them as bailee for the buyer; or (iv) handing over documents of title to goods, such as a bill of lading or railway receipt.

656. It is the seller's duty to deliver the goods. Unless otherwise agreed, delivery of goods and payment of price are concurrent obligations. The seller and buyer may agree about the time, mode, and manner of delivery. The seller is not bound to deliver until the buyer seeks delivery, unless otherwise agreed. The terms of the contract will determine whether it is for the buyer to take possession of the goods or for the seller to send them to the buyer.

The seller must bear the expense of putting the goods into a deliverable state. Apart from any contract, goods sold are to be delivered at the place at which they are at the time of the sale and goods agreed to be sold are to be delivered at the place at which they are at the time of the agreement to sell, or if not then in existence, at the place at which they are manufactured or produced. Even where the seller has agreed to deliver at another place at his own risk, the risk for deterioration incidental to transit falls on the buyer, unless otherwise agreed.

657. Delivery is not complete merely when the buyer receives the goods. The buyer has to accept them, and for that purpose has a right to inspect whether the goods conform to the contract. The normal place of inspection is the place of delivery.

A buyer need not accept delivery of goods of wrong quantity. If he does accept, he must pay for them at the contract rate. The buyer is also entitled to refuse to accept delivery of goods in instalments.

The buyer has accepted delivery if he intimates so to the seller, he deals with the goods delivered in a manner inconsistent with the ownership of the seller, or he retains the goods for more than a reasonable time without rejecting. If the goods do

622. Section 33 of the Sale of Goods Act 1930.

not conform to the contract, it is sufficient if the buyer informs his rejection to the seller and it is not necessary for him to return them to the seller.

A buyer failing or refusing to take delivery is liable for loss caused to the seller thereby.

II. Price

658. Price is the money consideration for the sale of goods. The parties may fix the price in the contract or may agree on a manner, for example, that it shall be fixed on valuation by a third party. The price can also be determined by the course of dealing between the parties.[623] Even otherwise, a buyer is bound to pay a reasonable price, and a contract of sale is not void for uncertainty merely because the price is to be determined later.[624] Price may be payable immediately or in instalments.

If new or increased customs or excise duty, or any sale or purchase tax is imposed after the making of the contract but before delivery of goods, the seller can add it to the price, unless otherwise agreed.[625] If it is reduced, the buyer can deduct it from the price.[626]

§3. Transfer of Property and Risk

659. Transfer of property means transfer of ownership. Risk prima facie transfer with transfer of property.

I. Transfer of Property

660. Property in goods is transferred to the buyer at such time as the parties intend it to pass. It may be the time of delivery, payment of price, making of contract, or any other time decided by them. Such intention may be express; otherwise it will be ascertained from the terms of contract, conduct of parties, and circumstances of the cases.

Sections 18–25 of the Sale of Goods Act give some rules to assist the courts to find out when the parties intended to pass property in goods to the buyer. These are but rules of construction, and in each case the intention of parties must be ascertained.

Goods must be ascertained before property can pass to the buyer. In a sale of unascertained goods by description, property will pass when the goods have been unconditionally appropriated to the contract. There is no particular mode of appropriation, but the most common mode is by delivering them unconditionally to

623. Section 9 of the Sale of Goods Act.

624. *M S Madhusoodhanan v. Kerala Kaumudi Pvt Ltd* AIR 2004 SC 909.

625. *Ravinder Raj v. Competent Motors Co. Pvt Ltd* AIR 2011 SC 1061.

626. Section 64A of the Sale of Goods Act.

a carrier. If the seller has to do something to the goods to ascertain the price, property will pass after that is done and the buyer is informed.

661. Specific goods must be in a deliverable state[627] before property passes. Unless a different intention appears, in an unconditional contract for sale of specific goods in a deliverable state, property passes to the buyer when the contract is made, irrespective of the time agreed for delivery or payment of price.

In a contract for the sale of specific goods or where goods are subsequently appropriated to the contract, the seller may reserve the right of disposal of the goods until certain conditions are fulfilled, in which case, property does not pass to the buyer until the conditions are fulfilled. Thus, where goods are shipped or delivered for carriage, and by the bill of lading or the carriage receipt, goods are made deliverable to the order of the seller, property does not pass on delivery of goods to the carrier.

662. Where goods are delivered to the buyer on approval or on 'sale or return' basis, property passes to the buyer when he gives his approval or acceptance, does any act adopting the transaction, or retains the goods without rejecting them beyond the period specified for return, and if no period is specified, beyond reasonable time.

II. Sale by Non-owner

663. The general rule is '*nemo dat quod not habet*', meaning that no one can transfer a better title than he himself possesses. Thus, no person can sell goods and give a good title to them unless he is the owner or someone having his authority or consent.

Although this rule protects the property to its owner, interest of trade and commerce demands that sale by others, especially those having authority, actual or apparent, from its owners, can confer good title on buyers, particularly those buyers who buy in good faith. The provisions in the Sale of Goods Act seek to balance these interests.

The Sale of Goods Act recognizes sale by a person who is neither the owner, nor has any authority from the owner of goods. In such a case, a buyer acquires no better title to goods than the seller had,[628] unless the conduct of the owner of those goods estops him from denying the seller's authority to sell. Any such sale is not binding on the owner, who can seek possession of the goods in a suit within three years from the time the owner first learns that it is in possession of the buyer.[629] If the seller has no title and the buyer is required to give up the goods to the owner, he is entitled to return of price as breach of condition.

---

627. Goods are said to be in a 'deliverable state' when they are in such state that the buyer would under the contract be bound to take delivery of them.
628. Section 27 of the Sale of Goods Act.
629. Article 68 of the Limitation Act 1963.

664. However, the following can confer good title on a buyer who buys goods for value in good faith without knowledge of defect in title or lack of authority:

(i) sale by mercantile agent having possession of goods or document to title of goods with consent of owner and acting in ordinary course of business;
(ii) sale by one of joint owners in possession of goods with consent of other owners;
(iii) sale by seller in possession under a contract voidable for lack of free consent, before its rescission;
(iv) sale by seller in possession of goods or documents of title of goods after sale;
(v) sale by a buyer in possession before sale.

§4. Risk

665. In a contract for sale of specific goods,[630] if the goods have perished or are damaged at the time of sale without the knowledge of the seller, the contract is void; and if they perish or are damaged after an agreement to sell, the agreement is avoided.

Risk follows property, but this is a prima facie rule. Ownership of goods can be separated from the risk, and the parties can decide that risk shall pass at some other time, or on some condition not necessarily passing of property.

The parties may expressly provide for the transfer of risk. If they have not, the goods remain at the seller's risk until the property is transferred to the buyer, irrespective of whether the goods have been delivered or not,[631] unless delivery has been delayed by the fault of the buyer or the seller, in which case goods are at the risk of the party at fault.[632] Thus, in a contract for sale on FOB (Free on Board) basis, the liability of the seller ceases as soon as he has placed goods on board.[633]

§5. Conditions and Warranties

666. A stipulation[634] in a contract of sale may be a condition if it is essential to the main purpose of the contract. Its breach gives a right to treat the contract as repudiated. If the stipulation is collateral to the main purpose of the contract, it is a warranty. For its breach, the buyer cannot reject the goods or treat the contract as repudiated, but can claim only damages. Whether a stipulation in a contract of sale is a condition or a warranty depends in each case on the construction of the contract. A stipulation may be a condition, though called a warranty in the contract. The buyer can waive the condition or elect to treat a breach of condition as a breach of warranty. Conditions and warranties may be express; otherwise they are implied by

630. Specific goods are goods identified and agreed upon at the time a contract of sale is made.
631. Section 26 of the Sale of Goods Act.
632. *Phulchand Exports Ltd v. OOO Patriot* 2012 AIR SCW 30, (2011) 10 SCC 300.
633. *Contship Container Lines Ltd v. D K Lall* AIR 2010 SC 1704.
634. See s. 12 of the Sale of Goods Act.

law.[635] For a breach of warranty by the seller, the buyer can set up the breach of warranty in diminution of the price or may sue the seller for damages for breach of warranty.[636]

A buyer is entitled to damages on breach of both conditions and warranties. But where a condition is broken, he has the option of the remedy of treating the contract as repudiated and rejecting the goods, provided he has not accepted the goods.

Conditions and warranties may be express. The Sale of Goods Act provides of certain conditions and warranties which will be implied unless a different intention appears from the contract. These are as follows:

667. As to title, enjoyment, possession – In every contract of sale there is:

(i) an implied condition given by the seller that he has a right to sell the goods;
(ii) an implied warranty that the buyer shall have and enjoy quiet possession of the goods; and
(iii) an implied warranty that the goods are free from any charge or encumbrance.

These conditions and warranties will apply only if the contract shows a different intention. The buyer buying goods sold in execution of decrees takes the risk of the execution warrant turning out invalid.

668. As to quality of goods – Where goods are sold by description, there is an implied condition that goods will correspond with the description and that they shall be of merchantable quality, that is, immediately saleable under the description by which they are known in the market, or that the goods fit for the ordinary purpose for which such goods are used. The condition relating to description affects the nature of the article, rather than its quality.

Where goods are sold by sample, the goods must correspond to the sample and be free from defects rendering them unmerchantable, and the buyer must have an opportunity to compare the goods with the sample.

Goods sold by sample and description must correspond to both.

669. Cavaet emptor – Even where the goods correspond with the description, a question arises whether the buyer is entitled to reject the goods or takes the risk of their quality or condition if they are of inferior quality, are damaged, or are unfit for his intended purpose. The Sale of Goods Act adopts the common law rule of *caveat emptor*, and states the exception. A buyer must rely on his own skill and judgment and purchase at his own risk, except when there is fraud. Otherwise he may require an express warranty from the seller if he does not wish to take the risk. The Act, therefore, clearly provides that there is no implied warranty or condition as to the quality or fitness of the goods for any particular purpose.

There are three exceptions to this rule:

635. See ss 13–17 of the Sale of Goods Act.
636. Section 59 of the Sale of Goods Act.

(i) there is an implied condition that the goods shall be fit for the buyer's purpose where (a) the buyer makes known to the seller the purpose for which the goods are required; (b) the buyer relies on the skill and judgment of the seller; and (c) goods are of a description ordinarily dealt in by that seller;
(ii) there is an implied condition that the goods will be of merchantable quality where the goods are bought by description from a seller who deals in goods of that description;
(iii) implied condition or warranty as to quality or fitness will apply by usage of trade.

§6. Remedies of the Unpaid Seller

670. A seller is unpaid so long as he has not received the whole price or if the buyer has given him a bill of exchange or negotiable instrument for the price, and it has been dishonoured.

I. Rights to Price

671. An unpaid seller has the right to recover the price of goods with interest.

II. Rights about Goods

672. He also has the following rights in respect of the goods.

A. Right of Lien

673. The seller can retain possession of the goods sold until the payment of price, if the goods have not been sold on credit, and if sold on credit, the term of credit has expired. He can also retain the goods if the buyer becomes insolvent,[637] which can be proved by the buyer's admission or by other sufficient proof that the buyer was unable to pay the price in reasonable time.

The seller loses the right of lien if the seller delivers the goods to the buyer, or to a carrier without reserving the right of disposal, or if the buyer lawfully obtains their possession. The right also comes to an end when the price is tendered. The seller cannot exercise the right if he has waived it, expressly or by implication. The right of lien is not affected by any sub-sale or pledge of goods by buyer unless the seller has assented.

The right extends only to the price and not other charges incurred by the seller. The right is only to retain the goods, and does not extend to their sale.

---

637. Section 2(8) of the Sale of Goods Act defines an 'insolvent' as one who has ceased to pay his debts in the ordinary course of business, or cannot pay his debts as they become due, whether he has committed an act of insolvency or not.

B. Right of Stoppage in Transit

674. Even after the unpaid seller has parted with possession of goods, he can stop them in transit (any time before the buyer takes delivery from a carrier), resume possession, and retain them until the price is paid or tendered. He can do so only when the buyer becomes insolvent, that is, unable to pay his debts as they become due.

This right enables the unpaid seller to gain priority in respect of the goods over the general creditors of the insolvent buyer. The carrier is also under an obligation to redeliver the goods to the unpaid seller. The seller can later also exercise power of reselling the goods.

Any sub-sale or pledge by the buyer does not affect the right, unless the seller has assented to it.

C. Right to Marshal Securities

675. If the buyer has pledged the goods, the unpaid seller can require the pledgee to satisfy the amount due to him from any other goods or securities of the buyer in the hands of the pledgee.[638]

D. Right of Resale

676. A seller can expressly reserve a right to resell the goods if the buyer commits default in paying the price. He has the right even after the property has passed to the buyer. Such resale rescinds the original contract of sale without affecting the seller's right to claim damages.

Otherwise than under such contract, an unpaid seller can sell the goods even after the property has passed to the buyer if:

(i) the goods are of a perishable nature; or
(ii) the seller has exercised his right of lien or stoppage in transit and given notice to the buyer of his intention of resale, and the buyer has not paid or tendered the price within reasonable time.

The seller must resell the goods in reasonable time, and if he has given notice, he can also recover from the buyer damages for loss caused by his breach. The buyer is not entitled to any profit occurring on resale.

A seller reselling having exercised his right of lien or stoppage in transit, confers on the buyer of such resale a good title to the goods as against the original buyer, even if the seller has not given notice of resale to the original buyer.

---

638. Section 53(2) of the Sale of Goods Act.

677. This right is independent of the right to sue for the price. The seller can decide not to sell the goods and to sue for the price, leaving the buyer to decide when to take delivery of goods lying with him.

E. Prior Charge of Unpaid Seller

678. A seller will have a charge over the goods sold for the price or any other amounts only if it has been created by express contract. If created, it will bind subsequent transferees of the goods, but not any bona fide transferee for value without notice.

III. Right to Rescind

679. The seller has the general right to rescind the contract if the buyer has repudiated the contract before the date of delivery.[639] This is the option available to any contracting party under the general principles of contract for repudiation of whole of the contract, to the extent is remains to be performed.

Mere default by the buyer to make payment does not entitle the seller to rescind. Nor is a sale rescinded by the mere exercise of the right of lien or stoppage in transit. The contract stands rescinded by the seller when he has, under powers given to him by the contract, resold the goods on the buyer's default.[640]

Where the contract gives to the seller this right to rescind the contract, it does not prejudice his right to claim damages.

§7. REMEDIES FOR BREACH OF CONTRACT

I. Seller's Rights

680. Sue for price – The seller can sue for the price if:

(i) the price has become payable; and
(ii) where property has passed to the buyer, the buyer wrongfully neglects or refuses to pay for the goods according to the terms of the contract; or
(iii) although the property has not passed to the buyer nor the goods appropriated to the contract, the price is payable on a specified day irrespective of delivery.

Interest on price – The seller is also entitled to interest as agreed, and in absence of contract, from date of tender of goods or the date on which the price was payable.

639. Section 60 of the Sale of Goods Act.
640. Section 54(4) of the Sale of Goods Act.

Damages for non-acceptance – If the buyer wrongfully neglects or refuses to accept and pay for the goods, the seller can sue him for damages for non-acceptance.

II. Buyer's Rights

681. Damages for non-delivery – The buyer can sue the seller for damages for non-delivery if the seller wrongfully neglects or refuses to deliver the goods to the buyer.

Specific performance – The buyer may sue for specific performance if specific or ascertained goods are not delivered, if compensation in money would not afford adequate relief, or of it is difficult to ascertain the actual damage caused. Specific performance is not granted if the goods are articles of commerce or are easily available in the market.[641]

Set-off against price – In case of a breach of warranty by the seller, the buyer can set up the loss arising out of breach of warranty against the price or may sue for damages.[642]

§8. Auction Sales

682. The Sale of Goods Act states special provisions for auction sales.[643] Each lot of goods put up for sale in an auction is deemed to be subject of a separate contract of sale. The sale is complete when the auctioneer announces it by the fall of hammer or any other mode. A bid can be withdrawn any time before such announcement. A seller cannot bid unless his right to bid is expressly reserved, nor his nominee or agent; nor can an auctioneer permit such bidding. An auction sale may be held subject to reserve price. If the seller uses pretended bidding to raise the price, the buyer can avoid the sale.

§9. Products Liability

683. Apart from liability for breach of warranty or condition, a person suffering loss caused by a defect in product can seek damages by showing that the trader or manufacturer is at fault.

Ordinarily, a buyer of goods has no recourse against the manufacturer for goods purchased from a seller or dealer. The buyer can enforce a warranty or guarantee given by a manufacturer in respect of goods he purchased from a dealer, which he does as a contractual remedy and subject to its terms. Apart from such contractual remedy, the buyer has recourse against the manufacturer in tort, especially that of negligence. Here the buyer sues the manufacturer to enforce a duty of care to avoid

641. See ss 10, 12 of the Specific Relief Act 1963.
642. Section 59 of the Sale of Goods Act.
643. Section 64 of the Sale of Goods Act.

foreseeable injury to others. The manufacturer will also be liable under the principles of strict liability in respect of goods hazardous to life.

684. The Consumer Protection Act 1986 gives to a consumer[644] remedies if the goods purchased suffer from any defect. A defect means any fault, imperfection, or shortcoming in the quality, quantity, potency, purity, or standard that is required to be maintained by or under any law for the time being in force or under any contract, express or implied, or as is claimed by the trader in any manner whatsoever in relation to any goods.[645] If the goods have a defect, the consumer can seek remedies against the seller and also its manufacturer, any packer, or any person who has assembled the goods or has put his mark on them. The consumer can seek refund of price.

But he can seek compensation only by proving negligence of the trader or manufacturer.[646] This liability arises only on proof of negligence. The consumer must show negligence, but negligence might be presumed from the nature of defect or the nature of circumstances in which the injury is caused by use of goods.

The Consumer Protection Act now provides that a complaint can be filed if goods hazardous to life and safety are being offered for sale in contravention of any safety standards or in circumstances that the trader could have known with due diligence that the goods so offered are unsafe to the public. The precise remedy that the consumer court can grant is not yet clear.

§10. Sale on Instalment

685. A hire-purchase is a transaction of hire at inception with an option to purchase. The possession of goods is delivered by its owner on condition that such person shall pay the agreed amount in periodical instalments. The ownership of goods will pass on payment of specified instalments, especially the last one. The 'buyer' has the option to terminate the agreement at any time before that time. The hirer is granted an option to buy, but is not, as under a contract of sale, under a legal obligation to do so. This option to terminate the agreement being reserved to the hirer is the true test of a hire-purchase agreement, and there is no compulsion to exercise it. A hire-purchase will often involve more than two parties, especially the financier who will finance the sale by the seller to the buyer.

It differs from an instalment sale, in which there is a binding obligation to buy, and hence the buyer can pass a good title to a purchaser or pledgee, dealing with him in good faith and without notice of rights of the true owner.[647]

644. A consumer means any person who buys goods under any system of purchase, but does not include a person buying goods for the purposes of resale, or one buying for a commercial purpose.
645. Section 2(f) of the Consumer Protection Act 1986.
646. Section 14 of the Consumer Protection Act 1986.
647. *K L Johar and Co v. Deputy Commercial Tax Officer* AIR 1965 SC 1082; *Instalment Supply Company v. STO Ahmedabad* AIR 1974 SC 1105.

686. Hire-purchase transactions are extensively used in transactions for purchase of motor vehicles, domestic appliances, and so on. However, there is no separate legislation dealing with these transactions.

The need for a separate law for hire-purchase transactions has been felt for a long time. This is because a buyer of goods requires protection against abuses prevalent in hire-purchase trading. The owner of goods also needs protection. An enactment made in 1972 was not brought into force, and was repealed in 2005. The Law Commission of India gave its 168th report recommending enactment of such legislation. Without such independent law, unfair terms, so widely prevalent in such transactions, are beyond challenge except under general principles of contract. Nor does the buyer have benefit of implied conditions and warranties available on sale, because the provisions of the Sale of Goods Act do not apply to hire-purchase transactions.

Chapter 5. Building Contracts, Hire of Work and Skills

§1. SERVICES

687. The term 'service' refers to a service of any description that is made available to potential users. It includes providing services in connection with the business of any industrial or commercial matters, such as banking, communication, education, financing, insurance, real estate, transport, storage, material treatment, processing, supply of electrical or other energy, boarding or lodging, housing construction, entertainment, amusement, repair, conveying of news or information, or advertising.[648]

I. Liability under a Contract for Supply of Services

688. Other than the law relating to consumer protection, there is no law specifically dealing with contracts for services. A contract for services is governed by the general principles of contract.

Under the Consumer Protection Act 1986, a person supplying services is liable to his consumer for any deficiency in services. The consumer can claim return of charges and can also claim compensation for any injury caused by negligence of the supplier.[649]

This Act is applicable only between consumers and suppliers of services to them. It is not applicable to services engaged or hired for commercial purposes.

II. Contract of Service and for Services

689. A difference is made between a contract of service and contract for services. Employees or servants in employment of their employers or masters are under a contract of service. They are subject to the command of their master as to the work and the manner in which they shall work. There is an obligation to obey the orders of the employer.

On the contrary, a contract for services is one in which the person rendering the service is an independent contractor, not subject to direct control in the performance of those services.

This difference is important, for example, to determine whether a copyrightable work created by an employee in the course of employment is owned by the employer. If an author has made a work in the course of his employment under a contract of service, the employer is the first owner of copyright in the work and not the author. This distinction has achieved importance under the law of consumer protection. The Consumer Protection Act 1986 applies to supply of services to consumers and specifically excludes from its operation a contract of personal service.

648. See various definitions under the Consumer Protection Act 1986, and the Trade Marks Act 1999.
649. See s. 14 of the Consumer Protection Act 1986.

III. Contract of Sale and Contract for Work and Labour

690. A contract of sale differs from a contract for work and labour. This distinction is a fine one, and quite often it falls on courts to decide the true nature of the transaction, especially to decide liability for sales tax or tax on works contracts.[650] The provisions in the Sale of Goods Act, especially those relating to implied conditions and warranties, would apply to a contract of sale of goods only.

The question whether a contract is for sale of goods (i.e., of material) or for applying work and labour on those materials, has often been raised in the highest courts in proceedings relating to payment of sales tax or works tax.[651] The court looks at the 'substance' of the transaction and not necessarily the form. If the contract is primarily one for supply of material at a price agreed, the work or service is being incidental to executing the contract, and the main object is transfer of ownership, it is a contract of sale. If the main purpose is applying work and labour on the article, it is a contract for work and labour. One important factor is whether the material has separate identity as a commercial article or obtains value only by doing work on it. Neither the ownership of material nor the relative value of the work or labour or skill applied is material. A meal supplied to a customer in a restaurant is a sale of goods, the element of service being subsidiary; but a meal supplied to a lodger or a resident hotel guest is part of a contract for services.

691. If goods are delivered to another for him to perform some work on the goods, it is a contract for bailment, that is, handing over goods for repairs. The bailee must take care of the goods as if they are his own and return them when the work is done. He can claim remuneration only if it is agreed, has a right of lien until it is paid, and can in any case claim expenses incurred by him for the purposes of the bailment.[652]

IV. Contract for Work and of Agency

692. An agent is to be distinguished from an independent contractor. The latter is entirely independent of any control or interference. He merely undertakes to produce a specified result, and for this he employs his own means. An agent is bound to exercise his authority in accordance with all lawful instructions given to him from time to time by his principal.[653] A person engaging an independent contractor is not liable to others in tort for acts of the latter or his servants.

650. *State of Gujarat v. Variety Body Builders* AIR 1976 SC 2108; *Hindustan Shipyard v. State of Andhra Pradesh* AIR 2000 SC 2411; *Kone Elevator India Pvt Ltd v. State of Tamil Nadu* 2014 AIR SCW 5362, (2014) 7 SCC 1.

651. State laws relating to tax on works contracts define works contract to include any agreement for carrying out for cash or for deferred payment or for any other valuable consideration, the building construction, manufacture, processing, fabrication, erection, installation, fitting out, improvement, modification, repair or commissioning of any movable or immovable property.

652. See para. 642 onwards.

653. *Lakshminarayan Ram Gopal and Sons Ltd v. Government of Hyderabad* AIR 1954 SC 364.

§2. BUILDING CONTRACTS

693. The term 'building contract' has not been defined by statute. It differs from other contract in that it deals with various types of contracts for the construction of buildings. Nor is there any special statute regulating the rights and obligations of parties under a building contract. These are governed by the general principles of contract. Some principles affecting such contracts have been laid down in case law.

A building contract, even with two parties – the owner and the building contractor, would involve and affect other persons in its performance. This poses a challenge to the doctrine of privity of contract.

I. Form

694. Building contracts to be executed for the government, organizations, or bodies such as trusts, will usually be made with a building contractor whose tender for that work has been accepted. Contract documents in such a case will be many and will be usually listed in the formal document signed by the parties. Many standard forms of building and engineering contracts are used in India, in government and in private contracts.

Whether it is for the owner to supply material to the builder, or the builder to procure it, depends on the terms of the individual contract.

The contracted building is rarely completed in time. Even where the parties have stipulated that time shall be of essence of the contract, it is presumed to be not of essence, especially where it provides for extension of time or levy of penalty for delay.[654] It is usual to provide for extension of time in stipulated circumstances,[655] to have provisions for liquidated damages for any delay in completion, or to provide for increased rates to cover rise in prices of materials during that period.

695. A building contract may be of various types:

A lump sum contract is a contract to complete the whole work for a lump sum amount. In this case the contractor is not entitled to payment until he has completed the entire work, that is, substantially. Any payment, if made during progress of the work is an 'advance' payment.

An item rate contract or a *value contract* is one in which the price to be paid is to be ascertained by measurement or various parts of the work, and the valuation of work is done with reference to a schedule of prices given in the contract. This is especially suitable for works for which the extent or scope of work are unknown or liable to alteration.

Cost plus percentage contract is one in which the owner contracts to pay the contractor the actual cost of labour and materials consumed in the works and overhead charges, and a percentage of profit based on that amount.

654. *Hind Construction Contractors v. State of Maharashtra* AIR 1979 SC 720.
655. *Anand Construction Works v. State of Bihar* AIR 1973 Cal 550.

II. Obligations and Rights

696. A building contract consists of reciprocal promises,[656] obliging both parties to fulfil their promises agreed expressly or impliedly, and in the order in which these arise under the terms of the contract.

III. Owner's Liabilities

697. The owner must extend full cooperation to the building contractor in the construction work. He must do the following:

(i) give possession of the site or allow the contractor entry in the premises, as is the case;
(ii) prepare and supply plans, drawings, and designs;
(iii) appoint architects, engineers, surveyors, and so on;
(iv) permit the contractor to carry out the work;
(v) give instructions from time to time;
(vi) not interfere in the progress of the work, planning and progress of the work being privilege of the contractor;
(vii) supply materials for the work, where so agreed;
(viii) make payments as agreed.

IV. Contractor's Liabilities

698. The building contractor must complete the work. His other obligations are as follows:

(i) to do the work undertaken with care and skill in a good and workmanlike manner;
(ii) if he is to supply materials, to use good and proper materials;
(iii) ensure the work and materials are suitable for the purpose for which they are required;
(iv) to maintain continuous and steady progress of work and complete the work within the stipulated time.

699. The contractor is liable to rectify defective work at his cost where he has not constructed according to the drawings, specifications, and directions. If he agrees to build a work for a specified purpose, it is implied that the completed structure will be reasonably fit for the intended purpose. Such contract may contain clauses making the contractor liable for remedying the defects even after completion of the work. Where any guarantee period is named in the contract, his

656. See paras 341–345, 499–504.

obligation extends only to defects discovered during this period, but not for any wear and tear. Even in the absence of any defect maintenance clauses, the contractor is liable for rectifying defects after completion. An owner does not waive his right to claim damages by taking possession of the works. If the defects are patent, the owner must take objection immediately.

A building contract will also provide that the opinion of the architect or engineer about improper work shall be final. The contractor will be liable for defects in the work even though the architect or engineer has inspected the work, unless the particular matter was brought to the engineer's attention and he gave approval. In any case, the contractor is always liable for latent defects that the architect or engineer was unaware of when he gave approval.

700. Housing is a service, and a contractor will be liable under the Consumer Protection Act 1986 for any deficiency in providing the service.

V. Variation

701. An element of uncertainty is inevitable in building contracts. Despite all planning and precautions, the scope and extent of the work requires changes in complex works as well as variation in the quantity of work and changes in drawings, designs, and specifications. Later, unforeseen events may also require changes. A clause enabling variations or alterations in the work is usually found in these contracts. The terms may also limit the range for variations.

Any additional work ordered by the owner beyond the original framework of the contract, if carried out by the contractor, is a new contract. Additional work required in the performance of the contract and falling within the original terms is subject to the same terms and conditions.

VI. Payment

702. The precise terms of payment will be provided in the contract. It is usual for payments to be made from time to time in instalments as certified by the architect or engineer appointed by the owner. The architect or engineer must nevertheless function independently while certifying payments or quality. A contractor who has completed the work according to contract can recover payment even if the architect or engineer has refused to certify payment.

VII. Resolution of Disputes

703. An arbitration clause is usually found in building contracts. This enables dispute resolution by an expert in building construction.

VIII. Breach and Rights Thereafter

704. An owner cannot terminate the contract unless (i) he has that power to do so under the contract, which must be exercised in the precise manner and circumstances provided in the contract; and (ii) if the contractor has repudiated his obligations, that is, refused to perform the contract in its entirety. Occasions to terminate the contract will be rare.

Often breaches are smaller, resulting in some loss or delay in completion. Compensation may be liquidated otherwise it will be determined by the arbitrator or court. Difficulties, strikes, unexpected expense or rise in prices, or non-availability of materials, does not provide any excuse to performance. Such events might be managed according to any force majeure clauses usually found in such contracts.

Ordinarily a contract requiring constant supervision cannot be specifically enforced. Yet, a contract for construction of any building or execution of any work on land can be specifically enforced where (i) the work has been precisely described; (ii) the plaintiff has substantial interest in the performance of the contract; and (iii) the contractor is in possession of property in pursuance of the contract.[657]

IX. Role of Architect: Responsibility

705. The owner will be required to have a qualified architect to supervise the construction, not only to prepare plans and specifications and to check and supervise the execution of the work, but also to certify its quality, that it has been completed according to the contract, and that it satisfies the requirements of the building regulations. He is not a party to the building contract, but may have a separate contract with the owner. Supervision of an architect is a mandatory requirement of building and town-planning regulations of local authorities. The architect will also in most contracts certify the payments of bills submitted by the building contractor. He might also be required to settle and decide differences between the owner and the contractor.

Parties can stipulate that the decision of an architect or engineer regarding specified matters like quality of materials, workmanship, financial claims, and so on, shall be binding on them. Parties are then bound by his determination.[658] The person so appointed as authority must act judicially, and the court, when the matter comes before it, can always examine whether such officer has acted judicially.[659]

X. Subcontracts

706. A contractor is required to appoint subcontractors to carry out some works. He may have to engage contractors nominated by the owner. The owner can retain

657. See s. 14(3)(c) of the Specific Relief Act 1963.

658. *South India Railway Co Ltd v. S M Bhashyam Naidu* AIR 1935 Mad 356; *Chief Administrator Dandakaranya Project v. Prabartak Commercial Corporation Ltd* AIR 1975 MP 152.

659. *Heavy Electricals (India) Ltd v. Pannalal Devchand Malviya* AIR 1973 MP 7.

control over the work if the contract requires the consent of the owner for any subletting or assignment of the work. A contractor who sublets or assigns despite such prohibition commits breach sufficient to entitle the owner to terminate the contract. The extent to which the contractor can sublet the work would depend on the terms of the contract. The contactor is liable for the acts of his subcontractor.

707. Even where subcontract is properly appointed, there is no contractual relationship between the owner and subcontractor, and neither of them can sue the other.[660] The owner can make payment directly to the subcontractor for his work only if the contract so provides.

§3. Regulation of Promotion of Building Schemes

708. Land and buildings is a subject on which only states can make laws. Many states have made laws for regulation and control of promotion of building schemes. These laws are made for protecting the interest of purchasers of units or flats in such schemes.

Such laws are usually applicable to urban areas. The promoter is the person who causes the building scheme to be constructed and the units disposed of to prospective purchasers of such units. He may be the owner of the land, a builder, or a developer of property.

Very soon, the Real Estate (Regulation and Development) Bill is expected to be enacted into law. It seeks to provide for a uniform regulatory environment across states, protect consumer interests, help speedy adjudication of disputes and ensure orderly growth of the real estate sector. It makes provisions for setting up a Real Estate Regulatory Authority and for registration of real estate projects and registration of real estate agents with it.

709. The promoter will be liable to disclose his authority and title to construct and sell or dispose of units, and to show all papers to the prospective purchasers. He must make an agreement for the disposal, and the law can provide for a form of agreement. He is liable to construct under the supervision of an architect, and according to plans sanctioned by local authority. He is bound to construct according to agreed specifications. He must hand over possession of the unit as agreed, otherwise, at the option of the buyer, return the price with interest. He will be liable for all defects in the construction of the building or the unit for the period specified in the statute. He is liable to obtain a certificate of occupancy from the local authority.

All these terms are not contractual, but statutory, and the promoter cannot contract out of them. A promoter thus cannot exclude his liability to repair defects arising after completion of the flat.

660. *Raj Kumar Bahal v. Food Corporation of India* AIR 1990 Raj 64.

Chapter 6. Lease, Commercial and Agricultural Leases

§1. Lease Belongs to Law of Property

710. A lease involves transfer of interest in property by the lessor.[661] Leasehold rights, therefore, are property and not mere personal obligations. A lessee can, therefore, transfer his leasehold rights in any manner property can be transferred, that is, sale (called assignment), lease (called sub-lease) or mortgage. A lease is good against the whole world, irrespective of notice, and is not affected by any subsequent transfer of property by the lessor.

All property, movable or immovable, can be leased. Chapter V of the Transfer of Property Act 1882 gives detailed provisions about leases of immovable property. Lease of movables is possible in Indian law. Although there is no statute governing leases of movables or the relationship of parties to a lease, these will be governed by similar principles. A 'financial' lease is made as a long-term lease on fixed assets. Made primarily as a financial arrangement, and for tax benefits it enables, such a lease is a disguised way of purchasing an asset with the help of a loan.

Legislations are in force in almost all states for protection of lessees of premises in buildings in urban areas and of agricultural lessees.

§2. The General Law

711. A lease of immovable property is a transfer of a right to enjoy such property, made for a certain time, express or implied, or in perpetuity, in consideration of a price paid or promised, or of money, a share of crops, service, or any other thing of value, to be rendered periodically or on specified occasions to the transferor by the transferee, who accepts the transfer on such terms.[662] The words 'transfer of a right to enjoy property' indicates that all rights of ownership are not transferred. It creates a right and interest in the enjoyment of the leased property, and the tenant is entitled to remain in possession of the property until the lease is duly terminated and eviction takes place by law.[663]

I. Formation

712. A lease of immovable property from year to year, or for any term exceeding one year or reserving a yearly rent, can be made only by a registered instrument. All other leases of immovable property may be made either by a registered instrument or by oral agreement accompanied by delivery of possession. Because a lease involves covenants by the lessor, as well as the lessee, a lease deed in writing must be signed by both.

661. See s. 105 of the Transfer of Property Act 1882.
662. Section 105 of the Transfer of Property Act 1882.
663. *Delhi Development Authority v. Durga Chand Kaushish* AIR 1973 SC 2609.

II. Duration

713. In India, a lease may be in perpetuity. A lease may be created for a fixed term or may be made year to year or month to month or with reference to any period of time. If the lessee continues in possession of the property after the period of term is over, it is considered as under the original deed. In the absence of any contract to the contrary, a lease of agricultural or manufacturing purposes is a lease from year to year terminable with a six-month notice expiring at the end of the year, and a lease for other purposes is a lease from month to month, terminable by notice of fifteen days expiring with the end of the month of tenancy.

The lease may provide for renewal, requiring a new lease, or for an extension.

III. Termination

714. A lease ends when its term expires, the interest of the lessor and lessee merge, or the lessee surrenders his interest to the lessor by mutual agreement. A lease from year to year or month to month can be terminated by notice as stated earlier.

715. The lessor can terminate the lease by forfeiture in the following circumstances:

(i) The lessee breaks an express condition that provides that the lessor may re-enter on breach thereof; or
(ii) the lessee sets up a title in a third person or claims title in himself; or
(iii) the lessee is adjudicated an insolvent and the lease provides that the lessor may re-enter on the happening of such event.

In these three cases, the lessor must give written notice of termination.

716. The lessee is relieved from forfeiture if the lease has been terminated for non-payment of rent, and the lessee has in the suit for possession paid the rent with interest and costs. In other cases, the lessor must give a notice specifying the breach, and requiring the lessee to remedy the breach. Forfeiture will follow only if the lessee fails to remedy the breach within reasonable time. There is no relief from forfeiture if the lessee has broken an express condition prohibiting assignment or transfer of the lessee's interest.

If the lessor accepts rent after he has right to forfeit, he waives his right to terminate.

Forfeiture also annuls all under-leases.

IV. Rights and Obligations of the Lessor and the Lessee

717. In the absence of contract or local usage to the contrary, the following are the rights and obligations of the lessor and the lessee:

718. Possession and use: The lessor is bound to put the lessee in possession of the leased property. If the property is destroyed or becomes unfit for use on account of fire, tempest, flood, violence, or other irresistible force, the lease does not automatically terminate; the lessee has the option to avoid it.

A lessee is bound to keep the property in as good condition as it was in at the time when he was put in possession of it, and on the termination of the lease to restore the property in that condition. He must make use of the property as a person would of his own and for the purpose for which it was let.

719. Rent: A lessee is bound to pay or to tender the agreed rent at the proper time and place. The lessee must seek the lessor and pay rent. So long as the lessee pays the rent agreed and performs the other terms, the lessee is entitled to possession of property without interruption. If the lessor fails to make any payment that he is bound to make, the lessee can pay it and recover it or deduct it from the rent with interest. He can also recover or deduct from rent any amount spent by him for repairs that the lessor is bound to carry out.

720. Disclosure: The lessor must disclose hidden defects as would affect use of property by the lessee. The lessee is bound to disclose to the lessor any fact about the property he is aware of, and the lessor is not aware, that materially increases the value of the property. A lessee being in actual possession of property naturally becomes aware of any encroachment on the property or proceedings relating to the property and must inform the lessor of such events.

721. Assignment: A lessor can restrict the right of a lessee to assign or transfer in any manner his leasehold rights. In the absence of any such restraint a lessee is entitled to transfer, mortgage, or lease further his leasehold rights, fully or in part.

A lessor can transfer the property. This has the effect of transferring to the transferee all his rights, but not the liabilities, unless the lessee assents. If the lessee pays rent to the lessor without knowledge of the transfer, he need not again pay rent to the transferee.

§3. Protected Tenants in Urban Areas

722. Migration to urban areas after the two World Wars created a shortage of accommodation and prompted legislatures to enact laws to control rent and prevent unreasonable eviction. Although these were supposed to be temporary measures, they still survive in all states in India. These state laws apply to premises in urban areas and building or structures let out for residential, business, industrial, commercial, trade, storage purposes. Some laws might not apply to letting of open land. Though the general scheme of the state laws will be similar, they differ in the types of accommodation covered by them, the grounds available to a landlord to evict the tenant, the control mechanisms, authorities, and so on.

723. The provisions of these laws govern the relationship between the landlord and tenant, also overriding the provisions of the express lease. There is, therefore, a new and peculiar class of tenants referred to as statutory tenants, that is, those residing beyond the determination of lease by reason of protection of these laws. The rights of a statutory tenant are not heritable, except in the manner provided in these laws.

These laws would generally provide that the landlord:

(i) cannot contract, demand, or realize rent more than the standard or fair rent fixed according to the provisions of the laws, which in the event of dispute will be fixed by the court or other authority;
(ii) cannot evict a tenant from the premises so long as the tenant is paying the standard rent and is observing the other terms of the tenancy;
(iii) irrespective of the agreed period of the lease or the agreed mode of its termination, cannot evict the tenant except by obtaining an order of possession passed by the court or other authority. Such an order will be passed only on certain grounds recognized for this purpose, that is, nuisance by tenant, requirement of landlord, the tenant acquiring separate accommodation, non-payment of rent, change of use, or unauthorized construction by tenant. The tenant has relief from forfeiture if he pays rent;
(iv) cannot cut off or disturb the essential services or supplies necessary for enjoyment of the premises;
(v) must keep the property in repairs and good condition.

724. The tenant obtains considerable protection from eviction and in the fixation of rent, but he is subject to disabilities. He cannot assign his rights or sublet the premises without the consent of the landlord. He is bound to use the premises for the purposes for which it is let. These laws also protect sub-tenants.

The tenant cannot contract out of the provisions of these laws that are made for his protection,[664] but a landlord can waive his rights.[665]

725. Some laws also regulate the letting of premises. An owner can be compelled to make available premises on rent to prospective tenants. The competent authority will have the power to pass orders of requisition and allotment to make premises so available.

726. Many owners of premises give their premises on license. A licensee has a personal right to occupy the premises. Some rent control laws have given protection to licensees too equal to that of a tenant. However, there is recognition that the laws must enable more freedom to the landlord and facilitate eviction. Some states have made it easy for licensors to evict licensees occupying premises. This step has enabled growth of investment in the housing sector. Some laws make easy eviction of tenants where the landlord requires the premises after retirement from service, is a retired member of the armed forces, and the like.

---

664. *Waman Shrinivas Kini v. Ratilal Bhagwandas and Co* AIR 1959 SC 689.
665. *Murlidhar Agarwal v. State of Uttar Pradesh* AIR 1974 SC 1924; *Lachoo Mal v. Radhey Shyam* AIR 1971 SC 2213.

§4. AGRICULTURAL TENANCIES

727. Even when the Transfer of Property Act 1882 was enacted, it provided that the provisions affecting leases would not apply to agricultural leases.[666] The state governments can apply any of these provisions to agricultural leases. Such leases were exempted because they were largely regulated by usage and governed by local or provincial laws that protected tenants.

728. Agriculture and land are subjects on which only state legislatures can make laws. Laws affecting agricultural tenancies are in force in each State in India. These laws are aimed at improving the economic and social conditions of farmers and ensuring full and efficient use of land for agriculture; such laws include the following provisions:

(i) restrict transfer of agricultural lands;
(ii) make general provisions regarding tenancies and their duration;
(iii) confer tenancy rights on cultivators;
(iv) prohibit assignment or subletting;
(v) give security of tenure to a tenant;
(vi) fix amount of rent;
(vii) prohibit receiving rent in terms of service or labour;
(viii) consolidate holdings to make them economically viable;
(ix) facilitate ownership of land to the tillers by eliminating absentee landlords.

666. Section 117 of the Transfer of Property Act 1882.

Chapter 7. Compromises

729. A compromise is an arrangement by which parties in dispute settle or agree to settle their disputes or differences by abandoning or their respective claims against each other. It is a contract and can and is required to be enforced as such. It does not have the effect of res judicata.

The principles of contract law also apply to compromise of disputes or differences made by parties pending litigation.[667] At the request of parties, a decree might be drawn in terms of the compromise. Such a compromise can be challenged on any grounds on which a contract might be challenged as void or voidable under the Indian Contract Act. This can be done by approaching the same court and establishing there is no compromise; it cannot be done in any other proceeding, appeal or revision.[668]

730. A compromise requires consideration, which takes the form of forbearance to sue. The concession may consist in giving up some liability existing or reasonably supposed to exist, or a reasonable claim, though doubtful. The basis of a compromise is that the party making it has a chance of succeeding in his claim and bona fide believes that he has a fair chance of success.[669] His forbearance is then good consideration.

A family arrangement is a settlement of existing or future disputes regarding property amongst members of a family. It is sufficient consideration if the arrangement is intended to preserve or promote peace among members, or avoid litigation or possible future disputes.[670]

731. Public interest requires that litigation be discouraged and that parties settle or compromise any dispute. Yet, any compromise must occur with full information and no party must take undue advantage of the other.

If a compromise were easily attacked for mistake, that would defeat the very purpose of making a compromise. Where it is based on settlement of doubtful rights or rights based on doubtful law or doubtful construction of a document, mistake of such rights is not grounds for setting it aside. But it may be set aside for mistake as to subject matter of agreement.

732. Settlement of criminal proceedings depends on whether the offence involved is compoundable.[671] Where the offence is non-compoundable, any compromise would be unlawful as tending to stifle prosecution.[672]

---

667. See Order 23 rule 3 of the Code of Civil Procedure.

668. *Pushpa Devi Bhagat v. Rajinder Singh* AIR 2006 SC 2628; *R Rajanna v. S R Venkataswamy* AIR 2015 SC 706 (not separate suit).

669. *Poornammal v. R Srinivasarangan* AIR 1956 SC 162.

670. *Kale v. Deputy Director of Consolidation* AIR 1976 SC 807.

671. The Code of Criminal Procedure lists offences which are compoundable by the parties, others which are compoundable only with permission of the court, and yet other serious offences which cannot be compounded. See s. 320 of the Code of Criminal Procedure 1973.

672. *Ouseph Poulo v. Catholic Union Bank Ltd* AIR 1965 SC 166.

Chapter 8. Suretyship

§1. Contract of Guarantee

733. A contract of suretyship, termed as a contract of guarantee in Indian law,[673] is a contract to perform the promise or discharge the liability of a third person in case of his default.

A contract of guarantee involves three parties – the 'surety' who gives the guarantee, the 'principal debtor' in respect of whose default the guarantee is given, and the 'creditor' to whom the guarantee is given; but it is really a contract binding the surety to the creditor. It is accessory to the main obligation of the principal debtor to creditor, which may be contractual or any other legal obligation. The surety usually undertakes personal liability, but may also charge his property. Anything done or any promise made for the benefit of the principal debtor is sufficient consideration for the surety's promise, for example, money lent or goods supplied to the principal debtor or even forbearance to sue.

734. A guarantee may be oral or written. It is not a contract *uberrima fidei*. As between the creditor and surety, either the surety knows the risk or is deemed to have ascertained it, being acquainted with the principal debtor. A guarantee obtained by misrepresentation of the creditor is invalid.

735. If the principal debtor is a minor, the surety is liable as a principal debtor; the surety's contract is not then collateral, but the principal contract. Where a contract is *ultra vires* (beyond the powers) of a company, its director who gives any guarantee remains liable to the creditor.

I. Contract of Indemnity and of Guarantee

736. A contract by which one party promises to save the other from loss caused to him by the conduct of the promisor himself or by the conduct of any other person, is termed a 'contract of indemnity'.[674] Such obligation to indemnify may arise out of contract, express or implied, from an obligation resulting from the relation of the parties, or by statute.

The promisor undertakes an original and independent obligation to indemnify, unlike a guarantee in which the promisor answers for the default of another person primarily liable to the promisee. Where a person undertakes to be directly liable and not collaterally or undertakes to discharge the liability in any event, the contract is one of indemnity. Where the promisor promises to indemnify the promisee against losses, claims, damages and costs suffered is an indemnity, though called a guarantee.[675]

---

673. Sections 126–147 of the Indian Contract Act deal with contracts of guarantee.

674. Section 124 of the Indian Contract Act.

675. *State Bank of India v. Mula Sahakari Sakhar Karkhana Ltd* AIR 2007 SC 2361.

Whether the contract is one of guarantee or of indemnity is thus a question of construction in each case. If it is a guarantee (i) the surety need not be called on to pay unless the principal debtor has committed a default; and (ii) the surety is entitled to the rights of discharge in certain circumstances described in the following section.

II. Relationship between the Creditor and Surety

A. *Privileged Debtor*

737. A surety is a privileged and protected creditor. The conditions of liability must be strictly fulfilled to make him liable. This is because he usually receives no benefit in the transaction. A surety will not be liable beyond the agreed limit of liability, nor beyond any date fixed before which the guarantee must be enforced.[676] Contracts of guarantee are also strictly construed.

B. *Discharge of Surety*

738. A surety is liable for the precise default or liability of the principal debtor. Any act of the creditor that changes this entitles the surety to a discharge, because 'this is not what the surety agreed'.

The Indian Contract Act provides for a number of circumstances discharging the liability of a surety.[677] The precise conditions for discharge and extent may vary in each case. The circumstances of discharge must be proved by the creditor. A surety is discharged under the following conditions:

(i) The creditor and principal debtor vary their contract without the consent of the surety.
(ii) The creditor, without his consent, unconditionally releases the principal debtor, or acts in a manner as to discharge the principal debtor.
(iii) The creditor contracts with the principal debtor to make a composition with him, promises to give him time, or promises not to sue him, (but mere forbearance to sue does not discharge the surety).
(iv) The creditor acts in a manner inconsistent with the rights of the surety or omits to do any act that his duty to the surety requires him to do, and as a result the surety's eventual remedy against the principal debtor is thereby impaired, for example, where by negligence of the creditor a security given by the principal debtor is lost.[678]
(v) The creditor parts with any security he had against the principal debtor at the time of making the contract of guarantee, regardless of whether the surety knew about the existence of such security.

---

676. *State of Maharashtra v. M N Kaul* AIR 1967 SC 1634.
677. Sections 133–139 and 141 of the Indian Contract Act.
678. *State of Madhya Pradesh v. Kaluram* AIR 1967 SC 1105.

A surety can waive all or any of the above rights.[679]

C. Revocation by Surety

739. A surety cannot revoke a guarantee, unless it is a continuing guarantee (extending to a series of transactions) that can be revoked as to future transactions only, unless the surety has expressly agreed that the guarantee shall not be revoked or cancelled.[680] Such a guarantee is also revoked by his death.

D. Creditor's Option to Sue Surety Directly

740. The creditor can sue both the principal debtor and the surety, or at his option, any of them, or even any one of the co-sureties. The surety's liability is conditional upon default by the principal debtor, but is immediate. No sooner than the principal debtor defaults, the creditor can sue the surety directly without first proceeding against the principal debtor,[681] unless the contract provides otherwise. A decree passed jointly against the surety and the principal debtor can be executed against the surety, and the surety cannot insist that the creditor first exhaust remedies against the principal debtor.[682]

III. Relationship between the Principal Debtor and Surety

741. A surety's liability is co-extensive with that of the principal debtor, but it may be limited or restricted by contract. It does not arise unless the principal debtor has made default. Upon such default, he is immediately liable to the full extent of his obligation. Unless the contract so requires, the surety is not entitled to any notice of the default, nor is the creditor liable to first call on the principal debtor to pay. However, an arbitration agreement between the creditor, debtor and one surety does not bind another surety.[683]

742. After the surety has paid to the creditor the amount due under the guarantee, the surety has a right of indemnity against the principal debtor, and to recover any sum he has paid rightfully under the guarantee. This right is not affected by the discharge of the principal debtor by the creditor.

No sooner than the surety has paid the guaranteed debt or performed whatever he was liable for, does he get subrogated to all rights that the creditor had against the principal debtor. This is automatic and does not require any transfer or written

679. *H B Basavaraj v. Canara Bank* (2010) 12 SCC 458.
680. *Sita Ram Gupta v. Punjab National Bank* AIR 2008 SC 2416.
681. *State Bank of India v. Indexport Registered* AIR 1992 SC 1740.
682. *Bank of Bihar Ltd v. Damodar Prasad* AIR 1969 SC 297.
683. *S N Prasad v. Monnet Finance Ltd* AIR 2011 SC 442.

assignment.[684] An indemnifier cannot sue in his own name under his contract of indemnity unless he has an assignment from the creditor; but a surety can.[685]

IV. Relationship between Sureties

743. Where a debt or duty is guaranteed by two or more persons, they are co-sureties.[686] If one of them pays more than his share of the guaranteed debt, he can compel contribution from the others, whether under the same contract or different contracts, and whether he knew or did not know at the time of making the guarantee about other co-sureties. If the creditor releases one of them, it does not discharge the others. The released co-surety continues to be liable to others. If the co-sureties are bound in different sums, they are liable to pay equally as far as their agreed obligation permits.

684. 2. *Amrit Lal Goverdhan Lalan v. State Bank of Travancore* AIR 1968 SC 1432.
685. *K V Periyamianna Marakkayar v. Banians & Co* AIR 1926 Mad 544.
686. Sections 146–147 of the Indian Contract Act.

Chapter 9. Pledge

§1. Bailment and Pledge

744. The bailment of goods as security for payment of a debt or performance of a promise is called 'pledge'.[687] This is on contract that when the debt is paid or the promise is performed, the goods bailed shall be returned or otherwise disposed of according to the direction of the pawnor. The bailor is the 'pawnor'. The bailee is the 'pawnee'.

The ingredients of a pledge are as follows:

(i) the property pledged should be actually or constructively delivered to the pawnee;
(ii) such bailment is by way of security;
(iii) the security is for payment of a debt or performance of a promise; and
(iv) when the debt is paid or promise performed, the goods are to be returned to the pawnor, or disposed of according to his directions.

I. Pawnee's Right

745. The pawnee does not become owner, but has the right to possess, and is said to have a special property. The Supreme Court states:[688]

> [T]he pawnbroker has special property rights in the goods pledged, a right higher than a mere right of detention of goods but a right lesser than general property right in the goods. … [T]he pawnor at the time of pledge not only transfers to the pawnee, the special right in the pledge but also passes on his right to transfer the general property right in the pledge in the event of the pledge remaining unredeemed resulting in the sale of the pledge. … [T]he pawnee who holds not only the absolute special property right in the pledge but also the conditional general property interest in the pledge, the condition being that he can pass on that general property only in the event of the pledge being brought to sale.

II. Delivery of Goods as Security

746. Delivery of the goods under a pledge and advance of money need not be simultaneous. The delivery may be made subsequent to the advance in pursuance of the contract of pledge.[689] Delivery is necessary to complete a pledge; it may be actual or constructive.

687. Section 172 of the Indian Contract Act.
688. *Karnataka Pawnbrokers' Association v. State of Karnataka* AIR 1999 SC 201.
689. *Lallan Prasad v. Rahmat Ali* AIR 1967 SC 1322.

III. Pledge by Persons Not Owners

747. One of several joint owners of goods in sole possession thereof with the consent of the rest may make a valid pledge of the goods. Other cases in which a person who is not the owner of goods may make a valid pledge thereof are (i) a seller left in possession after sale; and (ii) a buyer to whom possession has been delivered before payment of the price.[690]

§2. Rights and Duties of Pawnor and Pawnee

748. If the pawnor makes default in payment of the debt, or performance, at the stipulated time, of the promise in respect of which the goods were pledged, the pawnee may bring a suit against the pawnor on the debt or promise and retain the goods pledged as a collateral security, or he may sell the thing pledged on giving the pawnor a reasonable notice of sale.[691] The rights to retain or sell the pawn are not concurrent, but the rights to sue and to sell are concurrent rights.

A pawnee is entitled to retain the goods for expenses incurred by him for possession or preservation of the goods, in addition to the payment or the debt or performance of promise and the interest on the debt. The pawnee's right is presumed to extend to subsequent advances. The pawnee is entitled to receive from the pawnor any extraordinary expenses incurred for preservation of the pledged goods (but no right to retain the goods).

Once the pawnee, after reasonable notice to the pawnor of his intention to sell the goods pawned, sells them under section 176 of Contract Act, the pawnor's right of redelivery is extinguished.

The pawnor's right to redeem continues until the sale,[692] that is, at any moment up to the time of exercise by the pawnee of his power of sale by entering into a valid contract of sale.

The pawnee is not entitled to any interest on the principal amount from the date on which the pawnor seeks release of the goods pledged by satisfying the debt.

After sale the pawnee can recover the balance of the loan unsatisfied on the sale of the pledge.

749. In pledge, being essentially a bailment, the pawnee is bound to take care of the goods bailed to him as a man of ordinary prudence would under similar circumstances, take of his own goods of the same bulk, quality, and value as the goods bailed.[693] If he has taken such care and loses the goods without his fault, he can still recover the debt, without responsibility for the loss, and the loss of goods would fall on the owner.[694]

---

690. Section 30 of the Sale of Goods Act.
691. Section 176 of the Indian Contract Act.
692. See s. 177 of the Indian Contract Act; see also *Lallan Prasad v. Rahmat Ali* AIR 1967 SC 1322.
693. See s. 151 of the Indian Contract Act.
694. *Rampal Ramchand Agarwal v. Gourishankar Hanuman Prasad* AIR 1952 Nag 8.

If he fails to take such care, the goods are damaged, and he cannot return the goods to the pawnor in the same condition, the pawnee is not entitled to claim amounts in respect of which the pawn is offered as security, simply on the principle that a creditor cannot recover a debt for which security is given, when he cannot return it.[695] Negligence of the pawnee or hypothecatee resulting in the loss of goods given as security may also discharge the sureties for payment of that debt.[696]

§3. Pledge and Hypothecation

750. Hypothecation is a transaction under which goods are made available as security for a debt without actual transferring property or possession to the creditor. The owner must discharge the debt within the stipulated time, failing which the creditor can recover his dues, if need be, by the sale of the goods hypothecated.[697] The owner-borrower is entitled to use them for the purposes of his business subject to the terms of hypothecation-deed.

If the creditor has such power under the hypothecation agreement, he can take possession and also sell the hypothecated property without intervention of the court on default by the debtor or on breach by the debtor of any conditions of the agreement.[698] The creditor can enforce the charge also against the transferee of goods having knowledge of the hypothecation.[699] Similarly, a financer of goods on hire-purchase basis repossess the goods on default of payment, if the terms of the hire-purchase agreement so provide.[700]

§4. Pledge and Mortgage

751. The contract of pledge differs essentially from a mortgage. A pledge is a security intermediate or midway between a simple loan and a mortgage that wholly passes property in the thing conveyed. A mortgagee acquires general property in the thing mortgaged, subject to the mortgagor's right to redeem. A mortgage transfers a legal interest in the goods is assigned; a pledge gives only a special property to the pawnee, leaving the general property remaining with the pawnor. The property pledged is actually or constructively delivered to the pawnee, whereas on a mortgage possession need not be given to the mortgagee in every case. The pawnee holds possession of the property for the purpose of securing to himself the advance. He has no property in the goods pawned and hence no right of foreclosure; he has merely a right to sell. Whether a particular transaction is a mortgage of movable

695. *In re Travancore National Bank Subsidiary Co Ltd, D Sundaravaradan v. M K Mani Iyer* AIR 1939 Mad 915.
696. *State Bank of Saurashtra v. Chitranjan Rangnath Raja* AIR 1980 SC 1528.
697. *Bank of Baroda v. Rabari Bachubhai Hirabhai* AIR 1987 Guj 1.
698. *In re Sree Yellamma Cotton, Woollen and Silk Mills Co Ltd, Bank of Maharashtra Ltd v. Official Liquidator* AIR 1969 Mys 280; *State Bank of India v. S B Shah Ali* AIR 1995 AP 134.
699. *Eureka Forbes Ltd v. Allahabad Bank* 2010 AIR SCW 3429.
700. *Charanjit Singh Chadha v. Sudhir Mehra* AIR 2001 SC 3721; *Anup Sarmah v. Bhola Nath Sharma* (2013) 1 SCC 400; but see *Citicorp Maruti Finance Ltd v. S Vijayalaxmi* AIR 2012 SC 509.

property or a pledge depends on the intention of parties and other surrounding circumstances.[701] In India, even shares can be pledged or mortgaged.

§5. Pledge and Lien

752. A lien is merely a personal right, whereas a pledge gives to the pawnee a 'special property' in the goods pledged. A lien gives no power of sale or disposition of the goods, whereas a pawnee has the power to sell in case of default. Lien is not transferable, but a pledge is assignable. A pledge with a lien is a secured creditor.[702]

§6. State Control over Pledges

753. State laws may control or regulate pawn-broking.[703] These laws may require a pawnbroker[704] to take a license and provide punishment for pawn-broking without one. They make provisions concerning the seeking of business and the formalities of entry into a pawn agreement. The statutes require that account books must be kept and pawn receipts be issued. They provide for the various offences that may arise under a contract of pawn, redemption period and procedure for redemption, effect of failure to redeem, and realization of pawns, including the requirement of sale by public auction. Thus, if the pawnor fails to redeem the pawned goods within the stipulated time and the grace period allowed under the statute, the pawnbroker can sell the goods at a public auction conducted in the manner prescribed by the statute. Such sale must be conducted by an approved auctioneer. The statute may give to the pawnbroker the liberty to bid at such auctions.

---

701. *Sri Raja Kakarlapudi Venkata Sudarsana Sundara Narasayyamma Garu v. Andhra Bank Ltd* AIR 1960 AP 273.
702. *Bombay Stock Exchange v. V S Kandalgaokar* AIR 2015 SC 193, (2015) 2 SCC 1.
703. See for example the Tamil Nadu Pawnbrokers Act 1943, the Karnataka Pawnbrokers Act 1961, certain provisions of the Bombay Money-Lenders Act 1946.
704. A person carrying on the business of taking goods and chattels in pawn for a loan; the Bombay Money-Lenders Act 1946 defines a pawnbroker as a money-lender who in the ordinary course of business advances a loan and takes goods in pawn as security for payment of such loan.

Chapter 10. Loans

754. Under Indian law, the term 'loan' refers to lending money repayable after a stipulated period of time or on demand or on happening of any event. Lending of property is a type of contract of bailment.[705] If goods are kept as security for repayment of a loan of money, it is a pledge.[706]

§1. Loan

755. A transaction of loan is a contract under the terms of which a person lends money to another repayable at the time specified if any or on demand. A covenant to repay is implied in every transaction of loan. A loan is due as soon as it is made, and if no condition or time is specified for its repayment, it is payable forthwith. A creditor need not demand it. It is the obligation of the debtor to seek the creditor and offer payment at the place of the creditor.

I. Loan and Deposit

756. A loan must be distinguished from deposit. Both loan and deposit are monies lent and placed in custody of another. In case of a loan, money passes from payer to payee at the instance of and for the requirement or use of the payee. In case of a deposit, the payee receives the money at the instance of the payer; the requirement or use of the payee is not a relevant fact. A deposit is repayable only on demand by depositor, and there is no immediate obligation to repay. A loan is repayable as soon as it is incurred.

The true test has been stated thus: whether there was an obligation on the debtor to seek out the creditor and repay him or whether the debtor is to keep the money till the creditor asks for them.[707]

Whether a transaction is a loan or a deposit is not determined merely from the terms of the document, but from the intention of parties after considering the surrounding circumstances, the relationship of parties, the character of transaction, and the manner in which parties treated the transaction.[708]

757. This distinction is especially important for calculating the limitation period for filing a suit for recovery of amount lent, and there is no period specified for its return. Where money is 'lent' repayable on demand or without specifying any period for repayment, a suit can and must be filed within three years from the date the *loan is made*.[709] If it is deposit payable on demand, the suit can and must be

705. Discussed in Ch. 2 of part II, para. 642 onwards.
706. Discussed in Ch. 9 of part II, para. 744 onwards.
707. *Mohd Akbar Khan v. Attar Singh* AIR 1936 PC 171.
708. *Ram Janaki Devi v. Juggilal Kamlapat* AIR 1971 SC 2551.
709. Articles 19 and 21 of Schedule II of the Limitation Act 1963.

filed within three years from the date the *demand is made*.[710] The latter also applies deposits of a customer in the hands of a banker.

§2. Interest

758. Interest is a return on a loan or other monetary obligation. To the lender, it is the difference between the money now and money in the future, seen as profit. It is the return or consideration or compensation for the use or retention by one person of a sum of money belonging to or owed to another. Interest, whether it is statutory or contractual, represents the profit the creditor might have made if he had use of the money or the loss he suffered because he had not that use.[711]

759. The law relating to interest was substantially developed in India even before the British came, in regard to mode of repayment, rates of interest, rights of creditors, and so on.[712] In 1855, the laws against usury were repealed by the Usury Laws Repeal Act 1855.

The Usurious Loans Act 1918 seeks to regulate certain usurious transactions. It empowers the courts to reopen transactions of money or grain loans in cases where the court is satisfied: (i) that the interest or other return is excessive; and (ii) that the transaction is substantially unfair, to revise the transaction between the parties, and if necessary, to reduce the amount payable to such sum as the court, having regard to the risk and all the circumstances of the case, may decide to be reasonable. It can also reopen any account taken between the parties, or set aside or alter any security given for a loan if (i) interest is excessive and (ii) the transaction was substantially unfair.

There are Acts in force in states giving relief from indebtedness in agricultural debts and also regulating the business of money-lending. All such laws substantially affect the transactions of loans and rates of interest.

760. The Interest Act 1978 gives the general law of interest applicable in the absence of contractual or statutory provisions. It keeps the right to interest within narrow limits. One reason for such provision as stated by the Law Commission of India in its sixty-third Report is to induce the creditor to take prompt action to file a suit.

A number of other laws provide for charging interest in respect of transactions they govern.[713] A person who delays paying any amount to a micro or small enterprise for goods supplied or services rendered to him, is liable to pay compound interest with monthly rests to the supplier at three times the bank rate notified by

710. Article 22 of the Limitation Act 1963.
711. *Sham Lal Narula v. Commissioner of Income-Tax* AIR 1964 SC 1878; *RM AR AR RM AR Ramanathan Chettiar v. Commissioner of Income-Tax* AIR 1967 SC 657.
712. A good discussion is found in the 63rd Report of the Law Commission of India on the Interest Act.
713. See s. 61 of the Sale of Goods Act 1930; the provisions of the Interest Act 1978; ss 78–81 of the Negotiable Instruments Act 1881.

the Reserve Bank of India, irrespective of the rate of interest agreed or provided by any other law.[714]

I. Right to Claim Interest

761. As a general rule, interest can be awarded only (i) if it is payable by custom; (ii) if there is an agreement either express or implied to pay interest; or (iii) under the provisions of any substantive law entitling the plaintiff to recover the same.[715] It cannot be awarded where the parties have agreed that no interest shall be payable.[716]

If a contract, whether in writing or not, provides for payment of interest, it is payable accordingly. There is no prohibition against charging of any rate of interest.[717] If interest rate is exorbitant, it can be reduced by the court in the exercise of its powers under the Usurious Loans Act 1918, or under section 74 of the Indian Contract Act if it amounts to a penalty.

II. Interest on Loans and Deposits

762. The debtor must pay interest at the agreed rate. It is valid to agree a higher rate of interest from the date of default. Payment of higher rate of interest or at compound rate from the date of breach, might be in the nature of penalty and liable to reduction to reasonable amount under the principles of award of liquidated damages.[718]

If the contract expressly prohibits payment of interest, the creditor cannot recover any.

In all other cases,[719] in any proceedings for recovery of debt,[720] the court may allow interest until the date of institution of proceedings, at the current rate of interest in the following circumstances:

(i) if the debt is payable on a specified date under the terms of a written instrument that is silent about payment of interest, it can be ordered from that specified date;
(ii) if it is not a written instrument, the creditor must first give notice to the debtor that interest will be claimed. Interest will be awarded from the date mentioned in the written notice.

---

714. Section 16 of the Micro, Small and Medium Enterprises Development Act, 2006.
715. *Mahabir Prasad Rungta v. Durga Datta* AIR 1961 SC 990; *Bengal Nagpur Railway Co Ltd v. Ruttanji Ramji* AIR 1938 PC 67.
716. *Union of India v. Krafters Engineering and Leasing (P) Ltd* AIR 2011 SC 2620; *Tehri Hydro Dev Corpn Ltd v. Jai Prakash Asso Ltd* AIR 2013 SC 920 (arbitrator cannot award).
717. Barring exceptions relating to charging of interest rates by banks.
718. See s. 74 of the Indian Contract Act 1872; see para. 568 onwards.
719. Interest Act 1978.
720. Under the Interest Act 1978, debt means any liability for an ascertained sum of money but not a judgment debt.

763. Interest on loans given by or deposits kept with banks and other financial institutions is regulated by the Reserve Bank of India under the Banking Regulation Act.

764. Interest for the period after institution of proceedings until recovery of amount is governed by laws of procedure[721] and lies in the discretion of the court. If the parties have not specified any rate of interest, the arbitral tribunal[722] can award interest at a reasonable rate from the date of cause of action until the date of award. Interest on arbitral award must carry interest at the rate of 18% per annum (p.a.) from the date of award until the date of payment.

III. Interest on Negotiable Instruments

765. Interest is payable at the specified rate if interest has been specified on a promissory note or bill of exchange or other negotiable instrument. If no rate of interest is specified in the instrument, interest is payable at a fixed rate of 18% p.a. on the amount due on the instrument notwithstanding any agreement relating to interest between any parties to the instrument.[723] Because no rate is specified on a cheque, a plaintiff filing a suit on a cheque will be entitled to interest at 18% p.a., a rate much higher than the current rate of interest at which banks lend amounts.

IV. Interest as Damages

766. Interest can be recovered as damages for breach of contract,[724] though it may not be awarded for mere withholding of debt, unless the contract or any statute provides.[725] A defendant who fails to pay an amount agreed is liable to pay the amount with interest up to the day agreed for payment as general damages, not any remote loss caused to the other party because of non-payment, unless specific circumstances likely to cause such losses was within contemplation of parties. A promisor who has failed to lend money as agreed is liable to pay damages being the difference between the cost of the loan contract and cost of substitute loan, which will usually be calculated as the difference in the two rates of interest. But he will be liable to compensate for further losses, even loss of profits, if he was aware of the object of loan, or where he has undertaken to maintain the credit of the promisee.

767. Interest as damages has been awarded, for example, where money is obtained or retained by fraud,[726] or it is wrongfully withheld for a long time

---

721. See s. 34 of the Code of Civil Procedure 1908.
722. Section 31(7) of the Arbitration and Conciliation Act 1996.
723. Section 80 of the Negotiable Instruments Act 1881.
724. *Bengal Nagpur Railway Co Ltd v. Ruttanji Ramji* AIR 1938 PC 67.
725. *Mahabir Prasad Rungta v. Durga Datta* AIR 1961 SC 990; *Union of India v. Rallia Ram* AIR 1963 SC 1685.
726. *Trojan & Co v. RM N N Nagappa Chettiar* AIR 1953 SC 235.

unreasonably,[727] where the plaintiff has been deprived of the right to enjoy or use his money[728] or invest money in business,[729] on price of goods where delivery of goods was unreasonably delayed.[730]

727. *Sat Prakash L Tara Chand v. Bodh Raj L Bhagwan Das Khatri* AIR 1958 Pun 111.
728. *Executive Engineer v. N C Budharaj* AIR 2001 SC 626.
729. *United India Insurance Co Ltd v. MKJ Corporation* AIR 1997 SC 408.
730. *Union of India v. Steel Stock Holders Syndicate* AIR 1976 SC 879.

Chapter 11. Contracts with the Government and Other Public Administrations

768. The Indian Contract Act, which owes its origin to English common law, unlike that of France and other countries, has no special legal regime governing contracts made by public authorities.

769. The Union (government at the Centre) and each state have the executive power of making of contracts for any purpose.[731] Separate Central or state Acts will confer contracting power upon local authorities, other bodies, or authorities. Their powers will be determined by the relevant statute and its purpose.

§1. Form

770. A contract can be enforced by or against the Union or the states only if the formalities required by Article 299 of the Constitution of India are complied with.

In order to comply with Article 299, the contract:

(i) must be executed by a person duly authorized by the President or Governor, as the case may be;
(ii) must be executed by such person 'on behalf of' the President or Governor, as the case may be;
(iii) must be 'expressed to be made by' the President or Governor, that is, in the name of the President or the Governor.

Where a contract is made by tender and acceptance, the acceptance must be made by a duly authorized person and on behalf of the President.[732] All the conditions are mandatory,[733] and none of them can be waived.[734] There cannot be any implied contract with the government.[735]

771. A contract not complying with any of the conditions of Article 299(1) of the Constitution is not binding on or enforceable by the government and is absolutely void[736] and cannot be ratified.[737] However, a claim can lie for work done under such agreement in *quasi-contract* under section 65 or 70 of the Indian Contract Act.[738]

731. Article 298 of the Constitution of India.
732. *Union of India v. Rallia Ram* AIR 1963 SC 1685.
733. *State of West Bengal v. B K Mondal and Sons* AIR 1962 SC 779.
734. *Bihar Eastern Gangetic Fishermen Cooperative Society Ltd v. Sipahi Singh* AIR 1977 SC 2149.
735. *K P Chowdhry v. State of Madhya Pradesh* AIR 1967 SC 203.
736. *State of West Bengal v. B K Mondal and Sons* AIR 1962 SC 779.
737. *Laliteshwar Prasad Sahi v. Bateshwar Prasad* AIR 1966 SC 580.
738. *New Marine Coal Co (Bengal) Private Ltd v. Union of India* AIR 1964 SC 152.

772. Such strict requirement is because 'the State should not be saddled with liability for unauthorized contracts which do not show on their face that they are made on behalf of the State'.[739]

773. These formalities apply to a contract made in exercise of executive powers of the Union or of the state, not to one made by a statutory authority in exercise of its powers conferred by statute[740] or to a compromise by parties during pendency of a suit to which the government is a party.[741]

§2. Enforcement

774. The government is like any other litigant when it comes to enforcement of contracts or claims for damages for breach. It is subject to the ordinary law of contract,[742] and the rights and liabilities are determined by terms that have been agreed. It can sue and be sued in civil courts.[743] It has no special privilege, except that it has the benefit of a very long period of limitation. The government can file a suit within thirty years[744] from the date of cause of action, whereas an ordinary litigant has only three years to file a suit relating to contract.

775. It is usual for contracts to which government is a party, to have clauses requiring parties to refer matters to arbitration. Quite often, an arbitrator might be an officer of that government. Such person would be uninvolved and unconnected with performance of the relevant contract.

§3. Tender Procedures in Public Contracts

776. There is no obligation under Indian contract law before a contract is formed. There is no obligation to negotiate or to continue to negotiate. The offeror also enjoys the freedom to keep an offer open. He is entitled to withdraw the offer at any time before its acceptance is complete against him. The offeree has the absolute liberty to accept any offer or any particular offer.

777. However, exercise of power to contract during the stages of offer and acceptance, by the government or by local authorities or government bodies, officers, or authorities, is subject to judicial review under the Constitution. Judicial review in public contracts lies in connection with actions relating to the process of inviting and accepting tenders, an area in which a civil court or an arbitrator would not interfere in matters between private parties. This is a 'public law' remedy by

---

739. *Bhikraj Jaipuria v. Union of India* AIR 1962 SC 113.
740. *Karamshi Jethabhai Somayya v. State of Bombay* AIR 1964 SC 1714.
741. *State of Haryana v. Lalchand* AIR 1984 SC 1326.
742. *Har Shankar v. Deputy Excise and Taxation Commissioner* AIR 1975 SC 1121.
743. *C K Achutan v. State of Kerala* AIR 1959 SC 490; *Life Insurance Corporation of India v. Escorts Ltd* AIR 1986 SC 1370.
744. Article 112 of the Schedule of the Limitation Act 1963.

way of a writ petition under Article 32 to the Supreme Court or Article 226 to any of the High Courts. This extraordinary remedy of writs cannot be invoked unless there is violation of any constitutional provision.[745] Contractual obligations cannot be challenged in writ jurisdiction. For example, where the government exercises the power of unilateral termination in the manner provided by the contract, the constitutional court will not interfere in the termination.

778. The government must sell by public auction and must invite tenders when it has to make a contract, whether for procurement or sale of produce or in any other contract. This ensures fairness, legitimacy, and non-discrimination. Such process has a number of benefits – selection of competent contractors, obtaining the lowest costs or the highest price, and giving opportunity to all persons interested in taking up that work. Deviation from this rule can be made only in the rarest of rare cases, like natural calamities, emergencies, or where the supplier has exclusive rights.[746] A government contract is viewed as a privilege or a largess, and the government or public body must use its power of contracting in public interest, in regard to the person with whom it would contract, as well as terms of the contract.

779. Public authorities invite tenders and prescribe clear procedures for their acceptance. If a contract is made without ignoring the basic procedure and after objective consideration, the courts will not interfere with the selection.[747] Judicial review will be concerned in reviewing the decision-making process and not the merits of the decision made.[748] The public body can choose its own method for the tendering process and fix its own terms of tender. But it must adhere to the norms fixed by it and procedures laid down. Any departure must not be arbitrary. Nor will the court interfere in decisions taken by experts or technical persons in choosing a particular tender.[749] Judicial quest in administrative matters has to find a right balance between administrative discretion to decide contractual matters and need to remedy any unfairness.

780. Judicial review under the principles of Article 14 of the Constitution of India[750] is for preventing arbitrariness or favouritism. A decision of a public body relating to the tender procedure can be struck down if it is *mala fide*, biased, or arbitrary to the extent of perversity. While exercising such power, the court will also consider that the government must have freedom to lay down policy, the fact that costs of completing works would increase if work is hampered, and the public interest. If the decision awarding the contracts is bona fide and in public interest, courts

745. *Premji Bhai Parmar v. Delhi Development Authority* AIR 1980 SC 738; *Bareilly Development Authority v. Ajai Pal Singh* AIR 1989 SC 1076.

746. *Nagar Nigam v. Al Faheem Meat Exports (P) Ltd* (2006) 13 SCC 382; *City Industrial Development Corporation v. Platinum Entertainment* AIR 2015 SC 340.

747. *Sterling Computers Ltd v. M & N Publications Ltd* AIR 1996 SC 51.

748. *C K Achutan v. State of Kerala* AIR 1959 SC 490; *Ramana Dayaram Shetty v. International Airport Authority of India* AIR 1979 SC 1628.

749. *Raunaq International v. IVR Construction Ltd* AIR 1999 SC 393.

750. Article 14 of the Constitution of India provides: The State shall not deny to any person equality before the law or the equal protection of the laws within the territory of India.

will not interfere.[751] In contracts having commercial elements, greater discretion is conceded to authorities to enable them to augment revenue; they have the freedom of 'play in the joints'.[752]

§4. Statutory Contracts

781. A contract may be governed by statutory provisions, for example, by the provisions of an Act and Rules that provide for the terms and conditions of the contract. The statute governs the relations between the parties. The rights and obligations have to be ascertained as a matter of statutory construction and interpretation of the scheme of the Act and Rules alone.[753] Examples of such contracts are: licenses granted under statutes for liquor vending, manufacture of salt, petroleum supply, electricity supply, service conditions of teachers, and so on.

751. *B S N Joshi and Sons Ltd v. Nair Coal Services Ltd* AIR 2007 SC 437: summarizes the principles of judicial review in government contracts.
752. *Sterling Computers Ltd v. M & N Publications Ltd* AIR 1996 SC 51.
753. *Sunnam Sattiah v. State of Andhra Pradesh* AIR 1980 AP 18.

Chapter 12. Contract of Partnership

782. The Indian Partnership Act 1932 deals with the law of partnership.

§1. Partnership

783. Partnership is the relation between persons who have agreed to share profits of a business carried on by all or any of them acting for all. Such persons are the partners and are together called a firm. Their relationship arises out of contract. They will have a name under which they carry on business.

A partnership need not be in writing, but disabilities and difficulties arise out of non-registration of a firm. Also, the Income-Tax laws give advantages where the partnership contract is in writing.

A partnership with more than twenty partners is an illegal association, unless it forms and registers as a company.[754]

A minor cannot become a partner, but can be admitted into the benefits of partnership and hence entitled to the profits and property without being liable for losses. On attaining majority, he has the option to continue in partnership.

§2. Rights, Duties, and Liabilities of Partners

784. The Partnership Act provides for powers, mutual rights, and liabilities of partners in their relations with each other and their relations with third parties. Partners share profits and losses equally, unless otherwise agreed.

A partner is an agent of the firm for the purposes of business. He has an implied authority to bind the firm by any act done to carry on the firm's business in the usual way. This may be extended or restricted by contract. A third party is not bound by any restriction on implied authority, unless he knows it.

Every partner is liable, jointly with all the other partners, and also severally, for all acts of the firm done while he is a partner, which would include all acts of other partners within their authority.

Partners' liability to third parties is unlimited.

§3. Partnership Property

785. Each partner may contribute funds or property to the partnership. All property, rights, and interests brought into the firm and acquired or purchased by or for the firm, out of the money of the firm or for the purposes of business of the firm, are partnership property.

---

754. Also see para. 790.1 *infra*: LLPs.

§4. Reconstitution of Firm

786. A new partner can join the firm with consent of all partners. He is not liable without his consent for acts of firm done before his joining. So can a partner leave the firm, and he will not be liable for later acts of the firm to third parties who have notice of his retirement.

§5. Determination of Partnership

787. The contract of partnership may provide for its determination, for example, on expiry of a specified period of time, on completion of a venture, or on happening of certain contingency such as death or retirement of a partner. If there is no provision about duration or determination, it is a partnership 'at will' and can be dissolved by any partner at any time by giving notice or dissolution. A firm can be dissolved with the consent of all partners. It can also be dissolved by the court.

§6. Registration of Firms

788. The Partnership Act provides for registration of a firm, and imposes disabilities if it is not registered. Unless the firm is registered (i) it cannot sue to enforce against any third party any right arising out of contract; and (ii) its partners cannot sue each other or the firm for their rights as partners. An unregistered firm cannot initiate arbitration proceedings,[755] but can seek interim measures for preservation of rights in anticipation of arbitration proceedings.[756]

§7. Suits by and against Firms

789. A firm is not an incorporated body and does not possess legal personality. The partners collectively form it. A firm can sue and be sued in its own name under the provisions of the Civil Procedure Code. It is really a suit by or against all its partners.

790. Partners are personally liable along with the firm for all debts and liabilities of the firm. Their liability is unlimited.

§8. Limited Liability Partnerships

790.1. Under the Limited Liability Partnership Act it is now possible to register limited liability partnerships (LLPs) in India for any trade, profession, or

755. *U P State Sugar Corpn Ltd v. Jain Construction Co* AIR 2004 SC 4335; *Jagdish Chandra Gupta v. Kajaria Traders (India) Ltd* AIR 1964 SC 1882.
756. *Ashok Traders v. Gurumukh Das Saluja* AIR 2004 SC 1433.

occupation. An LLP shall be a body corporate and have perpetual existence separate from its partners. With a minimum of two partners, there is no limit on the maximum number. Liability of its partners is limited to their respective investment in the LLP. One partner shall not be liable for wrongful acts or omissions of any other partner. Mutual rights and duties of partners shall be governed by their agreement.

Chapter 13. Quasi-Contracts

§1. Preventing Unjust Enrichment

791. A *quasi-contract* is not a real or consensual contract. The obligation is imposed by law, without reference to or even against the tenor of the probable intention of parties. They do not arise out of contract, nor from delict, hence the term *quasi-contract.* Liability rests on the equitable doctrine of unjust enrichment, to compel the defendant to make restitution of the benefit that he ought not retain at the expense of the plaintiff.

792. Even as English law grappled with the appropriate remedies for situations demanding just solutions to situations of unjust enrichment, Indian law already provided for such remedies for situations that did not squarely fall within the limits of contract obligations, but demanded appropriate remedies. When these were formulated, they stated the law wider than the prevalent English law. Thus, although payment made under a mistake of law was recoverable under these provisions of the Act, it was recognized as recoverable under English law only in 1999.[757]

793. There are two main theoretical bases of quasi-contractual liability: (i) implied contract and (ii) unjust enrichment. These are of course irrelevant in the Indian context, because the circumstances giving rise to liability and the remedy would be governed by the precise language and interpretation of sections 68–72 of the Act dealing with such relations. It is, however, generally accepted that these provisions embody the principles of unjust enrichment[758] and are claims in restitution.[759]

§2. 'Quasi-Contracts' in Indian Laws

794. Chapter V of the Indian Contract Act provides for five situations and calls them 'certain relations resembling those created by contracts'. These are relations in which one or other essential element of a valid contract is absent. But the situation demands reimbursement of incurred expense or loss incurred or remedying of unjust enrichment. These are really *quasi-contracts*, but the Act does not use this term.

A person who is under an obligation under the provisions of sections 68–72 of the Act must perform the obligation as stated in the relevant applicable section; if he fails to discharge the obligation after it has been incurred, he will be liable to compensate the person injured by his failure to the same extent as if he had contracted to discharge it and had broken the contract.[760]

757. *Kleinwort Benson Ltd v. Lincoln City Council* [1999] 2 AC 349, [1998] 4 All ER 513.
758. *Nallaya Goundar v. Ramaswami Gounder* (1958) 2 Mad LJ 86; *Muppudathi Pillai v. Krishnaswami Pillai* AIR 1960 Mad 1, FB.
759. *Mafatlal Industries Ltd v. Union of India* (1997) 5 SCC 536.
760. Section 73(3) of the Act.

I. *Negotiorum Gestio*: Obligation of Person Enjoying Benefit of Non-Gratuitous Act

795. Section 70 of the Indian Contract Act, which deals with the obligation of a person enjoying the benefit of a non-gratuitous act, comes closest to the concept of *negotiorum gestio* under Belgian law. This Indian provision is not restricted to management of the interests of another. The obligation is directly enforceable, and there is no need to resort to the analogy of agency. If a person acts out of necessity to protect the interests of another, an 'agency of necessity' is created[761] and such person will be subject to all duties and liabilities and will have all rights and powers of an agent.

796. Section 70 provides that where a person does or delivers something to another without intending to do so gratuitously, he is entitled to receive compensation for the thing or restoration of the thing delivered if the other party has enjoyed the benefit of the thing done or delivered.[762] Thus, where A, a tradesman, leaves goods at B's house by mistake, and B treats the goods as his own, he is bound to pay A for them.

This provision applies when (i) the goods are to be delivered lawfully or something has to be done for another person lawfully; (ii) the thing done or the goods delivered must be done or delivered without intention to do so gratuitously, that is, without expectation of compensation; or (iii) the person to whom goods are delivered enjoys the benefit thereof. It contemplates that there was no proposal, promise, or request initially which prompted the act.

797. The person must have done or delivered the thing lawfully. This indicates that he must have lawful interest in making it[763] and that the payment has been made bona fide. Payment made or act done or delivery will not be lawful where it violates the express provisions of statute or the express wish of the other that the act should not be done or the thing delivered.

Recovery can be had not only for services rendered or thing delivered, but also for money paid, not where these are given with the object of benefiting the plaintiff himself. The thing must be done or thing delivered for the defendant.

798. The person who is sought to be held responsible must have had the opportunity or option to accept or not to accept the benefit.[764] The section will not apply where the defendant derives no benefit from the work done.[765]

799. The section does not apply where an act is done by one person at the *express* request of another, for example, where goods are supplied at the request of

761. See para. 612 *supra*.
762. Section 70 of the Indian Contract Act.
763. *Gobind Ram Sanchaiti v. Ram Kishore Choudhari* AIR 1953 Pat 145; *Nuli Kanaka Rao v. Tetali Sriranga Venkata Ramalinga Reddy* AIR 1966 AP 297.
764. *Jhala Umedsinghji Merubhabhai v. Indumati Markandray Trivedi* AIR 1971 Guj 214.
765. *M K Radhakrishna Iyer v. Secy of State* AIR 1936 Mad 930; *In re Ambica Textiles Ltd* AIR 1950 Cal 491.

another,[766] in which case payment will be ordered on the basis of an implied contract.

However, recovery has been allowed where a request was made by a person without authority, on the analogy that there is really no request.[767] This provision is also the basis of a claim where a contractor has provided goods or services to the government under an agreement, but the agreement does not comply with the formality requirements of Article 299 of the Constitution of India,[768] where the government has taken benefit of the performance.[769] The same principle would apply where benefit under an agreement is enjoyed by a statutory authority, but the agreement does not comply with formalities given by the statute.

800. This provision does not allow compensation in substitution of the thing delivered.

801. It is usual to apply this provision to compensate for services rendered beyond the scope of terms of the contract, benefit of which is availed of by the defendant. A person who does work or who supplies goods under a contract, if no price is fixed, is entitled to be paid a reasonable sum for his labour and the goods supplied. If the work is outside the contract, the terms of the contract can have no application; and the contractor is entitled to be paid a reasonable price for such work done by him.[770]

II. Unjust Enrichment

802. The principle of unjust enrichment is stated simply: 'A person who has been unjustly enriched at the expense of another is required to make restitution to the other'. Sections 68–72 of the Indian Contract Act represent the principles of unjust enrichment.[771] It is unjust to allow one person to retain a benefit received at the expense of another person. *Nemo debet locupletari ex aliena jactura*: No man should grow rich out of another person's loss. The principle of unjust enrichment has been stated to presuppose three things: (i) that the defendant has been enriched by the receipt of benefit; (ii) he must have been so enriched at the plaintiff's expense; and (iii) it would be unjust to allow him to keep the benefit.[772]

803. The Law Commission of India proposed in 1958 that a residuary section be inserted to cover other numerous situations of unjust enrichment which were not

766. *B N Elias & Co Ltd v. State of West Bengal* AIR 1959 Cal 247.
767. *J K Enterprise v. Prithviraj Ratanchand Mehta* (1990) 92 Bom LR 572; *State of Orissa v. Prathibha Prakash Bhavan* AIR 1995 Ori 62.
768. See para. 770 *supra*.
769. *Mulamchand v. State of Madhya Pradesh* AIR 1968 SC 1218.
770. *State of Punjab v. Hindustan Development Board Ltd* AIR 1960 Pun 585.
771. *Nallaya Goundar v. Ramaswami Gounder* (1958) 2 Mad LJ 86; *Muppudathi Pillai v. Krishnaswami Pillai* AIR 1960 Mad 1, FB; *Mafatlal Industries Ltd v. Union of India* (1997) 5 SCC 536; *Renusagar Power Co Ltd v. General Electric Co* AIR 1994 SC 860.
772. *Mahabir Kishore v. State of Madhya Pradesh* AIR 1990 SC 313.

specifically provided for. But the Act was not amended. Yet, apart from cases falling under sections 68–72 of the Act, relief in the nature of remedying unjust enrichment are granted in other cases, such as action for money had and received,[773] subrogation,[774] and contribution[775] and also in situations in which the contract was invalid for want of proper form or authority, rather than capacity,[776] at times by stretching the interpretation of sections 68–72.

804. Three situations are discussed under this category: (i) claims for necessaries supplied to incompetent persons; (ii) reimbursement of person paying money due by another in payment of which he is interested; and (iii) responsibility of finder of goods.

A. *Claims for Necessaries Supplied to Incompetent Persons*

805. If necessaries are supplied to a minor or a person of unsound mind, the supplier is entitled to reimbursement for the necessaries.[777] The supplier is not entitled to claim the price agreed, but only to reimbursement. The incompetent person is not personally liable, but only his property.

This applies also to supplies made to persons whom such incompetent persons are legally bound to support, for example, wife, minor son, minor and unmarried daughter, sister, younger brother. A minor being bound to support his sister, money advanced to a minor for marriage of his sister was recoverable under this section.[778]

Even if a minor or a person of unsound mind cannot be made liable under contract, a statutory claim arises under this section against his property. This section does not apply to contracts made by guardians of minors or managers of persons of unsound mind. Their powers as guardian or manager rest on provisions of other laws.[779]

806. The term 'necessaries' is not confined to necessities, but includes everything necessary to maintain an incompetent person in the state, station, or degree of life in which he is, and what is 'necessary' is a relative fact to be determined with reference to the fortune and circumstances of that particular person who is supplied necessaries.[780] Further, they must be things that the person needs; therefore, if he is

773. *Thomas Abraham v. National Tyre and Rubber Co of India Ltd* AIR 1974 SC 602.
774. *Oberai Forwarding Agency v. New India Assurance Co Ltd* AIR 2000 SC 855.
775. *Nawab Mirza Mohammad Kazim Ali Khan v. Nawab Mirza Mohammad Sadiq Ali Khan* AIR 1938 PC 169.
776. *State of West Bengal v. B K Mondal and Sons* AIR 1962 SC 779; *New Marine Coal Co (Bengal) Private Ltd v. Union of India* AIR 1964 SC 152; *Mulamchand v. State of Madhya Pradesh* AIR 1968 SC 1218.
777. Section 68 of the Indian Contract Act.
778. *Jai Indra Bahadur Singh v. Dilraj Kaur* AIR 1921 Oudh 14; *Shriniwasarao v. Baba Ram* AIR 1933 Nag 285.
779. See paras 223–224, 230 *supra*.
780. *Jagon Ram Marwari v. Mahadeo Prosad Sahu* (1909) ILR 36 Cal 768; *Sadhulaxmi Sadhu v. Suryanarayana* AIR 1950 Mad 274.

already supplied with things of that kind, a claim under this section will fail. The court would, therefore, consider the character of goods supplied, actual circumstances of the minor, and extent to which the minor was already supplied with them. Examples of necessaries are medical or legal services, costs incurred in defending a suit for protection of property, money advanced for a necessary purpose such as sister's marriage, repairs of house, saving property from compulsory sale, or charges for teaching and instruction.

It is for the creditor to prove that money was advanced or goods supplied, and that these were suitable to the condition in life of the minor, and that they were suitable to his actual requirements at the time, that is, the minor had not a supply from other sources.[781] Mere enquiries by the creditor into the existence of necessity, or mention in the transaction document that the amount was for necessaries, is not enough.

807. The supplier of necessaries is not entitled to claim the price agreed, but only to a reimbursement for the supplies. Therefore, it has been held in some cases that there cannot be a claim for interest on amount claimed.[782]

B. *Reimbursement of Person Paying Money Due by Another in Payment of Which He Is Interested*

808. A person who is interested in the payment of money that another is bound by law to pay, and who, therefore, pays it, is entitled to be reimbursed by the other.[783] This gives indemnity to a person who pays an amount legally payable by another. Though often the plaintiff would stand in some relationship with the person whose liability he pays, there need not be any privity between them.

Thus, where an owner of land is liable to pay the government land revenue for that land, and the tenant pays it to save proceeding for sale of land in revenue recovery proceedings, the tenant is entitled to recover the amount from the owner. Similarly, where property of A is attached by B in execution proceedings against B's debtor C, and A pays off the amount, he is entitled to recover it from C.

809. The requirements for the application of this provision are:

(i) The plaintiff has been compelled to pay this money to a third party. It is necessary that the plaintiff is compelled with the motive of protecting his own interest.[784] The plaintiff must not only be interested in the payment, but must be compelled to pay for protecting that interest, and must have paid it bona fide. This interest must be legal, but need not arise out of compulsion arising

781. *Sadasheo Balaji v. Firm Hiralal Ramgopal* AIR 1938 Nag 65.
782. *Umrao Singh v. Firm Banarsi Das-Dip Chand* AIR 1927 Lah 414; *Manmatha Kumar Saha v. Exchange Loan Co Ltd* AIR 1936 Cal 567; *Ramchandra v. Hari* AIR 1936 Nag 12.
783. Section 69 of the Indian Contract Act.
784. *Desai Himatsinghji Joravarsinghji v. Bhavabhai Kayabhai* (1880) ILR 4 Bom 643.

out of law. The plaintiff will be interested in payment where he seeks to protect some interest that would be lost to him, or when he has no alternative action. Such interest may be pecuniary, or related to property. But it must not be arising of mere sentiment or moral or social obligation. Voluntary payment cannot be recovered.

(ii) The plaintiff has made an actual payment of money. The plaintiff can claim the amount only after he has actually paid the amount. It is not available, for example, where the plaintiff has merely given a security or promissory note for the amount he is interested in paying.

(iii) The defendant was legally liable to pay the third party. Money paid cannot be recovered unless the person from whom it is sought to be recovered was bound by law to pay it, and at the time the payment was made. Where the defendant is under no legal liability to pay the money, the plaintiff cannot claim reimbursement, even though the payment may have indirectly benefited the defendant. This liability may arise under statute, but also that which lay under an agreement.

810. Moreover, the person making the payment must be a person who is not himself bound to pay the whole or any portion of the money. Such person cannot, therefore, claim contribution in cases in which he makes the whole payment for which he along with others is liable to pay. Claims of contribution between joint promisors, if arising out of contract, lie under the direct provisions of the Indian Contract Act,[785] otherwise may arise out of implied agreement of indemnity.

811. A liability to reimburse payment made on behalf of one may be contractual, in which case the provisions and terms and conditions of that contract will determine the obligation.

C. Responsibility of Finder of Goods

812. A person who finds goods of another, and takes them into custody, is liable as a bailee of the goods.[786] These would include the obligation to search the owner, and take care of the goods as any prudent person would take of his own. He possesses a right of lien for the trouble and expenses incurred by him in preserving it and can sue for reward, if announced, and to retain the goods until he receives the reward.[787] He also has the right to sell the goods in certain cases if the owner cannot with reasonable diligence be found or refuses to pay the lawful charges of the finder.[788]

785. Section 45 of the Indian Contract Act.
786. Section 71 of the Indian Contract Act; see para. 642 onwards.
787. Section 168 of the Indian Contract Act.
788. Section 169 of the Indian Contract Act.

III. Money Paid but Not Due

813. A person to whom money has been paid, or anything delivered by mistake or under coercion, must repay or return it.[789] This is also an application of the principle of unjust enrichment.

For example:

(i) A and B jointly owe 100 rupees to C. A alone pays the amount to C, and B, not knowing this fact, pays 100 rupees over again to C. C is bound to repay the amount to B.
(ii) A railway company refuses to deliver up certain goods to the consignee, except on the payment of an illegal charge for carriage. The consignee pays the sum charged to obtain the goods. He is entitled to recover so much of the charge as was illegally excessive.

814. Because this provision contains a rule of equity, equitable considerations are relevant in applying this rule. Certain circumstances may, therefore, disentitle a plaintiff from recovering, that is, estoppel, or that the payee has changed his position substantially. Nor are payments made in settlement or by way of compromise to be disturbed.

A. Payment Made under Mistake

815. The person who has paid money under mistake can recover under this provision in the following circumstances:

(i) He is under a mistake as to material fact, by mistake meaning lack of knowledge.
(ii) The mistake should be as to some fact causing a liability to pay.[790]

The 'mistake is in thinking that the money paid was due when in fact it was not due'.[791] But money paid voluntarily with full knowledge of all facts cannot be recovered on the ground of mistake.[792] The word 'mistake' used in this section has been held as wide enough to cover not only mistake of fact but also mistake of law.[793]

816. This being a recovery in restitution, the test of mistake is broader than that in contract. The mistake of fact need not necessarily be of the same fundamental character that makes the contract wholly void. Therefore, recovery has been allowed in cases of mistake as to creditworthiness or arithmetical mistakes.

789. Section 72 of the Indian Contract Act.
790. *O A P R M A E Adaikappa Chettiar v. Thomas Cook & Son (Bankers) Ltd* AIR 1933 PC 78.
791. *Sri Sri Shiba Prasad Singh v. Maharaja Srish Chandra Nandi* AIR 1949 PC 297.
792. *Anath Bandhu Deb v. Dominion of India* AIR 1955 Cal 626.
793. *Sales Tax Officer v. Kanhaiya Lal Makund Lal Saraf* AIR 1959 SC 135.

This provision is essentially different from the provision dealing with mistake invalidating a contract and its consequences. The mistake here lies in thinking that the money was due when in fact it was not. Payment 'by mistake' in section 72 must refer to a payment that was not legally due and that could not have been enforced: the 'mistake' is in thinking that the money paid was due when in fact it was not due.

A person to whom a bank has credited payment by mistake is bound to return the amount under this section.[794] A person can recover under this section any amount overpaid to the creditor;[795] and a buyer of goods can claim refund of the excess price paid by him because the weight of goods sold was wrongly calculated in the invoices.[796]

817. Under Indian law, a taxpayer can recover the amount paid under a mistake of law, even if payment of tax liability is voluntary.[797] It has been consistently held that payment toward tax or duty that is without authority of law is payment made under mistake within the meaning of section 72. Any tax that is not eligible under the law or the law under which it is imposed is declared unconstitutional is a payment under a mistake of law and the word 'mistake' in section 72 of the Contract Act includes a mistake of law, and the assessee paying the tax would be entitled to sue for refund.[798] However, such repayment will not be ordered where the plaintiff does not suffer having passed the burden of tax or duty to another person.[799] Whether the burden of the duty has been passed on to a third party is a matter within the exclusive knowledge of the claimant; he has the best evidence in his possession, and it is for the claimant to establish that he has not passed the burden of the duty to a third party.[800]

B. Payment Made under Coercion

818. The word 'coercion' in this section is used in its general and ordinary sense, and its meaning is not controlled by the definition of 'coercion' in section 15.[801] Payment under coercion under this section means payment under compulsion which the defendant has no right to claim.[802]

794. *S Kotrabasappa v. Indian Bank* AIR 1987 Kant 236; *Indian Bank v. Mocro Electronics* AIR 2005 AP 328.
795. *Badr-un-nisa v. Muhammad* Jan (1880) ILR 2 All 671.
796. *Nanak Chand Shadurain v. Tinnelvely-Tuticorin Electric Supply Co Ltd* AIR 1975 Mad 103.
797. *Sales Tax Officer v. Kanhaiya Lal Makund Lal Saraf* AIR 1959 SC 135; *Sri Sri Shiba Prasad Singh v. Maharaja Srish Chandra Nandi* AIR 1949 PC 297.
798. *Ballabhdas Mathuradas Lakhani v. Municipal Committee* AIR 1970 SC 1002; *Town Municipal Committee Amraoti v. Ramchandra Vasudeo Chimote* AIR 1964 SC 1166.
799. *Sahakari Khand Udyog Mandal Ltd v. Commissioner of Central Excise* AIR 2005 SC 1897; *Automotive Tyre Manufacturers Association v. Designated Authority* AIR 2011 SC (Supp) 481.
800. *Mafatlal Industries Ltd v. Union of India* (1997) 5 SCC 536.
801. *Seth Kanhaya Lal v. National Bank of India Limited* (1913) 40 IA 56.
802. *Petlad Bulakhidas Mills Co Ltd v. Union of India* AIR 1970 Guj 59.

819. Thus, if a person pays money to save his property that has been wrongly attached in execution, he is entitled to recover it;[803] so is it recoverable where money was paid as income-tax under threat of attachment;[804] person charged with non-compoundable offence induced to pay money to stifle prosecution;[805] amount paid on official demand as penalty to avoid prosecution;[806] or money paid by one joint owner to release property attached for purpose of realizing fine imposed on another joint owner.[807] Thus, where a consumer of electricity pays money to the supplier of electricity under protest on being threatened with disconnection in case of default, the amount is recoverable under the section,[808] as also a payment of water cess made under fear of coercive process of recovery.[809] If a seller refuses to deliver unless a certain additional amount is paid and the buyer demurs, the buyer can recover the amount.[810]

803. *Dulichand v. Ramkishen Singh* (1881) 8 IA 93.
804. *A H Forbes v. Secy of State* AIR 1915 Cal 621.
805. *Muthuveerappa Chetty v. Ramaswami Chetty* AIR 1917 Mad 607.
806. *Trikamdas Udeshi v. Bombay Municipal Corporation* AIR 1954 Bom 427.
807. *Bansraj Das v. Secretary of State* AIR 1939 All 373.
808. *Kaka Ram Tej Bhan Sekari v. Khattar Electrical Engineering & General Supply co Ltd* AIR 1939 Pesh 8.
809. *Secy of State v. Kannepalli Jankiramayya* AIR 1914 Mad 534.
810. *Shakoor Gani v. T S Sabapathy Pillai* AIR 1924 Mad 236.

Selected Bibliography

§1. Case Law

I. Cases

A B C Laminart Pvt Ltd v. A P Agencies, Salem AIR 1989 SC 1239, 273.
A H Forbes v. Secy of State AIR 1915 Cal 621, 819.
Abdul Hameed v. Mohd Ishaq AIR 1975 All 166, FB, 282.
Abdullah Bey Chedid v. Tenenbaum AIR 1934 PC 91, 549.
Afshar M M Tacki v. Dharamsey Tricamdas AIR 1947 Bom 98, 448, 451.
Alopi Parshad & Sons Ltd v. Union of India AIR 1960 SC 588, 448, 449.
Amrit Lal Goverdhan Lalan v. State Bank of Travancore AIR 1968 SC 1432, 433, 742.
Amteshwar Anand v. Virender Mohan Singh AIR 2006 SC 151, 427.
Anand Construction Works v. State of Bihar AIR 1973 Cal 550, 694.
Ananda Namdeo Kharde v. Pundalik Tukaram Chaudhury AIR 1936 Nag 225, 145.
Anant Das v. Ashburner & Co (1876) ILR 1 All 267, FB, 268.
Anath Bandhu Deb v. Dominion of India AIR 1955 Cal 626, 815.
Andheri Bridge View Co-op Hsg Society Ltd v. Krishnakant Anandrao Deo AIR 1991 Bom 129, 145.
Andhra Pradesh Tourism Development Corporation v. Pampa Hotels Ltd AIR 2010 SC 1806, 234.
Anup Sarmah v. Bhola Nath Sharma (2013) 1 SCC 400, 750.
Asaram v. Ludheshwar AIR 1938 Nag 335, FB, 293.
Ashok Kumar v. Union Territory Chandigarh AIR 1995 SC 461, 143.
Ashok Traders v. Gurumukh Das Saluja AIR 2004 SC 1433, 788.
Associate Builders v. Delhi Development Authority AIR 2015 SC 620, 565.
Attorney General v. Blake [2000] 4 All ER 385, HL, 542.
Automotive Tyre Manufacturers Association v. Designated Authority AIR 2011 SC (Supp) 481, 817.
BCPP Mazdoor Sangh v. NTPC AIR 2008 SC 336, 387.
B N Elias & Co Ltd v. State of West Bengal AIR 1959 Cal 247, 799.
B S N Joshi and Sons Ltd v. Nair Coal Services Ltd AIR 2007 SC 437, 780.
Babu Bhagwati Saran Singh v. Maiyan Murat Mati Kuer AIR 1931 Pat 394, 46.
Badr-un-nisa v. Muhammad Jan (1880) ILR 2 All 671, 816.
Ballabhdas Mathuradas Lakhani v. Municipal Committee AIR 1970 SC 1002, 817.

Selected Bibliography

Balwant Singh v. Rajaram AIR 1975 Raj 73, 346.
Banarsi Das v. Kanshi Ram AIR 1963 SC 1165, 598.
Bank of Baroda v. Rabari Bachubhai Hirabhai AIR 1987 Guj 1, 750.
Bank of Bengal v. Ramanathan Chetty AIR 1915 PC 121, 625.
Bank of Bihar Ltd v. Damodar Prasad AIR 1969 SC 297, 740.
Bansraj Das v. Secretary of State AIR 1939 All 373, 819.
Bareilly Development Authority v. Ajai Pal Singh AIR 1989 SC 1076, 777.
Bengal Immunity Co Ltd v. State of Bihar AIR 1955 SC 661, 85.
Bengal Nagpur Railway Co Ltd v. Ruttanji Ramji AIR 1938 PC 67, 761, 766.
Bhagwandas Goverdhandas Kedia v. Girdharlal Parshottamdas AIR 1966 SC 543, 109, 116.
Bharat Petroleum Corpn Ltd v. Great Eastern Shipping Co Ltd AIR 2008 SC 357, 3.
Bharati Knitting Co v. DHL Worldwide Express Courier Division of Airfreight Ltd AIR 1996 SC 2508, 322.
Bhikraj Jaipuria v. Union of India AIR 1962 SC 113, 772.
Bhimbhat v. Yeshwantrao (1901) ILR 25 Bom 126, 63.
Bihar Eastern Gangetic Fishermen Cooperative Society Ltd v. Sipahi Singh AIR 1977 SC 2149, 770.
Bombay Stock Exchange v. V S Kandalgaokar AIR 2015 SC 193, (2015) 2 SCC 1, 752.
BSNL v. Reliance Communication Ltd 2011 AIR SCW 525, (2011) 1 SCC 394, 570.
C K Achutan v. State of Kerala AIR 1959 SC 490, 774, 779.
C V Enterprises v. Braithwaite & Co Ltd AIR 1984 Cal 306, 143.
Carlill v. Carbolic Smoke Ball Co [1893] 1 QB 256, [1891–1894] All ER Rep 127, 26.
Central Bank of India Ltd v. Hartford Fire Insurance Co Ltd AIR 1965 SC 1288, 311, 527, 529.
Central Bank of India v. Grains and Gunny Agencies AIR 1989 MP 28, 210.
Central Inland Water Transport Corporation Ltd v. Brojo Nath Ganguly AIR 1986 SC 1571, 256, 289, 290, 319.
Chhanga Lal v. M C D AIR 2008 Del 146, 308.
Chhatra Kumari Devi v. Mohan Bikram Shah AIR 1931 PC 196, 60.
Charanjit Singh Chadha v. Sudhir Mehra AIR 2001 SC 3721, 750.
Chatterjee Petrochem Co v. Haldia Petrochemicals Ltd AIR 2014 SC (Supp) 699, 2014 AIR SCW 237, 145, 457.
Chidambara Iyer v. Renga Iyer AIR 1966 SC 193, 130.
Chief Administrator Dandakaranya Project v. Prabartak Commercial Corporation Ltd AIR 1975 MP 152, 705.
Chloro Controls India (P) Ltd v. Severn Trent Water Purification Inc AIR 2012 SC (Supp) 1017, 327, 375A.
Chotelal Lallubhai v. Champsey Umersey & Sons AIR 1923 Bom 75, 311, 474, 529.
Citibank NA v. Standard Chartered Bank (2004) 6 SCC 1, 414.
Cochin Port Trust v. Associated Cotton Traders Limited AIR 1983 Ker 154, 210.
Commissioner of Income-Tax v. Vazir Sultan and Sons AIR 1959 SC 814, 85.
Contship Container Lines Ltd v. D K Lall AIR 2010 SC 1704, 665.
Currie v. Misa (1875) LR 10 Ex 153, 130.

D Wren International Ltd v. Engineers India Ltd AIR 1996 Cal 424, 107.
Damodar Valley Corporation v. K K Kar AIR 1974 SC 158, 459.
Dan Kuer v. Sarla Devi AIR 1947 PC 8, 370.
Dargavarapu Sarrapu v. Rampratapu (1902) ILR 25 Mad 580, 145.
Deb Ratan Biswas v. Anand Moyi Dev AIR 2011 SC 1653, 632.
Debi Saran Koiri v. Nandalal Choubey AIR 1929 Pat 591, 135.
Delhi Development Authority v. Durga Chand Kaushish AIR 1973 SC 2609, 711.
Desai Himatsinghji Joravarsinghji v. Bhavabhai Kayabhai (1880) ILR 4 Bom 643, 809.
Dharshi Monji v. Chandulal Girdharilal AIR 1950 Kutch 84, 390.
Dhulipudi Namayya v. Union of India AIR 1958 AP 533, 107.
District Board of Ramnad v. Mahomed Ibrahim AIR 1933 Mad 524, 137.
Dulichand v. Ramkishen Singh (1881) 8 IA 93, 819.
Dwarka Das v. State of Madhya Pradesh AIR 1999 SC 1031, 561.
Dwarka Nath Pai Mohan Chaudhuri v. Rivers Steam Navigation Co Ltd AIR 1917 PC 173, 210.
Economic Transport Organisation v. Charan Spinning Mills (P) Ltd (2010) 4 SCC 114, 432.
Economic Transport Organisation v. Dharwad Dist Khadi Gramudyog Sangh, AIR 2000 SC 1635, 210.
Eureka Forbes Ltd v. Allahabad Bank 2010 AIR SCW 3429, 750.
Executive Engineer v. N C Budharaj AIR 2001 SC 626, 767.
Fateh Chand v. Balkishan Das AIR 1963 SC 1405, 572.
Firm Chhunna Mal Ram Nath v. Firm Mool Chand-Ram Bhagat AIR 1928 PC 99, 470.
Firm Hardayal Mal – Mohri Lal v. Firm Kishan Gopal Jhanji & Sons AIR 1938 Lah 673, 624.
Food Corporation of India v. Jagannath Dutta AIR 1993 SC 1494, 526, 527.
Food Corpn of India v. Surana Commercial Co (2003) 8 SCC 636, 128.
Forasol v. Oil and Natural Gas Commission AIR 1984 SC 241, 423.
Gaganmoyi Debi v. Troilucka Nath Chowdhry (1906) 8 Bom LR 375 (PC), 183.
Ganga Saran v. Firm Ram Charan Ram Gopal AIR 1952 SC 9, 349.
Geo-Group Communications INC v. IOL Broadband Ltd, AIR 2010 SC (Supp) 271, 211.
Ghaziabad Development Authority v. Union of India AIR 2000 SC 2003, 557.
Gherulal Parakh v. Mahadeodas Maiya AIR 1959 SC 781, 259, 277, 288, 289, 648.
Gobind Ram Sanchaiti v. Ram Kishore Choudhari AIR 1953 Pat 145, 797.
Godhra Electricity Co Ltd v. State of Gujarat AIR 1975 SC 32, 334.
Gokal Chand v. Parvin Kumari AIR 1952 SC 231, 88.
Grant Smith and Company and McDonell Limited v. Settle Construction and Dry Dock Company AIR 1919 PC 85, 442.
Gujarat Bottling Co Ltd v. Coca Cola Co AIR 1995 SC 2372, 265.
Gulabchand v. Kudilal AIR 1966 SC 1734, 283.
Gurmukh Singh v. Amar Singh (1991) 3 SCC 79, 286.
Gurunath v. Kamalabai AIR 1955 SC 206, 96.
H B Basavaraj v. Canara Bank (2010) 12 SCC 458, 738.
H M Kamaluddin Ansari & Co v. Union of India AIR 1984 SC 29, 511.

H V Rajan v. C N Gopal AIR 1975 SC 261, 63.
Hadley v. Baxendale (1854) 9 Exch 341, [1843-60] All ER Rep 461, 536.
Hajee S V M Mohamed Jamaludeen Bros & Co v. Govt of Tamil Nadu AIR 1997 SC 1368, 527.
Haji Mohamed Haji Jiva v. E Spinner (1900) ILR 24 Bom 510, 211.
Hanil Era Textiles Ltd v. Puromatic Filters (P) Ltd AIR 2004 SC 2432, 273.
Har Shankar v. Deputy Excise and Taxation Commissioner AIR 1975 SC 1121, 774.
Harichand Mancharam v. Govind Luxman Gokhale AIR 1923 PC 47, 125.
Haridwar Singh v. Bagun Sumbrui AIR 1972 SC 1242, 119.
Harinagar Sugar Mills Ltd v. Shyam Sundar Jhunjhunwala AIR 1961 SC 1669, 96.
Harnandrai Fulchand v. Pragdas Budhsen AIR 1923 PC 54, 349.
Heavy Electricals (India) Ltd v. Pannalal Devchand Malviya AIR 1973 MP 7, 348, 705.
Hind Construction Contractors v. State of Maharashtra AIR 1979 SC 720, 694.
Hindustan Corporation (Hyd) Pvt Ltd v. United India Fire and General Insurance Ltd AIR 1997 AP 347, 382.
Hindustan Shipyard v. State of Andhra Pradesh AIR 2000 SC 2411, 690.
Hungerford Investment Trust Ltd v. Haridas Mundhra AIR 1972 SC 1826, 525.
In re Ambica Textiles Ltd AIR 1950 Cal 491, 798.
In re Sree Yellamma Cotton, Woollen and Silk Mills Co Ltd, Bank of Maharashtra Ltd v. Official Liquidator AIR 1969 Mys 280, 750.
In re Travancore National Bank Subsidiary Co Ltd, D Sundaravaradan v. M K Mani Iyer AIR 1939 Mad 915, 749.
In the goods of Mulne (1906) 33 ILR Cal 625, 183.
Indian Bank v. Mocro Electronics AIR 2005 AP 328, 816.
Indu Kakkar v. Haryana State Industrial Development Corporation (1999) 2 SCC 37, 386.
Industrial Credit and Development Syndicate v. Smithaben H Patel AIR 1999 SC 1036, 430.
Instalment Supply Company v. STO Ahmedabad AIR 1974 SC 1105, 687.
InterGlobe Aviation Ltd v. N Satchinand (2011) 7 SCC 463, 104, 317.
Inuganti Kasturamma v. Chelikani Venkatasurayya Garu AIR 1916 Mad 605, 76.
Irrawaddy Flotilla Company v. Bugwandas (1891) 18 IA 121, 95.
Iswaran Pillai v. Sonnivevaru (1913) ILR 38 Mad 753, 371.
J G Engineers Pvt Ltd v. Union of India AIR 2011 SC 2477, 544.
J K Enterprise v. Prithviraj Ratanchand Mehta (1990) 92 Bom LR 572, 799.
J M Tagore v. G M Tagore (1872) 47 IA Supp 18, 60.
Jaffer Meher Ali v. Budge Budge Jute Mills Co (1907) ILR 34 Cal 289, 281.
Jagdish Chandra Gupta v. Kajaria Traders (India) Ltd AIR 1964 SC 1882, 788.
Jagon Ram Marwari v. Mahadeo Prosad Sahu (1909) ILR 36 Cal 768, 806.
Jai Indra Bahadur Singh v. Dilraj Kaur AIR 1921 Oudh 14, 805.
Jainarayan Ram Lundia v. Surajmull Sagarmull AIR 1949 FC 211, 152.
Janki Bai Chunnilal v. Ratan Melu AIR 1962 MP 117, FB, 283.
Jawahar Lal v. Mathura Prasad AIR 1934 All 661, 607.
Jethalal Nagji Shah v. Municipal Corporation, Greater Bombay AIR 1954 Bom 167, 389.

Jhala Umedsinghji Merubhabhai v. Indumati Markandray Trivedi AIR 1971 Guj 214, 798.
Joseph Darmanin v. Carmel Micallef AIR 1946 PC 50, 334.
K L Johar and Co v. Deputy Commercial Tax Officer AIR 1965 SC 1082, 687.
K Narendra v. Riviera Apartments (P) Ltd AIR 1999 SC 2309, 565.
K P Chowdhry v. State of Madhya Pradesh AIR 1967 SC 203, 770.
K V Periyamianna Marakkayar v. Banians & Co AIR 1926 Mad 544, 742.
Kaka Ram Tej Bhan Sekari v. Khattar Electrical Engineering & General Supply Co Ltd AIR 1939 Pesh 8, 819.
Kale v. Deputy Director of Consolidation AIR 1976 SC 807, 730.
Kalyani Breweries Ltd v. State of West Bengal AIR 1998 SC 70, 642.
Kamal Kant Paliwal v. Prakash Devi Paliwal AIR 1976 Raj 79, 245.
Kamal Narayan Shopowner Sitaram v. Baniram Shopowner Sheonarayan AIR 1923 Nag 332, 148.
Kandaswami Pillai v. Ramasami Mannadi AIR 1919 Mad 168, 63.
Karamshi Jethabhai Somayya v. State of Bombay AIR 1964 SC 1714, 773.
Karnataka Pawnbrokers' Association v. State of Karnataka AIR 1999 SC 201, 745.
Kedar Nath Bhattacharji v. Gorie Mahomed (1887) ILR 14 Cal 64, 137, 140.
Kedar Nath Motani v. Prahlad Rai AIR 1960 SC 213, 295.
Kesavulu Naidu v. Arithulai Ammal (1912) 36 ILR Mad 533, 254.
Keshavananda Bharati v. State of Kerala AIR 1973 SC 1461, 17.
Keshavlal Brothers & Co v. Diwan Chand & Co AIR 1923 PC 105, 449.
Keshub Mohindra v. Commissioner of Gift Tax (1968) 70 ITR 1, 130.
Khardah & Company Ltd v. Raymon & Co (India) Private Ltd AIR 1962 SC 1810, 453.
Khwaja Muhammad Khan v. Hussaini Begam (1910) 37 IA 152, 369.
Kleinwort Benson Ltd v. Lincoln City Council [1999] 2 AC 349, [1998] 4 All ER 513, 792.
Kone Elevator India Pvt Ltd v. State of Tamil Nadu 2014 AIR SCW 5362, (2014) 7 SCC 1, 690.
Krishna Lal Sadhu v. Promila Bala Dasi AIR 1928 Cal 518, 354.
Krishnawanti Puri v. Life Insurance corporation of India AIR 1975 Del 19, 244.
Kush Kanta Barkakati v. Chandra Kanta Kakati AIR 1924 Cal 1056, 645.
L C Golak Nath v. State of Punjab AIR 1967 SC 1643, 17.
Lachoo Mal v. Radhey Shyam AIR 1971 SC 2213, 724.
Ladli Parshad Jaiswal v. Karnal Distillery Co Ltd AIR 1963 SC 1279, 251.
Lakshmi Dass v. Rooplal (1906) ILR 30 Mad 169, 597.
Lakshmiayya v. Murahari AIR 1930 Mad 547, 304.
Lakshminarayan Ram Gopal and Sons Ltd v. Government of Hyderabad AIR 1954 SC 364, 610, 692.
Lala Man Mohan Das v. Janki Prasad AIR 1945 PC 23, 46.
Laliteshwar Prasad Sahi v. Bateshwar Prasad AIR 1966 SC 580, 771.
Lallan Prasad v. Rahmat Ali AIR 1967 SC 1322, 746.
Larsen and Toubro Ltd v. Mohan Lal Harbans Lal Bhayana AIR 2014 SC (Supp) 1366, 147.
Life Insurance Corporation of India v. Escorts Ltd AIR 1986 SC 1370, 774.
Liladhar v. R S Sunderlal AIR 1932 Nag 32, 296.

Nawab Mirza Mohammad Kazim Ali Khan v. Nawab Mirza Mohammad Sadiq Ali Khan AIR 1938 PC 169, 803.
New Marine Coal Co (Bengal) Private Ltd v. Union of India AIR 1964 SC 152, 771, 803.
Niranjan Shankar Golikari v. Century Spinning and Manufacturing Co Ltd AIR 1967 SC 1098, 265, 495.
Nirmala Anand v. Advent Corporation (P) Ltd AIR 2002 SC 3396, 493.
Nuli Kanaka Rao v. Tetali Sriranga Venkata Ramalinga Reddy AIR 1966 AP 297, 797.
O A P R M A E Adaikappa Chettiar v. Thomas Cook & Son (Bankers) Ltd AIR 1933 PC 78, 815.
Oberai Forwarding Agency v. New India Assurance Co Ltd AIR 2000 SC 855, 803.
Oil and Natural Gas Corporation Ltd v. SAW Pipes Ltd AIR 2003 SC 2629, 570, 324.
Ouseph Poulo v. Catholic Union Bank Ltd AIR 1965 SC 166, 732.
P B Bhatt v. V R Thakkar AIR 1972 Bom 365, 188.
P D'Souza v. Shondrilo Naidu AIR 2004 SC 4472, 493.
P R Transport Agency v. Union of India, AIR 2006 All 23, 110, 116.
P R Viswanatha Iyer v. A Muthukumaraswami Pillai AIR 1948 Mad 139, 389, 390.
P Radhakrishna Murthy v. NBCC Ltd (2013) 3 SCC 747, 544.
Pamulapati Bhushayya v. Kommareddy Chinnapareddi AIR 1960 AP 39, 283.
Percept D'Mark (India) Pvt Ltd v. Zaheer Khan AIR 2006 SC 3426, 265.
Perumal Mudaliar v. Sendanatha Mudaliar AIR 1918 Mad 311, 140.
Petlad Bulakhidas Mills Co Ltd v. Union of India AIR 1970 Guj 59, 818.
Petrofina (Great Britain) Ltd v. Martin [1966] Ch 146, 264.
Phulchand Exports Ltd v. OOO Patriot 2012 AIR SCW 30, (2011) 10 SCC 300, 665.
Poornammal v. R Srinivasarangan AIR 1956 SC 162, 730.
Prakash Chandra Pathak v. State of UP AIR 1960 SC 195, 85.
Pramada Prasad Mukherji v. SagarmalAgarwalla AIR 1954 Pat 439, 533.
Pratima Chowdhury v. Kalpana Mukherjee AIR 2014 SC 1304, 183.
Prem Singh v. Birbal, (2006) 5 SCC 353, 221.
Premji Bhai Parmar v. Delhi Development Authority AIR 1980 SC 738, 777.
Pure Helium India Pvt Ltd v. Oil and Natural Gas Commission AIR 2003 SC 4519, 422.
Pushpa Devi Bhagat v. Rajinder Singh AIR 2006 SC 2628, 729.
Quadricon Pvt Ltd v. Bajarang Alloys Ltd, AIR 2008 Bom 88, 116.
R Rajanna v. S R Venkataswamy AIR 2015 SC 706, 729.
Radhakrishna Agarwal v. State of Bihar AIR 1977 SC 1496, 527.
Radhamohan Thakur v. Bipin Behari Mitra AIR 1938 Pat 505, 188.
Raj KumarBahal v. Food Corporation of India AIR 1990 Raj 64, 707.
Raja Dhruv Dev Chand v. Raja Harmohinder Singh AIR 1968 SC 1024, 63, 443.
Rajkot Municipal Corporation v. Manjulaben Jayantilal Nakum (1997) 9 SCC 552, 50.
Ram Coomar Coondoo v. Chunder Canto Mookerjee (1876) 4 IA 23, 290.
Ram Dhan v. L Chauthmal AIR 1935 Oudh 496, 369.
Ram Janaki Devi v. Juggilal Kamlapat AIR 1971 SC 2551, 606, 756.

Ram Nath v. Mannu Lal AIR 1923 All 518, 148.
Ram Pratap Kamalia Mills v. State of Bihar AIR 1963 Pat 153, 46.
Rama Shankar Singh v. Shyamlata Devi AIR 1970 SC 716, 580.
Ramana Dayaram Shetty v. International Airport Authority of India AIR 1979 SC 1628, 779.
Ramayya v. Firm of Gulfarosh Mohdeen Saib Shaik Saib AIR 1958 AP 576, 448.
Ramachandra Narayan Nayak v. Karnataka Neeravari Nigam Ltd 2013 AIR SCW 5913, 528.
Ramchandra v. Hari AIR 1936 Nag 12, 807.
Rampal Ramchand Agarwal v. Gourishankar Hanuman Prasad AIR 1952 Nag 8, 749, 750.
Ranganayakamma v. K S Prakash AIR 2009 SC (Supp) 1218, 128.
Rani Kunwar v. Mahbub Baksh AIR 1930 All 252, 63.
Rashik Laf v. Ram Narain (1912) ILR 34 All 273, 63.
Ratanchand Hirachand v. Askar Nawaz Jung AIR 1976 AP 112, 290.
Raunaq International v. IVR Construction Ltd AIR 1999 SC 393, 779.
Ravinder Raj v. Competent Motors Co. Pvt Ltd AIR 2011 SC 1061, 658.
Renusagar Power Co Ltd v. General Electric Co AIR 1994 SC 860, 422, 802.
Rickmers Verwaltung GmbH v. Indian Oil Corporation Ltd AIR 1999 SC 504, 211.
Rivers Steam Navigation Company v. Choutmull Doogar (1899) 26 IA 1, 210.
RM AR AR RM AR Ramanathan Chettiar v. Commissioner of Income-Tax AIR 1967 SC 657, 758.
S Amarchand & Co v. Ramdas V Durbar AIR 1914 Bom 290, 63.
S Chatterjee v. Dr K L Bhave AIR 1960 MP 323, 52.
S K Jain v. State of Haryana 2009 AIR SCW 1934, 256, 319.
S Kotrabasappa v. Indian Bank AIR 1987 Kant 236, 816.
S N Prasad v. Monnet Finance Ltd AIR 2011 SC 442, 742.
S V R Mudaliar v. Rajabu F Buhari AIR 1995 SC 1607, 493.
Sachs v. Henderson [1902] 1 KB 612, 50.
Sadasheo Balaji v. Firm Hiralal Ramgopal AIR 1938 Nag 65, 806.
Sadhulaxmi Sadhu v. Suryanarayana AIR 1950 Mad 274, 806.
Sah Lal Chand v. Indrajit (1899) 27 IA 93, 188.
Sahakari Khand Udyog Mandal Ltd v. Commissioner of Central Excise AIR 2005 SC 1897, 817.
Sales Tax Officer v. Kanhaiya Lal Makund Lal Saraf AIR 1959 SC 135, 815, 817.
Sat Prakash L Tara Chand v. Bodh Raj L Bhagwan Das Khatri AIR 1958 Pun 111, 767.
Satgur Prasad v. Har Narain Das AIR 1932 PC 89, 306.
Satyabrata Ghose v. Mugneeram Bangur & Co AIR 1954 SC 44, 353, 439, 446, 448, 454.
Secretary of State for India in Council v. Augustus John Arathoon (1882) ILR 5 Mad 173, 348.
Secy of State v. Kannepalli Jankiramayya AIR 1914 Mad 534, 819.
Seth Kanhaya Lal v. National Bank of India Limited (1913) 40 IA 56, 818.
Shakoor Gani v. T S Sabapathy Pillai AIR 1924 Mad 236, 819.
Shakuntala v. State of Haryana AIR 1979 SC 843, 135.

Sham Lal Narula v. Commissioner of Income-Tax AIR 1964 SC 1878, 758.
Shriniwasarao v. Baba Ram AIR 1933 Nag 285, 805.
Sita Ram Gupta v. Punjab National Bank AIR 2008 SC 2416, 739.
Sita Ram v. Radha Bai AIR 1968 SC 534, 295.
Societe Commercial De Corealas & Financiers v. State Trading Corporation of India AIR 1998 Guj 94, 374.
Som Giri v. Ram Ratangiri AIR 1941 All 387, 67.
Sorabshah Pestonji v. Secretary of State for India AIR 1928 Bom 17, 246.
South India Railway Co Ltd v. S M Bhashyam Naidu AIR 1935 Mad 356, 348, 705.
Southern Roadways Ltd v. S M Krishnan AIR 1990 SC 673, 630.
Sri Raja Kakarlapudi Venkata Sudarsana Sundara Narasayyamma Garu v. Andhra Bank Ltd AIR 1960 AP 273, 751.
Sri Sri Shiba Prasad Singh v. Maharaja Srish Chandra Nandi AIR 1949 PC 297, 815, 817.
State Bank of India v. Mula Sahakari Sakhar Karkhana Ltd AIR 2007 SC 2361, 736.
State Bank of India v. Indexport Registered AIR 1992 SC 1740, 740.
State Bank of India v. S B Shah Ali AIR 1995 AP 134, 750.
State Bank of Saurashtra v. Chitranjan Rangnath Raja AIR 1980 SC 1528, 749.
State of Gujarat v. Memon Mahomed Haji Hasam AIR 1967 SC 1885, 643.
State of Gujarat v. Variety Body Builders AIR 1976 SC 2108, 690.
State of Haryana v. Lalchand AIR 1984 SC 1326, 773.
State of Karnataka v. Shree Rameshwara Rice Mills AIR 1987 SC 1359, 553.
State of Madhya Pradesh v. Kaluram AIR 1967 SC 1105, 738.
State of Maharashtra v. M N Kaul AIR 1967 SC 1634, 737.
State of Orissa v. Prathibha Prakash Bhavan AIR 1995 Ori 62, 799.
State of Punjab v. Hindustan Development Board Ltd AIR 1960 Pun 585, 800.
State of Tripura v. Bina Choudhary AIR 2007 SC 2169, 643.
State of West Bengal v. B K Mondal and Sons AIR 1962 SC 779, 770, 771, 803.
Sterling Computers Ltd v. M & N Publications Ltd AIR 1996 SC 51, 779, 780.
Subbu Chetti v. Arunachalam AIR 1930 Mad 382, FB, 371, 373.
Subrahmania Pattar v. Narayanan Nayar (1900) ILR 24 Mad 130, 624.
Sukkulal Sowcar v. A V Tirumala Row Sahib AIR 1919 Mad 200, 323.
Sukumar Bysack v. Sushil Kanta Banerjee AIR 1972 Cal 207, 188.
Sunnam Sattiah v. State of Andhra Pradesh AIR 1980 AP 18, 781.
Surasaibalini Debi v. Phanindra Mohan Majumdar AIR 1965 SC 1364, 296,304.
Syndic in Bankruptcy of Khoury v. Khayat [1943] AC 507, [1943] 2 All ER 406, 422.
T N S Firm v. V P S Muhammad Hussain AIR 1933 Mad 756, 219.
T P Petherpermal Chetty v. R Muniadi Servai (1908) 35 IA 98, 295, 296.
Tan Ah Boon v. State of Johore AIR 1936 PC 236, 549.
Tarapore and Co v. V/O Tractoroexport Moscow AIR 1970 SC 891, 513.
Tatia v. Babaji (1896) ILR 22 Bom 176, 63.
Teegula Babiah v. Mohammed Abuds Subhan Khan AIR 1954 Hyd 156 FB, 283.
Tehri Hydro Dev Corpn Ltd v. Jai Prakash Asso Ltd AIR 2013 SC 920, 761.
The Heron II, Koufos v. C Czarnikow Ltd [1969] 1 AC 350, [1967] 3 All ER 686, HL, 560.

Thomas Abraham v. National Tyre and Rubber Co of India Ltd AIR 1974 SC 602, 803.
Timblo Irmaos Ltd v. Jorge Anibal Motos Sequeira AIR 1977 SC 734, 549.
Toolsidas Tejpal v. M P Venkatachalapathy Aiyar AIR 1921 PC 46, 352.
Town Municipal Committee Amraoti v. Ramchandra Vasudeo Chimote AIR 1964 SC 1166, 817.
Town Municipal Council Athani v. Presiding Officer Labour Court AIR 1969 SC 1335, 598.
Trikamdas Udeshi v. Bombay Municipal Corporation AIR 1954 Bom 427, 819.
Triveni Oil Field Service Ltd v. Oil and Natural Gas Commission AIR 2006 Del 331, 109, 110, 116.
Trojan & Co v. RM N N Nagappa Chettiar AIR 1953 SC 235, 767.
Trustees of the Port of Bombay v. Premier Automobiles Ltd AIR 1981 SC 1982, 643.
Tulsi v. Chandrika Prasad AIR 2006 SC 3359, 193.
Turner Morrison and Co Ltd v. Hungerford Investment Trust Ltd AIR 1972 SC 1311, 587.
Tweddle v. Atkinson (1861) 1 B & S 393, 369.
Twentsche Overseas Trading Co Ltd v. Uganda Sugar Factory Ltd AIR 1945 PC 144, 440.
Tyagaraja Mudaliyar v. Vedathanni AIR 1936 PC 70, 188.
U P Co-op C U Federations v. West U P Sugar Mills Assocn AIR 2004 SC 3697, 653.
U P Co-operative Federation Ltd v. Singh Consultants and Engineers (P) Ltd (1988) 1 SCC 174, 513.
U P State Sugar Corpn Ltd v. Jain Construction Co AIR 2004 SC 4335, 788.
Umrao Singh v. Firm Banarsi Das-Dip Chand AIR 1927 Lah 414, 807.
Union of India v. Kishori Lal Gupta & Bros AIR 1959 SC 1362, 147, 453, 459.
Union of India v. Krafters Engineering and Leasing (P) Ltd AIR 2011 SC 2620, 761.
Union of India v. Rallia Ram AIR 1963 SC 1685, 766, 770.
Union of India v. Raman Iron Foundry AIR 1974 SC 1265, 553.
Union of India v. Sri Sarada Mills AIR 1973 SC 281, 432.
Union of India v. Steel Stock Holders Syndicate AIR 1976 SC 879, 767.
United Breweries Ltd v. State of AP AIR 1997 SC 1316, 642.
United India Fire and General Insurance Co Ltd v. Pelaniappa Transport Corporation AIR 1986 AP 32, 382.
United India Insurance Co Ltd v. MKJ Corporation AIR 1997 SC 408, 767.
UP Rajkiya Nirman Nigam Ltd v. Indure Pvt Ltd AIR 1996 SC 1373, 347.
Venkatasubbiah Chetty v. Govindarajulu Naidu (1907) 31 ILR Mad 45, 188.
Vishnu Agencies v. Commercial Tax Officer AIR 1978 SC 449, 653.
Vishwanath v. Sadashiva AIR 1932 Nag 1, 607.
Visweswaradas Gokuldas v. B K Narayan Singh AIR 1969 SC 1157, 99.
Waghela Rajsanji v. Sheikh Masludin (1887) 14 IA 89, 16, 36.
Waman Shrinivas Kini v. Ratilal Bhagwandas and Co AIR 1959 SC 689, 724.
Webb v. Macpherson (1903) 30 IA 238, 60.
Y A J Noorbhai v. S P L K R Karuppan Chetty AIR 1925 PC 232, 455.
Yarlagadda China Rattayya v. Donepudi Venkataramayya AIR 1959 AP 551, 550.

§2. Books

Atiyah, P.S. *Essays on Contract.* Oxford: Clarendon Press, 1986.
Datta, C.R. *Company Law.* 6th edn. Gurgaon: Lexis Nexis, 2008.
Jain, M.P. *Outlines of Indian Legal and Constitutional History.* 7th edn. Gurgaon: Lexis Nexis, 2014.
Khergamvala. *Negotiable Instruments Act.* 21st edn. Gurgaon: Lexis Nexis, 2013.
Krishnamurthy, K. *Indian Stamp Act.* 11th edn. Gurgaon: Lexis Nexis, 2011.
Kwatra, G.K. *Arbitration Made Easy: A Practical Guide.* 3rd edn. Gurgaon, Universal Law Publishing Ltd, 2011.
Lewison, K. *The Interpretation of Contracts.* 5th edn. London: Sweet and Maxwell, 2011.
Markanda, P.C. et al. *Law Relating to Arbitration and Conciliation.* 8th edn. Gurgaon, Lexis Nexis, 2013.
Mulla. *The Registration Act.* Updated 12th edn. Gurgaon: Lexis Nexis, 2013.
Mulla. *Sale of Goods and the Indian Partnership Acts.* 10th edn. Gurgaon: Lexis Nexis, 2012.
Mulla. *The Law of Insolvency in India.* 5th edn. Gurgaon: Lexis Nexis, 2013.
Patil, B.S. *Building and Engineering Contracts.* 6th edn. Pune: S B Patil, 2011.
Pollock & Mulla. *Indian Contract and Specific Relief Acts.* Updated 14th edn. Gurgaon: Lexis Nexis, 2013.
Ramaiya, A. *Guide to the Companies Act.* 18th edn. Gurgaon: Lexis Nexis, 2014.
Ratanlal & Dhirajlal. *The Law of Evidence.* 25th edn. Gurgaon: Lexis Nexis, 2013.
Ratanlal & Dhirajlal. *The Law of Torts.* Updated 26th edn. Gurgaon: Lexis Nexis, 2013.
Saharay, H.K. *Law of Carriage of Goods.* 2nd edn. Kolkata: Eastern Law House, 2013.
Salmond & Heuston. *Law of Torts.* 20th edn. London: Sweet and Maxwell, 1992.
Sarkar. *Law of Evidence.* 18th edn. Gurgaon: Lexis Nexis, 2013.
Sarkar. *Code of Civil Procedure.* 11th edn. Gurgaon: Lexis Nexis, 2006.
Sathe, S.P. *Administrative Law.* 7th edn. Gurgaon: Lexis Nexis, 2004.
Singh, G.P. *Principles of Statutory Interpretation.* 13th edn. Gurgaon: Lexis Nexis, 2012.
Sujan, M.A. *Law Relating to Arbitration and Conciliation.* 2nd edn. Delhi: Universal Law Publishing Co Ltd, 2001.
Tannan, M.L. *Banking Law and Practice in India.* 25th edn. Gurgaon: Lexis Nexis, 2014.
Venkoba Rao. *Law of Agency.* 3rd edn. Gurgaon: Butterworths, India, 2011.
Wadhwa D.P. & N.L. Rajah. *The Law of Consumer Protection.* 2nd edn. Gurgaon: Lexis Nexis, 2009.

§3. List of Acts

(in alphabetical order of subject matter)
The Advocates Act 1961.
The Arbitration and Conciliation Act 1996.

Selected Bibliography

The Act for Avoiding Wagers (Amendments) Act 1865.
The Banking Regulation Act 1949.
The Indian Bills of Lading Act 1856.
The Carriage by Air Act 1972.
The Carriage by Road Act 2007.
The Indian Carriage of Goods by Sea Act 1925.
The Charitable and Religious Trusts Act 1920.
The Charter Act of 1833.
The Citizenship Act 1955.
The Code of Civil Procedure 1908.
The Code of Criminal Procedure 1973.
The Commercial Documents Evidence Act 1939.
The Companies Act 2013.
The Consumer Protection Act 1986.
The Contempt of Courts Act 1971.
The Maharashtra Cooperative Societies Act 1960.
The Employees' Provident Funds Act 1952.
The Employees' State Insurance Act 1948.
The Indian Evidence Act 1872.
The Forward Contracts (Regulation) Act 1952.
The Guardian and Wards Act 1890.
The Hindu Maintenance and Guardianship Act 1956.
The Income-Tax Act 1961.
The Information Technology Act 2000.
The Presidency-Towns Insolvency Act 1900.
The Provincial Insolvency Act 1920.
The Insurance Act 1938.
The Interest Act 1978.
The Law Reports Act 1875.
The Legal Services Authorities Act 1987
The Limitation Act 1963.
The Indian Majority Act 1875.
The Marine Insurance Act 1963.
The Married Women's Property Act 1874.
The Micro, Small and Medium Enterprises Development Act, 2006.
The Mental Health Act 1987.
The Bombay Money-Lenders Act 1946.
The Motor Vehicles Act 1988.
The Negotiable Instruments Act 1881.
The Notaries Act 1956.
The Indian Partnership Act 1932.
The Indian Penal Code 1860.
The Karnataka Pawnbrokers Act 1961.
The Tamil Nadu Pawnbrokers Act 1943.
The Powers-of-Attorney Act 1882.
The Public Liability Insurance Act 1991.
The Railways Act 1989.

The Indian Registration Act 1908.
The Regulating Act of 1773.
The Maharashtra Rent Control Act 1999.
The Sale of Goods Act 1930.
The Securities Contracts (Regulation) Act, 1956.
The Specific Relief Act 1963.
The Indian Stamp Act 1899.
The Trade Marks Act 1999.
The Trade Unions Act 1926.
The Transfer of Property Act 1882.
The Indian Trusts Act 1882.
The Usurious Loans Act 1918.
The Usury Laws Repeal Act 1855.
The Employees' Compensation Act 1923.

§4. Websites

<http://goidirectory.nic.in/>, one-point source to access all Indian Government Websites.
<http:// indiacode.nic.in/>, INDIACODE India Code Information System (Bills and Acts of Parliament).
<http://egazette.nic.in/>, The Gazette of India.
< http://india.gov.in//>, National Portal of India.
<http://lawcommissionofindia.nic.in/>, Law Commission of India.
<http://lawmin.nic.in/>, Ministry of Law and Justice, Government of India.
<http://parliamentofindia.nic.in/>, Indian Parliament.
<http://eci.nic.in>, Election Commission of India.
<http://mea.gov.in/apostille.htm>, Ministry of External Affairs.
<http://supremecourtofindia.nic.in/scr.htm>, Supreme Court Reports.
<http://judis.nic.in/>, Judgment Information System of Supreme Court and other High Courts.
<http://www.airwebworld.com/>, All India Reporter Pvt Ltd (Private Reporter and Publisher).
<www.scconline.com/>, Online database of SCC.
<www.manupatra.com>, Manupatra (Private Reporter and Publisher).
<www.uncitral.org/>, UNCITRAL – United Nations Commission on International Trade Law.
<www.unidroit.org/>, UNIDROIT – International Institute for the Unification of Private Law.

Selected Bibliography

Index

The numbers here refer to paragraph numbers.

Index

Index

Index

Index

www.ingramcontent.com/pod-product-compliance
Lightning Source LLC
Chambersburg PA
CBHW072242240926
51846CB00012B/135
* 9 7 8 9 0 4 1 1 6 8 5 2 8 *